Developing through
Relationships

Developing through Relationships

Origins of communication, self, and culture

Alan Fogel

The University of Chicago Press

The University of Chicago Press, Chicago 60637
Harvester Wheatsheaf, a division of
Simon & Schuster International Group
© 1993 Alan Fogel
All rights reserved. Published 1993
Printed in Great Britain

16 15 14 13 12 11 10 09 08 07   2 3 4 5 6

ISBN-13: 978-0-226-25659-7 (paper)
ISBN-10: 0-226-25659-6 (paper)

Library of Congress Cataloging-in-Publication Data

Fogel, Alan.
    Developing through relationships : origins of communication,
self, and culture / Alan Fogel.
        p.   cm.
    Includes bibliographical references and index.
    ISBN 0-226-25658-8 (cloth : alk. paper). —
ISBN 0-226-25659-6 (paper : alk. paper)
    1. Interpersonal relations.   2. Interpersonal
communication.   I. Title.

HM132.F63   1993
302—dc20   93-20092
                                                    CIP

♾ The paper used in this publication meets the minimum
requirements of the American National Standard for
Information Sciences—Permanence of Paper for Printed
Library Materials, ANSI Z39.48-1992.

Contents

Preface

I began to consider the study of relationships as an intellectual vocation in 1970, the result of two years of college teaching that was part of my work as a United States Peace Corps volunteer in Bogotá, Colombia. After another year I began my doctoral training in the Department of Education at the University of Chicago, working on Kenneth Kaye's mother–infant communication studies and struggling to fill the gaps in my knowledge of developmental psychology left by undergraduate and master's degrees in physics and mathematics.

I am still struggling, as I believe all professionals struggle, with incompleteness and ambiguity, wavering between conviction and uncertainty. The work that follows is part of an ongoing learning process. Apart from what I have said about these limitations in the body of the text I can also add that it feels finished enough for now, ready for public scrutiny, but open to revision in the future. This book is the product not only of the year over which the writing took place, but also of the past twenty years of my professional development and of my personal life history.

Part of this life history is my relationship with many individuals who have in some way contributed to the production of this book. The most recent are those who were generous enough to give the time to read and critically review earlier drafts: Farrell Burnett, George Butterworth, Steve Duck, Jacqueline Fogel, Donna Gelfand, Wendy Haight, Penny Jameson, Kenneth Kaye, Andy Lock, Barbara Rogoff, Rudolph Schaffer and Esther Thelen. I accept their support and critiques with gratitude. Sandy Sommer's capable assistance in the preparation of the manuscript was invaluable. I recognize the more historically distant but no less influential contributions of my teachers and mentors, especially Kenneth Kaye, Starkey Duncan, Dan Freedman and John Knobloch. In addition, the graduate and postgraduate students with whom I have worked, the colleagues whose ideas I borrowed and those I reviewed, the subjects who participated in my research, and my parents, brothers and sisters, wife and sons are all part of me, therefore implicated in the work, and entirely without blame for its faults.

I am also grateful for the support of the universities in which I have spent significant amounts of productive time – in reverse and roughly chronological order, the University of Utah, the Free University of Amsterdam and the University of Groningen (Netherlands), Purdue University (Indiana), Nagoya, Kobe and Hokkaido Universities (Japan), the University of Chicago, Universidad Javeriana (Bogotá), Columbia University, and the University of Miami — and for the major sources of financial support that have been necessary to sustain my research efforts: the National Science Foundation, the National Institutes of Health, the Fulbright Foundation, and the Spencer Foundation.

Salt Lake City
July 1992

For Jacqueline

Part I

Communication processes

Chapter 1

Introduction and perspective

The purpose of this work is to address the problem of how individuals develop through their relationships with others. Both individuals and relationships, in the perspective taken here, are never fully defined; they are always dynamically constituted as part of a process. This process is described from three points of view – *communication, self*, and *culture* – each of which is conceptualized as an aspect of development through relationships.

Communicative connections to other people are fundamental to the workings of the human mind and self, and to the culture that enriches and sustains our spirits and achievements. The study of personal relationships has historically been in the provinces of philosophy, theology, art and literature. Contained in this cultural heritage are eloquent and passionate expressions of what I view as fundamental in relationships, insights I can only remind the reader about with considerably less poetry. More recently, the study of personal relationships has expanded into the late nineteenth-century scholarly upstarts of psychology, communications, sociology, linguistics, anthropology and the newly born field of cognitive science.

I offer this work at a time when the research and writing on personal relationships is already expansive and due to explode with new energy and productivity. It is therefore opportune to unite the historical insights about relationships with the profound contribution of scientific thought in the twentieth century: the concept of the dynamic open system.

The task I set out to accomplish is to describe relationships and their contributions to individual selves that is both humanistic and scientific, both philosophical and psychological, both literary and technical. As a field that bridges both arts and sciences, the study of personal relationships provides both intellectual challenges and deep personal gratification and I hope this is communicated through the writing.

I try to show that an attempt to comprehend the human mind and self that is not grounded in a theory of personal relationships may sprout and grow but is unlikely to yield edible fruit and attractive flowers. Human cognition and the sense of self are fundamentally and originally *relational*.

Relational perspective

Throughout the work I contrast an objectivist perspective on individuals and their development with a relational perspective. The objectivist tradition of Plato and Descartes is the basis of our current scientific methodologies. It is the view that perceptions and cognitions are characterized by their contents, contents that are more or less a direct copy of the way the world is structured. The cognitive contents are believed to be freed from the context in which one learns about the world. I refer to all such objectivist models as discrete state models of communication, self, cognition and culture. This work is one of several recent attempts to examine the implications of an undue reliance on objectivist thinking in various domains of scholarship.

I believe that cognition and perception are not mirrors of reality, but relational processes that reflect the ways in which we have experienced the world. Our initial cognitions and memories are in the form of direct action procedures, as the noted Swiss epistemologist and developmental psychologist Jean Piaget pointed out. Babies know objects because they are graspable and because of the texture, shape and color that can be perceived with the sensory systems of their bodies. Knowledge and memory are therefore encoded cognitively, not as representations of the abstract physical properties of objects, but as the form of the relationship between the individual's perception and action. I trace how such *embodied cognitions* in infancy lead to a sense of self and to the characteristic process of human cognition that never escapes its fundamental relational embodiment, even in the midst of the most abstract thought.

The human mind and sense of self must also be understood as evolving out of the historical process of personal relationship formation between the self and other individuals. Upon close examination, one finds that the workings of the mind and the ways in which we perceive and understand ourselves is remarkably like the form of our personal relationships. The life of the mind is a dialogue, most typically a verbal dialogue, between imagined points of view. The points of view of the mental discourse bear a close resemblance to positions taken by two different people in a discussion, or to the physically embodied positions of individuals engaged in non-verbal communication (as in sport, dance, and battle).

To continue treating the mind as a disembodied relationless computational machine, as an objective thing inside the head, is to be blind to the evidence of one's own cognitive experience. Cartesian objectivity is the embodied mind disguising itself as a ghost; wisps of thought trapped in a net of rules, floating above a sea of troubles.

To bring some life into the mind, life in the form of a bubbling and unpredictable dialogue with emotional force, I propose a continuous process model of communication, one that has general applicability to any form of live interaction between individuals and to the mental discussions we call thought. Suggestions are made throughout the book on applications of the model to many different forms of communication, including between adults, and adults with children, communication within other animal species, and communication between species, such as between humans and animals. I also discuss communication within the self, between various action alternatives and imagined points of view.

As a developmental psychologist I have come to understand that relationships, between people and in the mind, are alive and changing. Relationships develop by identifiable processes and in concert with the individuals that embody them. A theory of the mind and of personal relationships would be incomplete without a consideration of how humans enter into relationships early in life and how they develop through relationships.

Developmental perspective

The perspective taken here is that developmental change arises in everyday communication. The secrets of developmental change are not locked in some inaccessible area of the brain or the cell. Developmental change is as open to inquiry as the mundane encounters between individual and environment, and between individuals and social partners. A workable model of the process of communication between the components of a living system should also be a model of developmental change within that system. Models of communication and thought that do not develop are inadequate to the task of explaining the mind and its origins.

What might such a model of communication and development look like? Developmental biologists have discovered growth hormones, genes that regulate growth processes, genes that are instrumental in producing proteins that create the structure of new developmental forms. Psychologists have discovered pathways of developmental change in mind and body that seem nearly universal, that occur in a wide range of physical and cultural environments. Developmental biologists, however, have not discovered a genetic developmental plan or blueprint for the creation of organisms from zygotes. On the contrary, structure is created when particular genes and particular cells interact with other micro- and macro-biological entities via real embodied processes that take time, that are wet and warm. If any of the components of the genes' or cells' supportive environment are missing or deleterious the result is development that is thwarted or changed, regardless of the abstract contents of the genetic code.

Just because development is patterned, organized and universal does not mean that there is a map, plan or scheme for the creation of those patterns. As developmental biologists[1] and a small number of developmental psychologists[2] have been pointing out, developmental patterning can occur by means of the local interactions of biological components within the individual and between the individual and the environment. Systematic developmental change processes can emerge out of the mutual constraints imposed on components of the individual–environment system as they interact.

These mutual constraints are discussed in this book with respect to the concept of *co-regulation*. Co-regulation occurs whenever individuals' joint actions blend together to achieve a unique and mutually created set of social actions. Co-regulation arises as part of a continuous process of communication, not as the result of an exchange of messages borne by discrete communication signals. Co-regulation is recognized by its spontaneity and creativity and is thus the fundamental source of developmental change. Co-regulation, in social and mental life, allows the individual to participate in the discovery of the unknown and the invention of possibilities. If our genes provide us with any developmental guideline at all it is our ability to enter into co-regulated discourse.

The model of co-regulated communication proposed in this book is one that applies generally to communication between cells and genes, and also to social forms of communication. The model provides a focal point to answer the questions: What are the abstract features of communication that apply to all of its forms? Can these features of the communication process also be generalized to explain development? In particular, how does communication begin in infancy and how do infants develop into participants in a culture of communication?

Cultural perspective

A model of communication, mental life and personal relationships would also be incomplete without a consideration of culture. I do not mean culture only in the sense of belief systems, taboos and customs. Rather, culture is the set of tools, media, communication conventions and beliefs that mediate all of our relational experiences. When we think it is usually in words or in culturally available imagery. When we act alone we are using cultural tools – such as hammers, pens, computers, chairs and shoes – to amplify and extend the limits of the body into wider realms. When we interact with others we employ conventional means of movement and expression.

Cultural systems are not static. Like the mind and like personal relationships they develop, they shrink and expand, they are varied in their relation to the context and purpose of action. Cultures are relational and embodied, expressed as the actions and products of the participants. We can give a computer model of the mind a kind of culture: the programming language, the rules set forth in the expressions of that language, and the machine environment. Yet that mind will never develop in ways even close to what a human infant can do unless its links to its culture are co-regulated. The machine's static environment is a slavish regimen, not a genuine culture. Artificial intelligence will never occur in the form of a clever program of commands. The program must have a open relationship to its operating system and to the environment outside the machine. At the same time, a growing mind is imprisoned and retarded without access to culture in its broadest and most dynamic sense: as a complex system of co-regulated relationships.

About this book

The work described in this book is centered in the field of developmental psychology and is directed primarily to an audience of persons interested in issues of human development in the social context. The work is unique, however, because it weaves together theoretical ideas and empirical findings from a number of other major disciplines. These include social psychology, developmental biology, communications, linguistics, philosophy, cognitive and neural science, ethology, perception, movement studies (including training and performance, athletics, and rehabilitation) and anthropology.

This book proposes a model that encompasses the forms of com-munication in which infants can participate. However, the reader will not find an outline of the specific developmental changes that one might see in infants and children at any given age. This information can be obtained from other sources, including my own text on infant development.[3] There are a number of different accounts of the developmental changes in infant communication; some that focus on gestural, non-verbal or vocal/verbal forms; and some that emphasize the cognitive, emotional or functional features of communication.

I shall have a great deal to say that can be applied to the evaluation of such accounts of developmental stages in infant communicative competence. I also make concrete suggestions for how I think developmental change might best be conceptualized and studied. It is my view that a listing of developmental changes in infant communicative performance is not a theory of development unless it is also founded upon a generative process by which such changes come about. In this work, I provide the process, leaving for the future the work of evaluating whether the process can explain the observed data of communicative development in all its detail. Thus, I am not trying to prove a theory. My goal is a more modest one of making a theoretical model plausible by the following means.

I use a form of philosophical analysis in which the meanings of scientific metaphors are examined for their consistency within the technical language system used in developmental psychology. I apply ethnographic and historical analysis to examine the values implicit in the Western scientific culture as part of the heritage of ideas about communication during the last two centuries. I provide many examples of the type of continuous systemic communication process that forms the core of the theoretical model. I present concrete models, based on the theory, for the workings of communication in relationships, selves and cultures. Finally, I generate some implications for research and practice that seem to follow from my point of view.

Contrary to the tradition in psychology, I will not be bolstering my arguments with quantitative data and statistical calculations. The reader will find many references to psychological research using the traditional inferential methods, including research of my own. I am more concerned in this volume with a critical examination of what counts as data when one wants to preserve the dynamic integrity of the system under study. I shall focus on finding a consistent language with which to describe phenomena that are not fixed but fluid, not objectively specifiable but creatively emergent.

I recognize the difficulty of creating a science of relationships that is linguistically consistent and systemically open to the currents of thought and multiplicity of research methods available at the end of the twentieth century. In the novel of monastic intrigue during the Middle Ages in Europe, *The Name of the Rose*, by Umberto Eco, I found that the character most like the spirit of the last decade of the twentieth century – and the message of this book – was not the scientifically minded sleuth brother William nor the faithfully accurate reporter Adzo, but Salvatore the deformed polyglot.

Salvatore could not keep his tongues separate, his sentences were amalgamated from many languages, none of which he knew well enough to use on its own. He was painful to behold and difficult to comprehend. Was Salvatore sweeping a profound ignorance under the carpet of his glib patois? In a time that presaged the myth of the encompassing knowledge of Leonardo da Vinci, was Salvatore mocking the Renaissance ideal of universal thought, seen from the writer's historical vantage? Or was Salvatore a successful political strategist, able to make himself understood to many people at the linguistic crossroads of medieval Europe while avoiding words, both sacred and profane, that could be used to condemn and to kill? The brutalities of war and inquisition that Salvatore had witnessed in his life were undescribable in any single ordinary language.

Perhaps what Salvatore knew was unutterable in the culture of his time: that there is no single truth, no one correct means of expression, only a fluidity of cultural experience in which one can survive by grasping the bits and pieces of convention that surface in the turbulence of the living process. The myth of scientific objectivity is the modern inquisitory power that continues to repress this insight. The attempt in this and other related works to offer a non-Cartesian science may be seen by some as heretical.

Notes

1. The *American Journal of Anatomy*, one of the major developmental biology journals that publishes on embryological development, has just recently been renamed *Developmental Dynamics*. The purpose of the journal is to 'emphasize the dynamic and complex controls that regulate pattern formation in development' (quoted from a recent advertisement for the journal).
2. Butterworth (in press); Fentress (1976); Fogel (1992); Fogel & Thelen (1987); Oyama (1985; 1989); Sameroff (1984); Thelen (1989); Thelen & Fogel (1989); Thelen, Kelso & Fogel (1987); Thelen & Ulrich (1991).
3. Fogel (1991).

Chapter 2

The origins of communication, self, and culture

Laura, aged 12 years, informed her parents during the evening meal 'I never want to go back to school ... ever!'. Despite a lengthy discussion that evening, Laura could admit to little more than a stubborn unhappiness. Although certain of little else besides her determination to avoid school, her parents decided to allow her to stay at home the next day, giving them the opportunity to talk more with Laura and to telephone her teacher.

At the next evening meal, Laura's mother told her of the teacher's suspicion of Laura's disagreement with her best friend. They had come back from lunch the day before last with an icy silence between their desks, an obvious contrast to their more usual exchanges of glances, smiles and secret notes. Laura nearly exploded with the tale she had held inside for the past day and amid tears explained to her parents what had happened: a broken confidence of a shared intimacy, a chain of unbearable moments of shame hearing other girls talking about her most personal thoughts, and most of all her disappointment in the trust she had placed in her friend. In the ensuing conversation, feelings were aired and soothed, strategies were offered, and Laura returned to school armed with things to say.

One of the developmental tasks of children in their early teens in the Western world is the establishment of bonds of intimacy with others.[1] It is a world in which personal secrets and revelations occupy long hours of talk, in which acceptance of one's own and others' inner feelings dissolve suddenly into piercing judgements and just as quickly coalesce back into acceptance. In this world one's personal experience pours into another's consciousness, a flow of images as water from a broken dam, in the form of a story narrative.

The teller usually doesn't just say 'I'm sad,' or 'I'm in love.' These messages are communicated as the narrative unfolds. A meeting is described or every word of a telephone conversation is reported. Comments are added. The story is embellished and made dramatic. The listener asks leading questions or conspires in the drama with well-timed sighs and exclamations.

The listener takes the floor and reveals a related personal story. There is more elaboration, more discussion, and more intimacy.

This example highlights the themes developed in this book, themes related to communication and the self. Laura's case is an example of breakdown and repair of communication between Laura and her parents, and between Laura and her friend. Laura at first refuses to impart the information that her parents might need to help her through the crisis. That information is obtained from the teacher and it proves to be a key to unlock the gate to the information that Laura later relates.

Guiding principles

The relationships between communication, self, and culture

Communication illuminates the self's relationship to others. When individuals communicate, the actions, ideas and feelings of the individual are made known to others. Individuals define themselves to others via communication.[2] In some cases the individual is quite clear about who they are and what they believe, but in other cases, the very process of acting and speaking helps the individual toward increased self understanding. Laura's narrative is related to personal feelings and social relationships: it is about the boundaries between self and other, what Laura knows and what others know, and what they can and may tell each other. As she tells her stories to others and observes the effect of her stories on them, she understands herself and her relationship to others in new ways.

Communication that leads to renewed self-understanding is a creative co-construction of the participants. Laura's telling of her encounter with her friend seems to explode into a fully formed story of anger and disappointment, of confidence and betrayal. That's not how it actually happened, however. Laura needed to be assured of her audience's interest and sympathy before she even began to talk. Her parents' patience, the efforts they made to find out more from the teacher, and no doubt their expressed concern at Laura's sadness was what their daughter needed in order to unburden herself. Thus, even before the telling, Laura's tale is partly shaped by the perceived receptivity of the audience.

Laura's story was not completely formed before it was told; few personal stories are complete, save the well-worn tales heard in political speeches. In the actual telling Laura rose to the occasion. Supported not only by her parents' empathy, and also by their leading questions, nods, laughs and comments, Laura created her story as she told it. Her creation was partly spurred by her own experience and ability as a storyteller, and also partly attributable to the inventiveness of the audience in detecting ambiguities and following up on particularly meaningful parts of the unfolding narrative. No doubt Laura would have told it differently to another girl friend or to the teacher.

Laura comes to understand herself better as she composes the text of her story. She learns about her feelings and what sets them off, she is able to examine the meaning of friendship and how this particular friend relates to her values and needs. She could not have done this in the same way without the contribution of her parents. For one thing, they gave Laura the freedom to explore her feelings in an emotionally safe situation. More importantly however, they contributed concretely to the telling by giving Laura tools for self-examination: questions to probe with, narrative forms around which to bind experiences.

The parents were also creating something with their daughter. On the first evening they were unable to induce Laura to speak. How could they help her? What should they do next? Laura's pain challenged them to think of new ways to open communication with her. Even as Laura began to tell her story, it is unlikely that either parent was following a prepared script for being a good parent. Although their actions were based in part on personal goals and cultural values, their questions and responses were creative compositions. Laura was not weaving her own story, nor were her parents acting out a parental role. The story that emerged they created together.[3]

Communication creates knowledge. If Laura knew in advance how her story would come out, would there be much need for telling it? Based on prior discussions with her parents, Laura could predict that they would be responsive to her and that usually such talks ended on a note of relief, if not complete resolution. But could she have predicted exactly how she would understand herself after the conversation? Would she have known in advance what her parents would say?

For some people the answer to such questions might be 'yes.' Often, when we can foresee the outcomes of a social interaction with someone, it is usually with someone we wish to avoid. We learn nothing new about ourselves or about them, we don't enjoy the encounter, we perceive it as boring, frustrating or painful. In some types of relationship pathologies, as in dysfunctional family systems, ritualized and rigid interaction patterns become the norm and require intervention to restore their creative innovation.[4]

Creativity in social exchanges leads to changes in self-understanding and to enhanced feelings of closeness to the partner.[5] One might call such interactions playful in the sense that there is shared agreement to indulge in the freedom to explore the topic at hand. The topic need not be a happy one, but it might be. Feelings of closeness to others enhances our willingness to do things together, our sense of belonging to a partner, a family or a community.

Communication depends on community, the existence of a culture. Part of what we call culture is the set of conventions that define the type of discourse possible between individuals.[6] The culture of communication includes tools used for communication: the 'software' of language, gestures and symbols and the 'hardware' of books, radios, musical instruments, computers and telephones.[7] The culture of communication also regulates who can talk to whom and what can be discussed. Laura might tell her story differently to her teacher than to her parents in part because they are different individuals, and in part because such intimacies have a different cultural significance at home or in school.

The culture of communication influences the form of the narrative. In some cultures like Laura's, young people are permitted to engage in playful discourse with adults in which the boundaries of status are minimized. Laura can tell her story in her own manner, and is encouraged to be inventive and verbally skilled. In other cultures, status differences bar children from speaking freely to adults.[8] Culture regulates whether discourse is permitted between the genders or only within; whether topics such as spirituality, sexuality, fear, desire or uncertainty are allowed.

Laura's story of her friendship problems is also woven from a rich array of culturally accepted narratives related to childhood growing pains. These cultural narratives are available from adults or in books in the form of standard moral tales: Bible stories, fairy tales, popular children's literature, TV shows and movies. Children's self-understanding is enhanced by identification with the characters in the story, perhaps through creating an imaginary private narrative dialogue with the characters, or perhaps through discussion of the story with peers or adults.[9]

Culture reflects the history of the community. The tools of communication and the rules that regulate its occurrence have been maintained over time as a historical tradition. Cultural history can be very brief, as in a clothing fad by which participants communicate their membership in the group, or it can be relatively stable like language forms and national myths that can last for centuries.

Assumptions of this work

In this book I address the problem of how the micro-culture of the parent–infant relationship allows the infant to partake of the macro-culture of the larger community. Since parents are already members of the macro-culture and act with their infants in ways specified by the community for childcare, the micro-culture is not entirely independent of the macro-culture. Although all scholars of human development acknowledge the parents' role in the child's acquisition of actions that are acceptable in the macro-culture, this book offers a different view of how that happens.

First, I assume that children develop as part of their everyday interactions within the family. Culture does not impose itself on children via broad categories like 'right' and 'wrong.' Culturally accepted behavior arises spontaneously as part of children's interactions with others.

Second, I assume that culture does not exist as a codified set of rules, procedures and tools that children acquire and then apply to particular situations. Children acquire patterns of action and thought that work for them in particular real-life situations, when alone and in the company of others. Children discover those patterns of acting and thinking via their own activity with others; they are not explicitly learning, nor are they following, rules.

Third, I suggest that 'rule-like' behavior – such as language, social manners, learning to do arithmetic – emerges from a set of constraints available from the child's transactions with members of the community.[10] None of these constraints is an explicit rule. Rather, given the social constraints (I get into trouble if I do X. I will be understood if I say Y. I will feel better if I move like Z.) and the inherent structural constraints of the human body and brain, cultural activity will emerge via the child's own creative solutions to everyday problems.

The unique contribution of this book is my tracing the roots of communication, self and culture to their earliest origins. While most scholars begin such a search after the child acquires language (the most recognizable and historically significant cultural tool), I suggest that cultural communication originates much earlier, in the pre-verbal period.

Defining individuals

The relationships between communication, the self and the cultural community are fundamental to any understanding of our human nature. Certainly these three terms must be at the heart of any enlightened psychology of the human mind. People can only be comprehended in the context of their community, in the historical time in which they live, and in relation to the forms of communication by which they express themselves.[11] But are individual actions such as an athletic achievement or a musical skill done independently of communication, self and culture? Is a record-setting speed in a running race a purely personal achievement?

Self. In setting a racing speed record, talent and personal effort are important factors, but it is impossible to measure the scope of this achievement outside the historical and current community of runners. One's 'personal best' is always measured against some social comparison.

Culture. Running is a culturally constructed means of self-expression. People engage in forms of athletics as members of a community of athletes who define the rules of the sport, provide the tools for its execution (race tracks, running shoes, clothing, stop-watches). How far and fast one runs depends not only on the shape and strength of the body, but also on whether one runs barefoot, in leathers and cleats, or in computer-engineered ergonomic running shoes made of synthetic materials.

Communication. It is hard to imagine any kind of race without communication. One's pace and place on the track is determined by the speed and location of the other runners. Even if one runs alone, communication is an inescapable part of running. The runner may talk about running with others, or may have learned to run better from a coach or teammate. Running as a form of self-expression is enhanced by communication, communication is enhanced by talking about running with others who care about it and both self and communication are enhanced by the historical continuity of a cultural community that promotes and elaborates the activity.

Communication and development

This book is about developmental change in the relationship between communication, self and culture. In particular, I try to answer the following questions: How do infants during their first years of life become participants in a culture? How do they acquire culturally acceptable communication skills? When and how does the self emerge? I believe that communication, self and culture are present and inseparable from the beginning of the life course. If this is so, it leads to further questions. What is the form of communication, self and culture in a 3-day-old infant, in a 3-month-old, in a 3-year-old? How does this trinity evolve developmentally? These topics form the core of this book.

Unfortunately, many scholars and clinicians who deal with developmental change think that just because communication, self and culture are inseparably related for Laura and for athletes it does not necessarily mean that such a unity exists from the beginning of the individual's life. These entities are believed to shape children's action and thinking only later, after a sufficient period of acculturation, after the biological needs and functions are met and relegated to the background of cultural existence, after the psychological self is freed from the tremors and longings of the infantile flesh.

This means that some of my narrative will be created in response to and in interaction with these opposing viewpoints. I believe that many of these scholars have forgotten that action and thought in adults are lived in a real physical body, not only in the mind. Early infancy is important to our understanding of development because it is a period in which the body is salient, its limits obvious, its desires nearly overwhelming. All later action, all manifestations of culture including the highest forms of art, are set within the context of the body as much as they are set within the context of the society. What we can learn from babies is a more balanced view of humankind in which spirit and matter commingle to achieve recognizable forms of civilization.

Communication, self, and culture in infancy

I will present research evidence suggesting that infants are active participants in a cultural system from the beginning, that newborns have a sense of self, and that communication with the environment exists from conception. I also intend to show that the dynamic and creative aspects of interpersonal relationships and of self-understanding that were discussed in the Laura story can be seen in some form in early infancy. Indeed, it is the creativity of interpersonal transactions from which development springs.

The assumption of the unity of communication, self and culture in early life solves some of the persistent intellectual problems that have puzzled developmental psychologists for some time. If you assume that the infant has no sense of self and does not partake of culture, you are left with the problem of how to get culture into the baby, and how a self emerges from an infantile, autistic-like state.[12] If communication is a tool for revealing the self, and if it partakes of a cultural system, how can a pre-cultural infant have a self? Doesn't the self have to await the infant's acquisition of cultural forms of communication?

In my perspective, these problems are reframed. I ask, for example, how mature forms of cultural communication evolve from their rudimentary origins. In what sense is culture available to a newborn infant? How might a newborn's experience of itself differ from a 2-year-old's or from an adolescent's search for personal meaning and values? Do these early forms of communication, self and culture embody the seeds of later forms, or do later forms arise in discontinuous jumps as new factors are added developmentally?

Regardless of how one answers these questions, I begin with the assumption that these concepts – communication, self and culture – are not separate entities. Each one is a facet, a partial portrait of the developing individual. I make the claim that each of these facets develops in relationship to the other: each facet defines the other, each facet creates the other. Infants learn to communicate as they define themselves. They create culture for themselves as they communicate with more culturally skilled individuals. They define others in the process of defining themselves. Development arises from being a participant in a dynamic discourse with other people.

Example 1

In this example, Paul (a British baby who is 6 months and 19 days old) sits alone in the living room of his home. He begins to cry as his mother enters the room.

> *Mother:* Oh, now what's up, hey? Oh dear, oh dear, what's the matter? [She picks Paul up.]
> *Mother:* Are you thirsty, is that what it is? Do you want a drink? [She goes and picks up his bottle and offers it to him. He refuses it and continues crying.]
> *Mother:* Hungry? Are you? Do you want something to eat? No? Sleepy then, do you want to go to sleep? [She puts him in his pram but he continues to cry. She picks him up again and walks about comforting him. She stops at the

window. Paul apparently looks out but continues crying. Mother tries to attract his attention and then to direct it.]

Mother: Look, there's a pussycat, can you see him? Do you know what pussycats say? Do you? They say 'miaow' don't they, yes, of course they do. [Paul stops crying during this speech.]

Mother: There, that's better, down you go then. [She places him back on the floor.]

This example[13] has some obvious similarities to the example of Laura. The child is upset about something and the parent can only guess the nature of his problem. Paul is sitting in the middle of the room with no visible cues about what he wants or needs. Perhaps Paul does not have a particular want or need. Perhaps like Laura there is a non-specific desire to communicate with another person, expressed as a general malaise. Perhaps Paul, like Laura, is not entirely certain about what the problem really is.

The parents play a similar role in these two examples. They operate from a state of relative uncertainty. The child is distressed, but with no visible cause. They must proceed with some guesswork, thinking about probable causes for the upset and perhaps doing some further investigation. Laura's parents called the teacher. Paul's mother might have checked the diaper or looked at the clock to see the time since the last meal.

Thus, both parties enter the discourse with incomplete information. Continuation of the discourse is based upon the subtle changes in the cues given by each partner. If Paul had increased the intensity of his cry, mother might have taken other steps. As it was, his gradual calming allowed her to settle Paul back down with his toys on the floor. For both Paul and Laura, the result was at least a partial resolution of the distress. In what sense can we consider this an example of communication, self and culture from the infant's point of view?

Communication occurs because the infant's cry serves as a source of information for the mother to enter the room and to begin asking questions about the source of the distress. The mother behaves *as if* the child were actually trying to communicate something to her, although it is highly probable that Paul's cry arises more from his own distress than from his intention to communicate about it.[14]

The mother's behavior is also a source of information for the infant, since after a while Paul calms down in her company. The question here is: if Paul doesn't obtain any information from his mother's words, what sort of information is he picking up? From the description of this example, it is not easy to answer this question. In later chapters will review research studies showing that Paul is likely to acquire information from the way his mother moves his body when she picks him up and moves him, from the way in which she touches Paul, and from the tone and cadence of her voice rather than from the meaning of her words. Some other examples may make this more clear.

Example 2

In this example, a mother reaches out to help pull her 4-month-old baby into a sitting position.

> The child is on his back on the floor and the mother takes hold of his hands, pulling gently. She pauses expectantly and the child strenuously pulls himself upward against the hands, using his arms and legs to effect this. The mother then completes the infant's actions and pulls him to a sitting position.[15]

The type of information echanged between mother and infant can be seen more easily in this example. Here mother and infant are communicating about how much force each has to exert to achieve a sitting position, and about when one or the other has to do the pulling. At first both mother and infant increase the contraction of their arm muscles and pull together. Then the infant's effort increases relative to the mother's, after which the mother pulls harder, and finally the pulling of both tapers off as the infant gets into a sitting position.

The information in Example 2 is in the continuously varying level of force intensity as a function of time, as shown in Figure 2.1. In this case, information about how much force to apply can be obtained from the kinematics of the action, that is, the time course of intensity changes. In the example, as the mother feels the infant begin to exert himself, she reduces her effort in exact proportion to his increase and as the infant's effort wanes, mother compensates by pulling harder. The result is that the total amount of force exerted by both of the partners is a smoothly changing function of time (Figure 2.2).

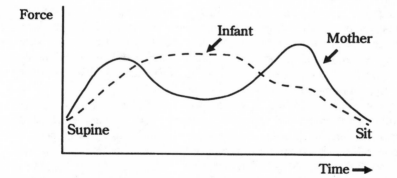

Figure 2.1 The force exerted by mother and infant in a pull-to-sit episode is shown as a continuously changing function of time. In this example, mother and infant are continuously exerting force, but the relative amount waxes and wanes in a co-regulated manner. Infants can perceive the self-generated contribution to the force when the curves diverge.

In this book, the concept of *co-regulation* will refer to the dynamic balancing act by which a smooth social performance is created out of the continuous mutual adjustments of action between partners. In co-regulated communication, information is created between people in such a way that the information changes as the interaction unfolds. Co-regulated communication is created as it happens, its process and outcome is partially unpredictable.

As in the other example, neither mother nor infant knows in advance the precise outcome of this pulling episode. Perhaps they know that the infant will end up sitting, but the way in which that is to be achieved is determined in the process of communication. Co-regulated communication is not ritualized, perfunctory or over-controlled by one or the other partner. Each time the infant is pulled up a different dynamic balance is struck. If on the other hand, the mother exerted a constant force without regard to the infant's input, the interaction would be imposed on the infant who would not be a participating communicative partner.

Self. The pull-to-sit example also suggests a way in which pre-verbal, pre-conceptual infants might experience the self. Certainly a 4-month-old infant cannot recognize herself in the mirror, nor be self-reflective, nor have even a rudimentary conceptual understanding of the self.[16] Her sense of self is rooted in the body and its relationship to the surround. Infants of this age can easily feel their own muscular exertion in relation to the mother's and they can detect their own movements in relation to their spatial location. The self is not unitary, but always perceived as related to something.[17]

I will propose in this book that the original sense of self arises from one's physical and social relationships.[18] In Figure 2.1, the infant becomes aware of self-exertion and self-movement at the times when the two curves diverge. In the first segment, when mother and infant are pulling together with the same

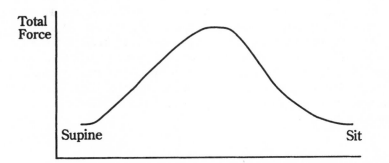

Figure 2.2 The summation of the curves in Figure 2.1. When the forces of the partners are added together, the result is a smooth function of time. Thus, even though the individuals are changing their own activity, the dyad appears to be seamlessly co-regulated.

force, the infant cannot distinguish self from other. As soon as his exertion exceeds that of the mother, or falls below that of the mother, there is a heightened awareness of precisely those aspects of the interaction that are in his control or not in his control. In other words, the infant becomes aware of self in relationship to another person, as a *dialogue* between self and other.

Looking back to the example of Paul we might presume that he and his mother had a co-regulated communication and that as a result Paul could experience the self. The ways in which Paul's mother picked him up and carried him probably led to interaction dynamics such as those in the pull-to-sit example. Most salient for Paul, however, is the mother's speech: not her words, but the changes over time in the intensity, pitch and timing of her speech.

Go back to Example 1 and try to read it imagining that you are talking to a real baby. The speech you are thinking about probably has a lot of changes from low to high pitch or from loud to soft intensity. It is lilting, somewhat musical in parts, and abrupt and staccato in other parts. Research evidence suggests that infants are acutely sensitive to this type of information contained in speech. In the company of infants adults from all over the world tailor their voice to make these characteristic speech patterns, called 'motherese.'[19]

In Example 1, changes in the mother's speech dynamics probably interfaced with changes in the infant's cry dynamics – intensity, pitch and timing – in such a way that the cry was modulated at the same time that the mother's voice changed. Imagine the difference between the staccato, 'Hungry? Are you? Want something to eat? No?,' spoken while Paul was crying, and the more sweetly flowing, soothing sound of 'Look, there's a pussycat, can you see him?,' spoken while Paul was calming down and stopping his cry.

If this episode was co-regulated, as I suppose it might have been, the mother's speech does not directly calm the infant. Rather, mother and infant mutually alter each other's vocal dynamics in a creative, exploratory manner. The infant, through such discourse dynamics, may begin to sense the boundaries of self-control over cry vocalizations as he perceives the sounds he feels himself make in relation to those he hears but does not make himself. In effect, he is able to use his perception of the similarity of the mother's changes in her vocalization with respect to his own as a tool for self-calming and self-monitoring.

Example 3

I suggest that even continuously changing forms of information in communication are inherently cultural, as suggested by this final example in which a 1-year-old infant hands an object to the mother. Infants begin taking objects from their caregivers earlier in the first year, but have a harder time giving away the prizes that they have won. The series of photographs in Figure 2.3 shows Andrew, one of the American infants that my students and I videotaped playing with his mother at weekly intervals since the first month of life. In the photos, Andrew is seen at 1 year. Note that the images were made with two cameras superimposed using a split-screen generator. The mother, who is to the right of the infant in the right-hand portion of the frame, is pictured in the left-hand portion of the frame. In our collection of tapes, this is the first time this infant voluntarily released an object into his mother's hand.

Andrew's action has two separate motor components. First, his arm extends (frames 1–6) and then he releases the object (frames 7–10). In past weeks, Andrew has extended his arm many times toward his mother without releasing the object. Once Andrew's arm is extended his hand remains relatively stationary and gradually opens as mother's hand moves underneath his hand. The fork gently leaves Andrew's hand as it is pulled only by the slightest contact with the mother's moving palm.

This object release, therefore, is not entirely due to Andrew's initiative. Since the child does not actually drop the object into the mother's hand and the mother does not actually take hold of the object, the object transfer seems to be jointly constructed by both, a genuinely co-regulated activity. Thus, *communication* is present in this example in the form of shared information about the position of the object relative to each person's hand and body, and the intensity and timing of hand opening and closing.

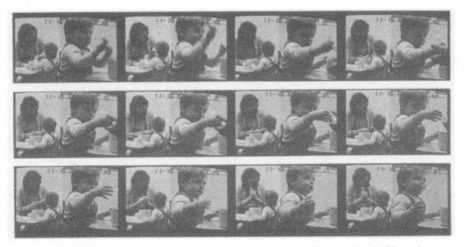

Figure 2.3 First instance of a successful object transfer. (*Source*: Bloch, H. and Bertenthal, B. *Sensory-Motor Organizations and Development in Infancy and Early Childhood*, 1990, reprinted by permission of Kluwer Academic Publishers.)

The *self* also makes an appearance, as Andrew no doubt feels the differences between his own hand opening and his own movement of the fork in relation to those movements of the fork for which he is not responsible. Indeed, the relative slowness of this sequence, lasting almost seven seconds, may assist Andrew in perceiving the relationship between his own and others' actions. Andrew's continuing gaze at the object after he releases it, his hand poised in space as if still holding on to the object, suggests that although the physical contact is broken the infant may perceive the object's motion as still related to *his own* activity. This is similar to an adult's follow through upon the release of a bowling ball or after hitting a golf ball.

Culture. There are several ways in which culture is relevant to the infant's actions as seen in Example 3. The transfer of objects in the form of an offering gesture (as opposed to just grabbing the object from the infant), the type of object transferred, and the smile in the final frame are the most obvious cultural aspects of this sequence.

In the entire sequence in Figure 2.3, the infant is for the first time showing a culturally accepted way of transferring objects, that is, by signalling the offer with an extended arm and then letting it go when mother accepts it.[20] An activity is cultural if the form of the action is *similar enough to an accepted community standard* that it can be *recognized and interpreted by other members of the community.* Earlier the infant would extend his arm but not release the object.

There are other aspects of this sequence that are also cultural by this definition. For example, sitting in a chair at a table, remaining there for the entire fifteen minutes during which the videotaping took place, using an object that has a cultural origin (a fork), and participating in cultural play with an adult. We could find communities in which none of these activities would be considered culturally acceptable for infants.

Another aspect of culture goes beyond the form of the action to include the timing of the performance of the action with respect to other actions. From the perspective of culture, it is important that Andrew smiled at a particular time in the sequence of activity that a member of the culture, the mother, can recognize as appropriate. There may be many reasons why Andrew smiled at that moment, perhaps as an expression of accomplishment or to return the mother's smile. Some evidence from studies of the development of infant gesture and expression of emotion suggest that Andrew's smile could be a spontaneous action that results from an inner feeling of completion and that Andrew at 1 year may not be aware of the communicative function and meaning of his smile to other people.[21] On the other hand, even at the age of 1 year, infants smile more frequently and with broader smiles in the company of other people, suggesting that some types of smiles are already cultural acts.[22]

Regardless of why Andrew smiled, the fact is that the smile occurred at just the point in this sequence when a Caucasian adult in North American society might expect it to happen. *An activity is cultural when one does it at the 'right' time and place*, regardless of whether one means it or not, or whether one even understands why one is doing it. Children and adults frequently participate in culturally accepted activities without understanding them. For example, children learn to sing songs even when some of the words and refrains do not make sense to them.

People do not need a shared understanding or a common sense of purpose in order to be members of a community. However, they must at least share the means of communication in order to determine if their understanding is indeed shared. Community members can differ in their goals and ideas so long as they can communicate using commonly accepted means. Arguments and fights are typically conducted in culturally specified ways – wrestling, duels, debates, arguments – and a good deal of communication between parents and children involves negotiations of disagreements and miscommunications.

Like grammar in a language, there is a culturally acceptable sequence of actions, a cultural *frame*, that assists members of a community to recognize the possible meaning of another's behavior. If Andrew had smiled at the beginning of the sequence shown in Figure 2.3, this smile might have had a different meaning to his mother – a desire to play, a request for cooperation – than the smile that follows the sequence.

An activity is cultural if it is done according to a shared intensity-by-time contour. Culture defines how loudly or sharply a child or an adult may speak to each other, whether drawn-out affectionate tonal patterns are permitted or discouraged, and whether adults should enter into co-regulated 'dances' with infants around particular childrearing issues.

For example, the soothing sequence in Example 1 would not have occurred in this way in a different community. In tribal cultures living in warm climates, infants are rarely physically separated from adults and they enjoy nearly continuous skin-to-skin contact day and night.[23] For a mother in the Fore tribe in New Guinea[24] the thought of leaving her infant alone in a room (Example 1) would be as bizarre as an urban mother who remains topless and carries her baby around on her hip at all times, such as to work or to the grocery store.

It is important and culturally accepted for the Western infant to cry loudly and for several minutes or more in order to attract and hold adult attention. The Fore babies rarely cry because during their close physical contact with the adult, the slightest movements can be detected by the mother who acts quickly to relieve the infant. Among the Fore, and other groups with similar infant care patterns, loud and prolonged infant crying is not culturally acceptable. One does not expect to hear more than a rustle and a fussy noise before the infant is relieved.

In early infancy, neither the British baby in Example 1 nor the Fore baby have any idea that their actions are communicative. Yet, from the early weeks of life, the intensity-by-time contours of their crying have a culturally specific sound: one cries long and loud, the other does not. Not only are their actions contoured in culturally recognizable ways, their budding senses of self are different. With a heightened level of crying, the experiences of self-movement and self-action are different since the Western infant must get more aroused in relation to the adult than the Fore infant.

From this general perspective, infants are participants in a cultural community right from birth, and perhaps earlier. The tools and devices of infant care (cradles, cribs, diapers and the like), what they eat or what their mothers eat (prenatally or postnatally if breast feeding), how and when they eat, the sights and sounds to which they are exposed, and the ways in which infants can be talked to, touched, held and smiled at: these form the culture of early childcare. They are part of the history of the community, and by virtue of co-regulated communication, become incorporated into the communication process and the actions of the infant.

Proposals for a relational perspective on infant development

By way of summarizing the points of this chapter, I list below a number of proposals that guide my own thinking about early human development. These proposals will be elaborated in the remainder of this book.

Proposal 1. Culture and self can arise from spontaneous co-regulated communicative activity well before the individual is self-consciously cognizant of culture or self. Communication, self and culture arise in the infant's experiences of the body, via feeling and movement. Communication, self, and culture are just different ways of talking about relationships, different points of view on the same phenomenon.

Proposal 2. No human action is acultural. Cultural frames permeate infant activity from before birth and hold people in their grip for the entire life course. The forms of human cultural action change developmentally. The cultural experience of infants is different from later childhood in part because of the differences in the patterning of infant care and childcare in the same community.

Proposal 3. Communication has the possibility of enhancing the perception of the self. Variability across individuals in their experience of the self depends on the form of their communication with others, its cultural basis and the extent to which it is co-regulated. Developmental changes in the sense of self emerge from changes in the infant's body and brain, changes that themselves arise from communication with others.

Proposal 4. Human developmental changes – in the self, in action and skill, in communication and cognition, in motivation and emotion – originate in the dynamically changing relationship between communication, self and culture. Human developmental change springs from social relationships and their cultural frames. Culture is not static any more than action or the self. Culture changes for us as we develop and it changes historically over generations.

Notes

1. Damon (1989).
2. Mead (1934).
3. Fogel (1992); Fogel, Nwokah & Karns (in press); Lock (1980).
4. Rigidity and spontaneity will be discussed in Chapters 6 and 7 as characteristics of relationships.
5. Fogel, Nwokah & Karns (in press).
6. Mead (1934); Tooby & Cosmides (1990); Valsiner (1989).
7. Vygotsky (1978).
8. Befu (1985); Kojima (1985); Morsebach (1980); Valsiner (1989).
9. Bettleheim (1976); Dyk (1938); Sindell (1974); Sommerville (1983).
10. A more complete definition of constraints and rules is given in Chapter 2.
11. Gilligan (1978); Kegan (1982); Mead (1934); Rogoff (1990); Valsiner (1989); Vygotsky (1978).
12. The idea of infantile autism, a lack of consciousness at birth, originates with Freud (1926). Later psychoanalytically oriented thinkers who were able to rely on their own observations and on the results of infancy research dispelled this notion and connected the infant to the environment via perception and action. These thinkers include Spitz (1965), Stern (1985) and Winnicott (1971), although other recent psychoanalysts retain the autism notion (cf. Mahler, 1968).
13. Lock (1980, pp. 50–1).
14. Kaye (1982); Lock (1980); Newson (1977)
15. Clarke (1978, p. 246).
16. Harter (1983); Lewis & Brooks-Gunn (1979)
17. This will be explained in detail in Chapter 6.
18. The perceptual and motoric aspects of solitary activity also contribute to a sense of self (Butterworth, 1992; Stern, 1985). I argue in Chapters 6, 7 and 10, however, that even solitary activity for infants is embedded in a social and cultural context. Most infants are surrounded by cultural tools and by caregivers who regulate their access to the physical environment.
19. Fernald *et al.* (1989); Papousek, Papousek & Bornstein (1985).
20. At least this is the first time a successful object transfer occurs in our weekly video recordings of this mother and child.
21. Sroufe (1979).
22. Dedo (1991); Jones & Raag (1989).
23. Sorensen (1979); Super (1981); Valsiner (1989).
24. Sorensen (1979).

Chapter 3

The communication system: co-regulation and framing

The usual manner of thinking about communication is in terms of a sender and a receiver exchanging information in the form of signals. We know that communication has taken place if the receiver changes its behavior following the transmission of the signal.[1] This definition also applies to physical communication, such as when a moving ball strikes a stationary one, communicating information in the form of momentum and direction of travel. The stationary ball leaps into action following the impact.

Biological and social communication can also be described in this way. Communicative information travels between neurons in the central nervous system via chemical and electrical signals. One dog approaches or avoids another depending upon the position and movement of the first dog's tail and ears. People communicate information to each other via language. In the process, the receiver's feelings, thoughts and behavior may change as a result of that information.

Most forms of communication are not simply one-way transmissions. Typically, the sender and receiver change roles as communication proceeds. As a result of striking the stationary ball, the moving ball experiences a reaction that changes its own speed and direction. Most biological communication occurs as a series of exchanges of signals going in both directions between the sender and receiver. Thus, even the simplest forms of communication are composed of sequences of signals, exchanged between communicating partners, occurring over some determined period of time.

But does this way of talking about communication – in terms of senders, receivers, and signals – reflect what actually transpires in a social situation? A glance back to the examples given in Chapter 2 suggests that the answer to this question would be negative.

Recall the object exchange sequence shown in Figure 2.3. At any moment in this interaction sequence, it seems impossible to determine who is the 'sender' and who is the 'receiver.' In fact, the actions of both participants are changing continuously. And what is the 'signal' in this case? If both the mother's and infant's hands are moving at the same time and the movement is continuous, how can we isolate segments of the movement and call them communication 'signals?'[2]

On the other hand, information is certainly transmitted or exchanged between the partners since they manage to act cooperatively. Their hands meet at a particular spatial location, the object is actually transferred between them, an act has been performed that requires the participation of both. Thus, information is exchanged even though we cannot clearly divide the roles of the partners into sender/receiver, nor can we identify any specific signals.

Senders, receivers and signals are terms that apply to *discrete state communication systems*. In such systems, the partners can be in only one of several clearly defined discretely different states, for example, positive and negative. In addition, while one partner is sending a message, the other must be in a state of readiness to receive the message. The partners cannot both be transmitting messages at the same time. One listens while the other talks. Messages have information content that may change the behavior of the receiver, but the receiver's change only becomes apparent when that individual takes the role of the sender. Exchanges of written communications such as letters, or formal oral communications such as debates, have this form.

As a participant in such forms of communication one often feels constrained. Why? Because there is no opportunity to give feedback to the speaker during the speech, no opportunity to interrupt or to nod in agreement, no opportunity to judge how the audience is reacting in order to be able to monitor and adjust your own speech.

Most forms of social communication are *continuous process communication systems*, rather than discrete state systems. In a continuous process system both partners are continuously active and continuously engaged in the communication. There are opportunities to modify the actions of partners as they occur, without the need to wait until they are finished.

One of the founders of modern research on human communication was the anthropologist, Ray Birdwhistell. Birdwhistell was one of the first to use filmed records of social behavior as the basis for scientific study. Because of the complexity and continuously varying nature of social interactions, films and videotapes have since become part of the communication researcher's basic tool kit. After thousands of hours of tedious and difficult transcriptions of social behavior made from film, Birdwhistell concluded that an individual

does not originate communication; he participates in it. Communication as a system, then, is not to be understood on a simple model of action and reaction, however complexly stated. As a system, it is to be comprehended on the transactional level.[3]

In other words, when one examines communication in some detail, it is nearly impossible to say who initiates a communication, nor who responds to whom.

Nevertheless, people frequently talk about social interactions as if it were possible to define social roles clearly and social actions as unambiguous signals. What is the meaning of a smile? From the perspective of a discrete state model of smiling there are many different meanings of a smile, each discretely different from the others. There are smiles that communicate messages of joy, of achievement, of friendliness, of politeness, and of embarrassment. The message is presumed to be in the smiler, who employs subtle differences in facial expression, gaze direction and body movement to enhance the probability of sending the message unambiguously.

We obscure our understanding of the workings of communication by treating smiles as discrete signals and ignoring the continuous process by which the smile is generated. Smiles, indeed all expressive movements, almost always occur in a social situation in which the partner is an active participant. That participation may contribute to the smile at the very moment when the smile is spreading across the person's face. A sudden change in the partner's actions could, conceivably, alter the form of this expression. For example, the smiler may be feeling enjoyment, begins to smile while looking toward the partner who at that moment appears distant or disapproving. The enjoyment fades to shame.

In Sylvan Tomkins'[4] theory of emotion, he proposes such a process to explain the origins of certain kinds of emotional pathologies in childhood. If parents are consistently disapproving of the child's spontaneous expressions of enjoyment, children begin to experience shame about the very sources of their own pleasure. Freud uses the concept of the superego, the internalized harsh parent, to explain the origins of repressed feelings of pleasure in certain individuals. Both Tomkins and Freud had a discrete state model of the emotions and their expression, and in their explanations of pathology they envisioned a process by which discrete emotions went underground and lay closeted for years.

My point is that in normal situations, one's emotions and expressions are not discrete entities encased in the individual, but they are socially constructed, dynamically created out of the fabric of the present.[5] Pathology arises when individuals cannot participate in this creative dynamic process, which may sometimes arise in the company of a parent who refuses to be a co-participant. We need not assume that psychopathology is the festering of a repressed collection of discrete states. It is a way of acting in the present, a stance with respect to how open one is to the creative possibilities of discourse.

It could be argued that smiles and other expressions are discrete by virtue of their universality across cultures and because they are immediately recognizable as meaningful configurations of facial action. On closer analysis, however, the apparent discreteness of the smile is actually a perceptual illusion. A smile reflects the action of at least four different facial muscles in the lower and middle part of the face and the corresponding actions of the eyes, head and body. Although the contractions of these muscles are relatively rapid and mutually coordinated, muscles do not contract instantaneously. The smile must be assembled from its parts as a continuous process of movement, even though we perceive it as a fully formed discrete package.

In order to understand how infants become communicators using culturally recognized actions that are interpreted by others as discrete signals, it will be important throughout this book to focus attention on the continuous aspects of social action. This is because infant communication is at first entirely within the realm of continuous processes. Later, infants acquire the skill to mold the form of these actions to resemble the categorical units of cultural communication. Adults are highly skilled at shaping the contours of their speech and non-verbal actions into forms that are culturally clear; nevertheless, words and gestures are composed out of continuous action processes.

Mutual social coordination requires that there be a continuous unfolding of individual action that is susceptible to being continuously modified by the continuously changing actions of the partner. I call this continuous mutual adaptation process *co-regulation*.[6] The systematic description of co-regulation and its role in the formation of social relationships and developmental change is complicated, in fact it takes up most of this book. Actually entering into co-regulated communication with a partner is so easy that newborn human infants are capable of doing it, and it is commonly observed in many animal species.

Co-regulation

Examples of co-regulated communication processes

One of my favorite examples of co-regulated communication comes from the work of Greg Moran and his colleagues[7] on patterns of ritualized fighting between adult wolves. The wolves enter into a repeatable pattern of co-regulated action of the sort shown in Figure 3.1. In this pattern, called circling, one wolf walks past another seated wolf who gets up and begins to move in the opposite direction. Instead of walking past and away from each other, the wolves begin to move in a head-to-tail circle pattern.

If we look at the wolves from above, and if we rotate at the same speed the wolves are walking, we would see two animals who maintain a constant distance from each other, and mirror-image body shapes curved so that each wolf seems to be following the other's tail.

The circling is a wonderful example of the impossibility of determining who is the sender or receiver, or of isolating a signal. Furthermore, the wolves are not immobile, they are constantly moving. Thus, the circular configuration is a dynamically created co-regulated system. The wolves don't have to plan this out, they don't have to say to each other, 'let's make a

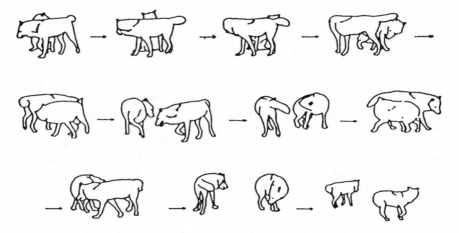

Figure 3.1 The initiation and conclusion of a pattern of wolf-circling. In the first frame, one wolf passes close to a seated wolf. In the second frame, they turn their heads towards each other, after which the seated wolf begins to move in the opposite direction. By the fourth frame, the wolves are circling. They break out of the pattern only when the distance between them is safe enough to preclude any sudden attack. (*Source*: Moran, G. *et al* 'A description of relational patterns of movement during "ritualized fighting" in wolves', in *Animal Behaviour*, 1981, **29**, 4, reprinted by permission of Academic Press Inc. (London) Ltd. and the authors.)

circle.' Nor does each wolf have to have encoded procedures in its brain for circling around with another wolf. Nor would it be correct to say that the pattern is created because the wolves are copying each other. The pattern is a consensual, negotiated system of action.

This co-regulated pattern emerges from the dynamics of the interaction and the constraints on the communication system. What are the constraints? Probably each wolf needs to be moving to maintain optimal readiness to attack and to respond to attack. Each must keep the other fully in view, and without turning its broadside or back toward the mouth of the attacker. In addition to these constraints imposed by the potential threat of aggression, the shape and flexibility of each animal's body (long from head to tail, four-legged, bendable, eyes on the side of the head rather than in front, teeth used as main weapon of initial attack), it is not hard to see how a circling pattern could emerge spontaneously and without any planning or design.[8]

Adam Kendon observed a similar kind of pattern among humans. When any group of standing individuals orient themselves toward each other for the purpose of engaging in a conversation, the group tends to form a circle pattern with individuals facing toward the center. Kendon calls this the F-formation, and suggests that it emerges spontaneously as participants create 'an orientational relationship in which the space between them is one to which they have equal, direct, and exclusive access.'[9] The F-formation is dynamic since individuals continuously move: they shift their heads and postures, they may change places, the entire configuration may rotate or reassemble in different locations.

Thus, co-regulated interactions are continuous processes, created out of the dynamics of action, the results of which are *emergent*, that is, occurring without an explicit plan, without a scheme or program inside each animal's nervous system that guides the action. The circling pattern emerges from the dynamic interactions of the partners with respect to the constraints within the system. It is impossible to understand how such patterns emerge by only considering the goals of the participants. We have to allow for the shape of their bodies and the kinds of actions their bodies are capable of performing.[10] If we want to understand continuous communication processes and their development we must place the body at center stage in psychological inquiry.

We must also place *creativity* at center stage since the most salient aspect of co-regulated interchange is the emergence of something novel, something that was not there before. According to Ernest Schachtel,

> The *quality* of the encounter that leads to creative experience consists primarily in the openness during the encounter and in the repeated and varied approach to the object, in the free and open play of attention, thought, feeling, perception, etc. . . . In characterizing this activity as play I do not mean that it is playful rather than serious, but that it is not bound by rigorous rules or by conventional schemata of memory, thought or perception.[11]

Thus, creativity is characterized by a stance of openness to the partner, a willingness to allow events to unfold and to be shaped by the process.

Wolf-circling is one example of a more general pattern of animal threat displays. In potentially aggressive situations, most animals show a threat display as opposed to immediately fleeing or actually engaging in a fight. Ethologist Robert Hinde[12] raised the question of why animals might threaten before attacking. If an animal is concerned about the risk of injury or worse, why not turn and run? On the other hand, if the animal intends to defend an offspring or some territory, the best strategy may be to attack immediately, depriving the opponent of the opportunity to defend the attack.

Hinde concluded that threat displays, like the vigilance seen in the circling wolves, were ways of assessing the intentions of the rival. Once the threat posture begins the animals enter into a co-regulated interaction in which each individual sizes up the other, creating the conditions for a mutual withdrawal of hostilities or, for that matter, their escalation. It turns out, however, that after such interactions the probability of withdrawal is much higher than the probability of a fight. Thus, although the animal's initial posture suggests an internal state of fear or the intention to stand ground,

> such signals are thus to be seen as involving negotiation with the rival as well as expression of an internal state. The term *negotiation* does not necessarily

imply *manipulation* but emphasizes the continuous interaction between the two individuals involved.[13]

Indeed, negotiation is closer to creativity, an openness to being co-regulated in the encounter, than to manipulation.

Human teasing is similar to ritualized fighting in wolves. For example, African-American male teenagers have been observed to exchange ritual insults, like 'Your mother eats dog food.' These insults typically do not lead to a fight, but rather to continued trading of insults and laughter. This happens in part because the insult has both a playful aspect as well as a serious or personal aspect. Both parties know that the statement is in the form of an insult, but both also realize that it is not true.[14] Other forms of teasing have more of a sting of truth in them. In these cases, the playfulness of the tease is largely determined by the reactions of the recipient. Whether the participants go on to trade teases and smiles, or whether the conversation ends in annoyance and rejection depends on a co-regulated mutual negotiation process regarding the meaning of the teasing.[15]

Interactions do not have to be aggressive to involve co-regulated negotiations. Research on human courtship interactions has revealed a rich array of verbal and non-verbal negotiation strategies. These include glances, nods, leans toward partner, invitations, stroking the hair, looking 'sexy,' coy smiling and the like.[16] They are displayed in order to assess the partner's interest and intentions; they convey one's interest, but not necessarily commitment. In other words, these gestures are used for the purpose of co-regulation.

Once a degree of intimacy is established, negotiations continue to be salient in the regulation of courtship interactions. This is illustrated by Adam Kendon's study of non-verbal interaction during a kissing episode between a male and female sitting on a park bench. In the following description, M = male, F = female, and Fa B = a facial expression involving a smile with mouth closed.

> it can be seen that each time M kisses F, M waits before finally approaching her until she shows Fa B, as if the appearance of Fa B is the signal that gives M clearance for his final approach. Whenever M kisses F, he always proceeds in two steps: he turns to face F and then approaches her. On each occasion ... M does not begin his approach until *after* F has shown Fa B ... M turns to F and remains still, F part-turns to M with parted lips. Her lips then close to produce Fa B and only when she has completed this does M begin his approach.[17]

In this example, the male makes a move toward the female and then waits until the female's face changes from lips parted to closed smile before proceeding. Of course, the female in this example also waits until the male has completed the first part of the approach before changing her facial expressions. Thus, each partner's actions are continuously regulated by the actions of the other partner.

Other research on adult communication shows that partners mold their communication to each other in very flexible ways. Figure 3.2 shows a representation of a small segment of conversation between a doctor and a patient.[18] The solid lines represent gazing at the partner. The patient begins a sentence, during which the doctor looks down at something he is reading. The patient elongates the next word (errr), becomes silent, and shifts his posture. Finally the doctor looks at the patient who resumes the sentence with the same word, again drawn out (herrr). The reshaping of the word 'her,' the silence and the posture shift are all ways of capturing the listener's attention, of assuring co-regulation.

It is as if words and sentences can be shaped like clay around the contours of the social situation, as if they are genuinely creative actions. If words were mere signals containing discrete units of information, this would not be possible or even necessary. In Figure 3.2, the word 'her' has a certain culturally prescribed meaning. Because 'her' or any other word is composed of continuous movements of the mouth, throat and tongue, the person talking is free to alter the intensity-by-time contour of the sound, and does this as a means of co-regulating with the social partner. Thus, even in a rather ritualized doctor–patient discussion, there is room for a great deal of creative variation. Once again we see that the dynamics and constraints of the body are crucial ingredients in understanding the workings of communication in everyday situations.

In ordinary conversations we don't notice or think about the fact that speech is constructed dynamically out of movements of the body. We hear words and

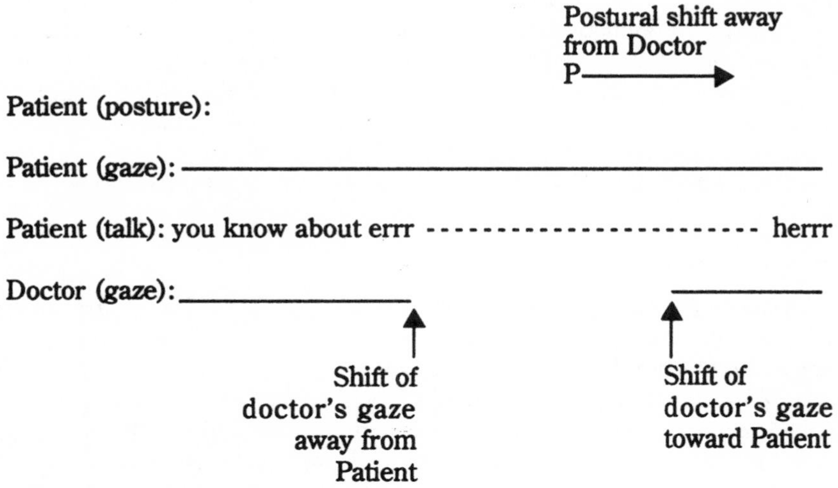

Postural shift away
from Doctor
P————————▶

Patient (posture):

Patient (gaze): ————————————————————————————————

Patient (talk): you know about errr - herrr

Doctor (gaze):_____   _____

                       ↑   ↑

Shift of   Shift of
doctor's gaze   doctor's gaze
away from   toward Patient
Patient

Figure 3.2 Stretching out a word, pausing and posture shifting are devices used here to attract the listener's attention. These devices depend on the speaker's ability to regulate the intensity of each action as a function of time in a continuous way.

translate them into particular meanings. However, speakers routinely use their bodies to vary the dynamics of speaking to achieve communicative goals, such as waiting for the partner to look or listen, adding emphasis or emotion, or changing the communicative function of the word or phrase. If 'her' is said with a rising intonation, the speaker seems to be asking a question. If it is said with a flat intonation, the speaker appears to be giving an answer or making a statement. In any case, co-regulated communication rests on the communicator's freedom to manipulate creatively the dynamic aspects of their actions with respect to the continuous changes in the partner's action.

These dynamics, which typify communication between partners of similar age and status, also occur during tutorial interactions in which a more skilled individual is working to educate another. According to Barbara Rogoff,[19] adult guides must tailor their actions to those of children and they do so by picking up on subtle cues about the child's attention and skill. Such cues include pausing and hesitation, glances, postural adjustments, and missed opportunities for taking a turn. Children also use adult non-verbal actions – nods, head shakes or hesitations – to gauge their own performance.

A similar process of mutual coordination is observed in successful animal training. According to Vicki Hearne[20] the most trainable animals, such as dogs and horses, are particularly good at reading human non-verbal actions to detect signs of pleasure or displeasure, approval or rejection, seriousness or ambivalence. The best trainers can detect subtle shades of meaning in the animal's movements. In order for training to work, a mutual understanding must arise between the animal and the trainer. Not only does the trainer have to recognize when animals are trying to mean something, but they have to take the animal seriously and enter into discourse on the animal's terms. In both tutoring and training, the essential ingredient for success is a co-regulated communication in which each partner is open to be influenced by the other. To be influenced by another is to take the other seriously, to respect the mutual influence as a pact of agreement, and to recognize and reward the other's contribution to the creative evolution of the relationship.[21]

Defining co-regulation

Co-regulation is a social process by which individuals dynamically alter their actions with respect to the ongoing and anticipated actions of their partners. During co-regulated discourse the individual's actions are emergent from the constraints imposed by their own body (its shape, size and possibilities for movement), by their expectations, by the actions of the partner, and by the cultural setting.

As a consequence of co-regulated interaction, a consensual social pattern is created and elaborated over time. Co-regulated patterns are recognized by their repetition and their coherence over time. A social game like peek-a-boo is recognizable by its repeating theme of hiding and revelation. The game has a coherence because of the preferred order in which the events occur: hiding is typically followed by revelation. Nevertheless, the game is also creative because it is being continuously elaborated by the participants. Partners change roles either by being the one who hides or the audience. A person can cover their own face with an object or they can cover the partner's face. The timing of the hiding and revealing changes subtly from turn to turn. Sometimes one lingers behind the hiding object, and at other times jumps out immediately. Changes are made in where one appears: from over the top of the object, from the side, or from underneath. Each of these variants on the game can be combined creatively so that the partner is never totally sure when, where and how the hider will emerge.

This creative variability within a patterned, ordered theme accounts for the heightened attention and enjoyment of the game.[22] The part of the game that is consensually patterned also explains how partners can adapt their behavior to the anticipated actions of the partner, even though those actions may be novel. I might vary the time or the place of revelation in part because my partner is currently looking at me, and in part because I anticipate my partner's laughter and continued participation in the game.

Co-regulated processes are emergent from the constraints on individual action. Co-regulated processes exhibit patterning and ordering. Such regularities suggest that there are underlying rules that individuals are following in the execution of their actions. I take the controversial view that the rules of the game are not really there, not really guiding the behavior. Rules are inferred by observers, they are convenient metaphors that help us describe or label the regularities. Once a rule is inferred by a participant, it may serve as one component of the system that guides action, but it is never the only explanation.

I can illustrate my view with a quote from a book chapter on social play that I wrote with colleagues Eva Nwokah and Jeanne Karns.

> So long as we think of play in the abstract, as the ideal expression of its 'rules,' there can be little to contradict this notion. However, when one observes real individuals playing – in any species in which play occurs – the subtle variability and emergent creativity leap out almost in mockery of the supposed rules of the game. An entire game may contain several successive subroutines each with new elements added, or the content of a person's turn suddenly changed. Do we have to have rules for strategies, and rules for breaking the rules, and rules for repairing the rules that were broken? Do we have to include rules to manage the emotional and linguistic forms of communication in which play is embedded, and all the rules by which these intrapsychic factors interact with the play of the game? Try writing down all the rules that would be necessary to play a game of checkers with a ten-year-old: for the game itself, for the banter, for the friendly advice about strategy, for the one-upmanship and protecting against it, and for processing the range of emotions during and after the game . . .
>
> We are not denying that individuals can cognitively represent games and their apparent rules. Anticipation based on prior expectations is certainly part of the enjoyment and engagement. The existence of such cognitions, though a

component of the play, does not mean that those cognitions are constitutive of the game, any more than a coach's game plan and score card and each player's knowledge of the 'rules' regulates the specifics of the encounter between two opposing teams.[23]

To focus only on the apparent 'rules' as an explanation of consensual activity means limiting one's view to the regularities of the sequence, ignoring the variability. It also suggests that the rules are reified and exist independent of action and are merely being followed by the participants. A complete understanding of communication and its development requires us to keep in mind both the regularities and variabilities. It is the continuously changing features of action, the dynamics of action in the social situation, that hold the key to understanding how we can connect so gracefully with another individual, and how infants develop such abilities.

The concept of co-regulation has been used so far to describe the process of mutual negotiation and the emergence of consensual agreement. The patterns of consensual agreement are called consensual frames. Consensual frames must exist even before partners can actually engage in a focused communication about something. They have to arrange themselves in such a way as to take best advantage of the information derived from the communication process.

Consensual frames

Webster's unabridged dictionary gives several meanings of the verb *to frame* that are particularly relevant to the communication process:

> (1) To shape, to fashion, to construct; to fit and unite together the several parts of (to *frame* a constitution, to *frame* a building); (2) To compose, to invent, to put into words (For thou art *framed* of the firm truth of valour. – Shak.); (3) to utter (his lips *framed* the words); (4) to shape, to fit, to regulate (the law was *framed* to equalize the tax burden); (5) to surround or provide with a border, as a picture.[24]

In this case there is no need to frame a new word, since in ordinary English, as well as in communication research, frame has a precise meaning and refers to a well-known aspect of the communication process: the need for communicators to establish a working definition of the communication situation. A frame is a *co-regulated consensual agreement* about the scope of the discourse: its location, its setting, the acts that are taken to be significant vs. those that are irrelevant, and the *main focus or topic*.[25]

The concept of frame combines its ordinary language sense of a border, with its ordinary sense of creation and regulation. Frames are mutual agreements about the limits of what is to be communicated between partners, about when and how interactions take place and for how long. Frames establish that some actions are to be taken as communicative, while others are less important. Frames also regulate the main topic of discourse; 'Social frameworks provide background understanding for events.'[26]

The notion of frame was first employed by the anthropologist Gregory Bateson[27] to describe how individuals let each other know how their actions are to be taken. When two children or two young animals play at fighting, their actions look very much like those used in actual fights: raised fists, yells, screams, bites and the like. When examined more closely, these actions stop short of actual harm to the partner. In human children, the actions are accompanied by smiles and laughs. These gestures of enjoyment, and the abbreviated forms of the fighting gestures, reveal a mutual agreement with the partner that 'this is pretend,' 'this is play, not real.' Framing is a meta-communication; a communication about the way the communication is to occur.[28] The consensual frame, therefore, is subject to the same process of co-regulation as negotiations around the main topic.

When frames are being negotiated, they become the main topic of discourse. Suppose a preschool child is engaged in solitary play in a classroom area devoted to free play. Another child wishes to invite the first to play together. The other child might say, 'Let's play house.' For the first child to accept the invitation, the two have to agree that this is what they want to play. Then they have to decide together where this will be done, in what part of the room. They must agree on what objects will 'count' as part of the play, on what roles each one has in the play, and on whether to let other children join in.

Two adult friends decide to get together for conversation. Where will they meet? At what time? For lunch or a tennis match? Once they get together, further framing must occur. What is permissible to discuss? Can they talk to each other about problems at work or at home? Do they only talk of their achievements and successes? Can they talk about serious things or only humorous stories? Framing, like the ensuing discussion, is consensual and co-regulated. Even if one takes the lead, sets the tone, is more directive than the other, the partner assents to these conditions in some manner.[29]

Constituents of frames

Adam Kendon has specified a number of factors that typically constitute communicative frames in face-to-face interaction.[30] These include attention direction, spatial location, postural orientation, and topic. Participants must achieve a consensus about some or all of these factors before further communication can occur.

Attention Direction. We must first recognize that communication between individuals in live encounters (ignoring for the moment electronic communication, letters, voice-only communication and the like) can be extremely complex. There are a large number of features that can be taken as communicative, not only actions but features of appearance such as clothing, grooming, respiration, intestinal noises, skin color, body secretions and odors.[31]

When two people meet for the purpose of interacting, how do they know that the communication is about the content of their speech and not about whether one's tie is straight, whether one has a nervous tic or some other distracting mannerism? When toddlers speak they mispronounce words, are poor articulators, and are unable to use adult grammatical constructions. Yet, in thousands of hours of observation done in many countries by many investigators, it is rare to hear a parent correcting a toddler's speech or refusing to continue on the topic until the toddler gets it right. Instead of attending to errors, adults seem to respond to the apparent meaning of the child's utterance. They interpret the child's meaning using their knowledge of this child and the particular context in which the utterance occurs.[32]

In some way the parent and child have a consensual agreement that the focus of mutual attention is the referent, not the form, of the utterance. Because communication is inherently multidimensional, participants must frame attention direction, agreeing to attend to some features and not to others.

Spatial Location. Agreement about the location of an interaction is essential, since the quality of a face-to-face interaction changes depending on the distance between partners and the physical setting. To begin an intimate encounter with someone, we would seek a quiet and private location. Level of intimacy can also be adjusted according to the distance between people and the amount of physical contact that is permitted.[33]

Postural orientation. We can stand, sit, recline or lie. We can face each other, our bodies can be oriented in an 'L' configuration, back-to-back or side-by-side. There are also different degrees of postural co-orientation. The orientation of the trunk is most salient, the upper body next, and then the head. If I sit facing you my upper body and/or head can also be facing you or be turned partially away. Each configuration has a different communicative significance.[34]

Sigfried Frey and his colleagues at the Max Planck Institute for Psychiatry in Munich, Germany asked people to rate their feelings toward the painting *La Giaconda*, otherwise known as 'Mona Lisa,' painted by Leonardo da Vinci in 1507. People were given a list of adjectives (sympathetic, dreamy, proud, cheerful, arrogant, honest, naive, etc.) and rated their feeling toward the original painting, as well as toward a picture of the painting in which the head was altered slightly to the left, away from her direction of gaze, and one oriented more to the right, toward her direction of gaze. When the famous lady had her head oriented toward the viewer and in the direction of her gaze, she was rated as dreamy, friendly, sensitive, involved, honest and inviting. When she was oriented away from the viewer she was called proud, tense, unsympathetic, arrogant, cold and detached.[35]

Research by Kendon and Ferber[36] shows that during a greeting sequence, individuals move through a series of head orientation changes: up, down, away and toward the other person. Each movement of the head reflects a different phase in the process of framing what kind of interaction will take place during and after the greeting.

Posture of the body and head in adults can communicate a wide variety of information related to framing an interaction. For example, dominant males in US high schools hold their bodies in a more erect posture than less dominant males.[37] During psychotherapy sessions, a higher rapport between client and therapist is associated with a higher incidence of leaning the upper bodies towards each other and holding the limbs in mirror image postures, and similar results have been found in experimental situations between both friends and non-friends.[38]

Topic. This refers to establishing a mutual focus on a topic, independent of the elaboration of the topic that we have discussed in earlier examples of co-regulation. An example of topic framing is given in Figure 3.2, in which the patient draws out his speech and adjusts his posture to assure the doctor's continued attention to the topic of discourse. The postural and pausing devices are attempts to co-regulate the frame of the discourse. Listeners can also contribute to topic frames by indicating their continued participation and attention to the speaker using *back channel* communications such as gazing, nodding, saying 'yeah,' or 'uh-hum.'[39]

Co-regulated framing processes

When beginning any interaction the negotiation of a frame is required. Yet how can two people co-regulate consensus about a frame even before interacting together to achieve it? Here's how Kendon states the problem:

> *P* is in something of a bind. He cannot formulate a line of action unless he knows how *Q* will take it. Yet he cannot know how *Q* will take any line of action he may produce, except by seeing how *Q* is indeed taking his line of action.[40]

In other words, someone has to make the opening move and there are always some risks involved in doing so: risks in whether the discourse will occur, in when and how, and about what.

The problems are similar to those in the co-regulation during the main discourse topic itself, except for the fact that a different dynamic may be needed to get things started than to keep things going. One resolution of the problem is easy: partners may rely on a cultural system and a history within their relationship to establish the bounds of discourse. One simply uses the cultural frame for how to, say, approach a teacher or ask someone for a date. Or, one relies on expectations built up with a particular partner. Even here, however, the cultural frame is only one component of the system. How does it apply to this person with whom I want to interact? Even within established relationships not everything is worked out, and each new encounter calls for some risks, some guesswork.

In these situations, individuals often lead by making movements that partially announce their intention, but not entirely. For example, in trying to leave a party one might finish a drink, button a jacket, make small moves in the direction of the door, talk about fatigue or the like. One hopes that the host will pick up on these cues and enter into a frame appropriate for departing. On the other hand, none of these moves by themselves clearly announce the intention to leave, so the actor is open to establishing frames for continued conversation if that is what the host seems to desire. In other words, by varying the *explicitness* of the action, one opens it to co-regulated negotiation about the new frame.[41]

Shared activity or consensual framing?

In the sense that frames are consensual agreements about some feature of the communication process, they can be described as shared between the participants. Kendon's concept of framing is related primarily to the actions of the partners, to what is needed to establish a communicative discourse. In order to communicate, at a minimum individuals need to share at least the means of communication in a shared space and with a shared focus of attention. Individuals could also share a good deal more than the means of communication.

There are several problems from my point of view with a description of communication as made up of episodes of shared activity. The term 'shared' suggests that each individual has a fixed representation of something that can be communicated to and expected by another person.[42] I argue in Chapter 8 that fixed representations are terms in discrete state models of cognition, and that they lead to assumptions of a discrete state model of communication by which these discrete cognitions are transmitted as messages. I prefer the term 'consensual frames,' because it implies a negotiated and dynamic process in which whatever is shared is earned through co-regulation. Jerome Bruner uses the term 'format' in the same way as I use consensual frame, that is, a social patterning that results from a negotiated co-construction.

Chapter 8 also elaborates a perspective in which cognitions like intentions, memories and meanings are active and creative processes. Often they are created through co-regulated negotiations with others and are formed in the very process by which they are communicated. I further suggest, therefore, that intention, memory and meaning are inevitably inherent in all forms of interpersonal communication, even between a parent and a very young infant. Although the intentions, memories and meanings become developmentally more complex and expressed increasingly through cultural communication frames, these mature forms of sharing evolve out of more rudimentary cognitive precursors present from the very beginning.

In this book, I intend to demonstrate that consensual frames partake of complex perceptual and cognitive processes from the beginning of human life and in most forms of communication in and between other animal species: every time there is co-regulation it must involve an intention, a memory and a meaning. I will not trace how the communication system develops over the course of human infancy because this could easily take up another volume. Rather, I offer a set of theoretical constructs and a model of communication from which a more precise picture of human development could be drawn, one that may guide future research at the interface of the individual and society.[43]

In summary, communication is a complex system in which multiple processes of co-regulation are required. To become an effective communicator in a culture, the child must acquire the skills not only to use the conventional gestures and symbols in meaningful ways, but also to establish or to break frames for communication. Although this level of complexity of communication is not typically considered in infant studies because infants are believed to be naive to these processes, I contend that we must consider the whole communication system of which the infant is a member in order to understand the acquisition of self and culture.

The essence of communication, in my view, is mutual creativity. It is from creativity in communication that we inherit creativity in personal action. Communication that is co-regulated occurs when both partners feel free to contribute to the process and when each respects the other's right to do so. When we are focusing on the regularities of communication, packaging actions into discrete units, formulating the supposed rules of discourse, or ignoring variability and playful creativity, we miss the core of the process and the excitement that keeps us involved.

Notes

1. Smith (1977).
2. Wertsch (1991).
3. Birdwhistell (1970, p. 104).
4. Tomkins (1962).
5. Fogel, *et al.* (in press).
6. Fogel (in press).
7. Moran, Fentress & Golani (1981).
8. It is likely that the circling pattern would occur in other species with similar body shapes, but I'm not aware of any cross-species data on this.
9. Kendon (1990, p. 209).
10. From an evolutionary perspective, the body shape and muscular configurations for social action may have evolved as a result of the success of those movements for individual fitness (Gouzoules, Gouzoules & Marler, 1985; Smith, 1977). In other words, upright postures, eyes in the front of the head, and a highly articulate set of facial muscles may have evolved in primates and

in humans because these features facilitate the face-to-face communication and mutual negotiation that enhance cooperative activity.

11. Schachtel (1959, pp. 241–2). *See also* Ochs, Smith & Taylor (1988); Rogoff (1989).
12. Hinde (1985).
13. Hinde (1985, p. 111).
14. Labov (1972).
15. Kochman (1970); Pawluk (1989). Similar patterns of mutual negotiation occur in conflicts between mothers and pre-school children (Eisenberg, 1992).
16. Grammer (1989).
17. Kendon (1975).
18. Heath (1984).
19. Rogoff (1990).
20. Hearne (1987).
21. Hearne (1987) points out that when interacting with animals or with other humans, entering into relationships of mutual coordination entails acceptance of the other as an individual with rights, privileges and responsibilities. In the second half of this book I follow her lead to suggest that co-regulation has profound consequences as the origin of a sense of self-in-relation to others, and of a responsibility to self and to others.
22. Stern, *et al.* (1977).
23. Fogel, Nwokah & Karns (in press).
24. Webster (1979, p. 727).
25. Bateson (1955); Garfinkel (1967); Goffman (1974); Kendon (1985).
26. Goffman (1974, p. 22).
27. Bateson (1955).
28. See also the concept of grounding in communication (Clark & Brennan, 1991).
29. Coregulation is absent, however, from interactions that are coercive and abusive. I will not be discussing this type of communication here.
30. Kendon (1985).
31. Danzinger (1976); Ekman (1965); Kendon, Harris & Key (1975); Poyatos (1975).
32. Austin (1962); Bruner (1983); Searle (1969).
33. Efran & Cheyne (1973); Hall (1964).
34. Bull (1987); Mehrabian (1969); Scheflen (1964).
35. Frey *et al.* (1983).
36. Kendon & Ferber (1973).
37. Weisfeld & Beresford (1982).
38. Charny (1966); La France & Ickes (1981); Maxwell & Cook (1985); Mehrabian (1968); Trout & Rosenfeld (1980).
39. Duncan (1973); Shegloff (1981).
40. Kendon (1985, p. 231).
41. Kendon (1985).
42. Kaye (1980).
43. See Chapter 11.

Chapter 4

The communication system: history and metaphor

The place is Paris, on the evening of the début of Igor Stravinski's ballet, *Le Sacre du printemps* (The Rites of Spring) on 29 May 1913 at the newly constructed Théâtre des Champs-Elysées. The French audience was genuinely aroused by the anticipation of seeing this exotic ballet, composed, choreographed and staged by Russians.

> Many in the audience were exceptionally elegant that evening as they arrived for the 8:45 curtain. All were excited. For weeks rumors had circulated about the artistic delights that the Russian ballet company had prepared for the new Paris season. Advance publicity talked of the 'real art,' the 'true art,' an art not confined by space and time. . .
>
> Regardless of attire, the audience on that opening night played, as Cocteau noted, 'the role that was written for it.' And what was that role? To be scandalized, of course, but equally, to scandalize. The brouhaha surrounding *Le Sacre* was to be as much in the reactions of the members of the audience to their fellows as in the work itself. The dancers on stage must have wondered at times who was performing and who was the audience.[1]

The half-naked dancers, the frenzied movements, the dissonant and disturbing music, carried the audience into an emotional battle between excitement and fear, pleasure and disgust. Insults were exchanged, not just hurled at the performers, but between members of the audience. There were reports of duels arranged, and fist fights.

> The boisterous evening rightly stands as a symbol of its era and as a landmark of this century . . . that opening of *Le Sacre* represents a milestone in the development of 'modernism,' modernism as above all a culture of the sensational event, through which art and life both become a matter of energy and are fused as one.[2]

Within months of this performance World War I would blacken the fields and destroy the evidences of a great physical culture all across Europe. Homes, churches, offices and museums containing countless historical treasures were obliterated. With them went the view of the world as a collection of essences of pure forms, of art and beauty as self-contained, of monarchs having the right to rule, of people having fixed horizons and paths in life preordained by heredity.

Systems and interdependence

Modernism and the idea of interdependence in Western thought

The first two decades of the twentieth century shook political practice and human consciousness to their foundations. Near the end of the nineteenth century, the political world of kings and popes, dynasties and empires – where power was passed on by heredity and divine succession – was continuing to give way to the right of individuals to govern themselves. Centralized leadership, passed on by heredity, was yielding in national cataclysms[3] to a more distributed and representative system of government in a process that began in the eighteenth century and continues today through the breakdown of the Soviet empire.

The New World Order of this century's final decade is an elaboration and extension of this continuing revolution in world governance. Having lost faith in the institutions that seemed as immutable as the rocks and the air, people were forced to define themselves. Where before the primary relationships were between a person and a central authority (God, religious leader, political leader) people's relationships to each other took on greater importance.[4] Part of this change is reflected in the scholarly studies in psychology and philosophy,[5] in literature and arts, of this time.[6]

A change also occurred for the common people of Western Europe and North America. In the battlefields, the scope of killing was unprecedented. For whom should one fight and die in the cold mud of the Belgian winter? Letters home from men suffering the horrors of trench warfare on the fronts of World War I revealed a retreat from the intolerable into the personal, a recognition that to obey blindly meant suffering or death. There seemed to be a liberation of the self, an affirmation that personal meaning is all we have in a decaying world, and paradoxically a commitment to enter into the social stream and as an individual to take part in the shaping of history.[7]

The legacy of the early twentieth century for the Western world was the Great War. It was the dictatorial embodiment of German philosopher Karl Marx's spirit of community in the Russian and later Chinese communist revolutions. At the same time in the West, this century saw the rise of the belief that freedom and wealth could be had by all. It heralded a century remarkable for its elevation of the self above all, the self to the point of violence, and at the same time remarkable for the rise of communist ideals intended to span the globe.

Without recounting the successes and failures of this revolution, it seems important to place the progenitors of our current view of human development into this historical context.[8] The idea of human interdependence, of social relativity, of people and their products as individuals who construct the social order, of freedom from hereditary predestination and from the constraints of centralized leadership, cannot be traced to a single individual but to a socio-historical process that shaped the character of Western science and thought.

Principles of systems thinking

Although American politicians have painted it otherwise, both capitalism and communism in the twentieth-century flow from the same socio-historical spring and share similar ideas. While communism was more oriented to community values and capitalism to the self, both of these political and economic philosophies are founded on the notion of the interdependence of members of a social and economic system. The Soviet Union and the West borrowed from each other, and were shaped in fundamental ways by a co-regulated discourse of international proportions. Modern capitalism was defined in part as a reaction to communism, and vice versa.

The concept of *system* is the main intellectual advance common to these political philosophies, and the central contribution of twentieth-century thinking.[9] This intellectual change arose from the Cartesian and later Enlightenment eras in which scientists and philosophers believed that they could reduce things to their elementary constituents and describe the world in terms of its objective reality. During this period in the eighteenth and nineteenth centuries the notion of the responsible individual, of the self created and independent from a divine being, was born as Descartes' *cogito* (I think), Rousseau's journey into self-discovery with *Emile* and John Locke's rational citizen, self-constructed from a *tabula rasa*. These philosophical and literary ideas were accompanied by a science which had the goal of making entirely objective measurements and discovering universal laws that governed all of nature.[10]

Thinkers in the era of scientific objectivity rejected the notion of divine control over human affairs and seemed to set the individual free from a life of dependency and obligation. The revolution that brought about systems thinking placed the now godless individual back into a context, this time a secular context of other humans and their cultural inventions. This revolution actually began in the mid-nineteenth century along a number of different scholarly fronts.

The dialectical process of Hegel and Marx suggests that change emerges from the transaction between opposing forces, the outcome of which cannot be set in advance. The global explorers who emerged from the hubris of individual conquest and self-fulfilment dragged nineteenth-century scientists in their wakes across the Atlantic and Pacific oceans, scientists who brought back an emerging view of a world of interdependent relationships.[11] On his voyages to the Pacific, Darwin saw that species evolved, not by some divine plan, but rather by their transactions with the local context of their environmental niche. Ernst Haeckel, a German disciple of Darwin, coined the term *ecology*, the 'science of the relations of living organisms to the external world.' Alexander von Humboldt from Europe and John Wesley Powell from America were among the first to see the western United States as a vast ecology, dependent upon the subtle balance of earth, wind and water and not amenable to unhindered growth. They were a stark contrast to the developers and exploiters of the arid lands east of the Mississippi River.[12]

Somewhat later, in the early decades of the twentieth century, Einstein's theory of relativity is founded on the view that the observer does not have a privileged position, that the world looks and acts differently depending on where one is standing, on the context of events. Pavlov construed behavior as having inexorable links to the situation in which it occurred. Freud explained psychopathology as emerging from the transactions between parent and child during development, and not necessarily due to the influence of a 'poor family,' a nineteenth-century euphemism for a belief in the genetic determinism of poverty and wealth, sickness and health, unruliness and manners.[13] The science of ecology arose in its modern form out of the drought of the American Dust Bowl of the 1930s.[14]

In the first half of the twentieth century many insights such as these from the sciences of biology, physics and psychology were codified into what has come to be called *General Systems Theory*. Some of the basic principles of systems theory are: complexity, organization, self-stability, equifinality, and hierarchy.[15]

Systems are complex, that is, they contain many parts, each of which may be different. The difference between a collection of parts and a system is that in the latter each of the parts bears some relationship to at least some of the other parts. Parts, in other words, are not independent of each other. Parts could be people in a society who are each different and who have a unique set of relationships to other members of the society. Changes in any single part of a system will create *corresponding changes in other related parts* of the system.

Systems are organized in the sense that the behavior of the system as a whole can be described in its own terms, terms that may not apply to the descriptions of the parts and their relationships. We can talk about phenomena that apply to the organization of a whole society, such as capitalism or communism. A society as a whole can tend toward capitalism regardless of whether some individuals in that society live in communes while others in that society acquire great wealth. Out of a large number of everyday transactions, a social order can emerge. In other words, systems can be described by their *collective behavior*, independent of the relationships between their component parts.

Systems are self-stabilizing and self-organizing. The collective properties of the organization are generally stable tendencies maintained over time by the transactions of the individuals and their relationships. In a societal system it is unlikely that there would be frequent changes between capitalism and communism. Typically, systems have a tendency to remain in one or another mode most of the time. The 'structure' of the system, whether it is capitalist or communist, is both created and stabilized by everyday transactions. When systems make changes between one major mode of organization and another, the transitions tend to be sudden and catastrophic. In a society, they feel like revolutions in which all individuals and their relationships undergo sudden and drastic changes. Most viable systems quickly settle into new modes of stable functioning following such transitions. The *stability* of a collective organization is maintained by *dynamic fluctuations of activity between its component individuals*, not by a static structural framework.

Systems exhibit equifinality. There are many different dynamic processes that can lead to similar system organizations. For example, capitalism can arise and maintain itself in different ways as it evolves in different nations. Thus, similarities between systems can arise because the dynamics of the process naturally lead to *a small number of collective forms* – in spite of the complexity of the dynamics – and not because systems are adhering to a blueprint that from the start specifies the end result.

Systems form hierarchical patterns. Higher and lower orders within the same system are the natural result of system dynamics. Although hierarchies are relatively independent of each other, they can and do influence each other. Thus, in most political systems there are local, regional and national levels of organization. Each level has its own rules, actors and relationships, yet there are transactions both within and between the levels of the organization. There is no particular level of a system that is more fundamental than any other. Lower orders do not cause or generate the higher orders of the system and vice versa, but rather *all the orders are part of the same system and are the natural result of the system's dynamics*.

Many of these properties of systems are nicely summarized by the biologist Paul Weiss:

> life is process, not substance. A living system is no more adequately characterized by an inventory of its material constituents, such as molecules, than the life of a city is described by the list of names and numbers in a telephone book ... The systems concept is the embodiment of the experience that there are patterned processes which owe their typical configuration not to a prearranged, absolutely stereotyped, mosaic of single-tracked component performances, but on the contrary, to the fact that the component activities have many degrees of freedom, but submit to the ordering restraints exerted on them by the integral activity of the 'whole' in its patterned dynamics.[16]

In the political system, each individual has many degrees of freedom in their behavior. One can buy or sell, vote or not vote, speak up or remain silent, support or criticize leaders, and the like. Yet, in spite of these degrees of freedom for each individual, now multiplied by the large numbers of individuals in the society, there is an overall tendency for people to 'submit to the ordering restraints' of the whole, that is, to behave in ways consonant to the maintenance of the social order.[17]

Participation in a complex social system reduces the number of degrees of freedom for the individual on the one hand, and at the same time creates the conditions for the ordered and self-stabilizing behavior of the system on the other. Selves and social systems define each other; each is a manifestation of the dynamic processes that form the basis of social organizations.

There are not an infinite variety of social orders, as might be suggested from the complex interactive possibilities of so many parts with so many degrees of freedom. As Hegel and Marx suggested, economic systems tend toward stable patterns of exchange between members by virtue of the operation of the dialectic of conflict between opposites. Stated more generally, complex systems are more likely to be *ordered* than disordered, to settle into a small number of relatively stable modes of functioning, in which only particular degrees of freedom are permitted to the component parts.

The ordered nature of systems is perplexing and paradoxical to many current thinkers. From the perspective of discrete state models, complex wholes are built up from rule-governed, logical relationships between the elements. Self-organization in complex systems is impossible from the perspective of logical combinatorial models of discrete elements.

Systems require a different kind of logic, a *dia*-logic, or *co-genetic* logic in which relationships are the main elements of thought.[18] One must view the whole in terms of the parts, the parts in terms of the whole. Unfortunately, it is just this sort of mysterious-sounding language that turns many scholars away from systems thinking. To make it concrete with respect to the example of a society, one has to imagine the relational constraints imposed by individuals upon each other, and at the same time imagine how those constraints are shaped in part by the emerging social order as a whole, which itself is shaped in part by the relationships between individuals. To comprehend a dynamic system, the mind must proceed with a flexible and dynamic logic that is not easily specifiable in terms of linear combinations of logical rules.

Systems thinking and ideas about human development

I have organized the preceding part of the chapter with respect to the organization and development of political systems for several reasons. The first I have already mentioned: ideas in science were part of the political changes that altered our daily lives and senses of self in fundamental ways. Second, by thus wooing you (I hope) into some tentative agreement about the worth of these systems concepts, I hope to get you on my side. My side of what? These ideas, when applied to biology and psychology – the fields to which we must turn to understand the origins and development of social communication – turn out to be extremely controversial. While systems concepts have fared extremely well in biology, they are not generally accepted by psychologists whose journals and conferences are clogged with debates in one way or another related to the worth of systems thinking compared to the well worked-out models and theories based on more mechanistic world views.

In some ways we are all caught up in these psychological controversies because they occur to most people in the process of their own development of self-understanding. These ideas touch how we think about ourselves, the origins of our own personalities and abilities, our attitudes toward our relationships with others, our own beliefs about how we and others become who we are. I can make this clearer by drawing the analogies between political beliefs and beliefs about biological and psychological processes, listed in Table 4.1.[19]

The systems perspective suggests that transactions within and between cells, within and between components of the body and environment including the brain, must be involved in the regulation of developmental change either in body structures or behavior. This view democratizes the process of developmental change. The body, its parts and their actions, are no longer subject to the tyranny of the genes and the brain. Instead, these emperors have been dethroned. They may still occupy their seats at the center of the skull and the middle of the cell, but they are now merely one part of a dynamic system. They depend on the sustenance of their supporting environment simply to live and in order to function.

In systems thinking, the genes are no longer viewed as existing before anything else and as creating everything else. The genes are part of an ongoing living process. It is true that children inherit their parents' genes but children also inherit the environment of the genes: the original cell (the zygote) in which the genes live, the biological environment that supports the life of that cell and its progenitors in the father's and mother's gonads and reproductive passages, the sources of nourishment of that cell. The genes actively interact with these environments, which actively regulate the actions of the genes. Thus, whole systems are passed between generations. Developmental processes are inherited and not simply genetic units.[20]

Similarly, systems thinking secularizes the brain, makes it one among many other essential components of the living body that contribute to the development of behavior. The body does not always need to look to the brain as a source of inspiration (intention), or of guidance (central commands), or of growth and change (brain maturation causes behavioral development). The brain is shaped and supported by the rest of the body. Mind and body are inseparable parts and levels of a single living system.

Finally, and most importantly, infants and young children develop communicative skills in relation to their social contexts, but the social

Table 4.1. Implications of systems thinking in three different fields

Political systems	Biological systems	Psychological systems
Relationships between individuals have equal status as those between each individual and the group leader. *Relationships between the individuals and the leader cannot by themselves determine the workings of the society, and the leader's effectiveness depends on the group's support.*	Interactions between cells and between component parts within each cell are as important as the relationships of the genes to the cells and their constituents. *The genes do not control all the processes in the body, and their operation depends on the functioning of the cells in which they live.*	Relationships between components of an action, such as the connections between the muscles in the face, are equally important in determining the pattern of action as each muscle's connection to the brain. *By itself, the brain cannot control all the body's activities, nor can the brain exist without its containment within a living body.*
The collective behavior of the system – capitalist or communist – is maintained by the dynamic transactions between individuals within, and between different levels of the hierarchy of, the system. *The leaders are not completely in control over each individual, but rather act to regulate the form of the relationships permitted between individuals.*	The structure of the organism is not created entirely by the genes, but by the multiple transactions within and between all the levels of the system. The chemicals, forces and electrical potentials exchanged between the cell and its neighbors are just as important in determining its structure and the genes in its nucleus. *The genes do not completely control the formation of body cells and structures, and they encode only what is not already determined by the dynamics of the system.*	The constraints and processes acting on the body, both from within (hormonal, neural, skeleto-muscular) and without (other people, gravity, surfaces and supports, tools, culture) are just as important in determining the final form of an action as information coming from the brain. *The brain does not completely control action and its operation can be economized by affecting the dynamic relationships between parts of the body, rather than trying to control each component unit on its own.*
These dynamics make political systems stable over long periods. Revolutionary changes require the active participation of members of the society in addition to the cooperation of the leaders. They occur when the dynamic transactions between individuals move beyond the normal range of fluctuation and variation. *Revolutions are the result of the active participation at all levels in the social system.*	Cell structures remain highly stable until their local transactions change the environment in such a way that a different set of genes becomes active in those cells, feeding back into the transactions between them, such as occurs during embryonic development or in cancer. *Developmental changes in cell organizations are as much determined by the interactions between cells as by genetic control.*	Coordinated actions develop in part due to changes in the brain, and in part due to changes in the components of the action, including changes in the environment that supports the actions. Changes in the body and in the environment can influence the development of the brain. *Developmental change is as much the result of changes in the body and its environment as it is of brain or cognitive re-organizations.*

context is not the sole determiner of how communication develops. In a systems perspective we would have to admit that adults are not faultless moral and intellectual guides, not dispassionate arbiters of right and wrong, not all-knowing experts in the workings of the culture. Adults may have more knowledge and experience and a broader view of human life than the child, but adults' actions must also be affected by the children's. Adults are members of social organizations and thus are a part of a complex flow of social transactions in which the child is embedded.[21]

Systems thinking applied to the process of communication is outlined in Table 4.2. These ideas apply to all forms of animal and human communication, including those between adults and children. This table summarizes notions about communication that have already been introduced in this book.

Perhaps because I was initially trained in physics[22] and because I read current work in developmental biology, systems thinking is intuitively appealing to me. In fact, I can hardly imagine thinking any other way. It surprises me, therefore, that many of my colleagues in psychology persist in talking about genes and environments as if they were solid objects, unaffected by each other, unassailable in their empires of control over behavior and development. I get puzzled when developmental psychologists speak of cognitions or emotions as the central and primary 'organizers' of behavior and developmental change. I am perplexed when people speak as if neural information processing, neural circuits and neural networks are all we need to study when it comes to explaining cognition and language, as if animals were computers rather than flesh-and-blood species living in real environments. I am confused when parental behavior or misbehavior is talked about as the primary cause of children's happiness or emotional

Table 4.2. Implications of systems thinking for the process of communication

---

Relationships of communicative actions between individuals are of equal importance to the relationships and organization of actions within the individual. Language, for example, cannot be understood only by examining the motor system for the production of words and gestures, nor only by examining the linguistic relationships that create syntax and semantics. Communicative actions are embedded in dynamic transactions with other individuals in such a way that no single individual has complete control over either the process, structure or outcome of communication.

Communication is not guided entirely by a plan or script within the brain of any individual. Nor is most everyday communication guided by a script for the actions and behavior of the partners. Individuals share in the regulation of communication, rather than its complete control. Regulation occurs when individual actions alter the information on which the partner's actions are based, rather than by affecting the other's actions directly.

Stability over time in a communication system occurs by virtue of a co-regulated process. The course of interaction between individuals is never identical across occasions, yet a theme or ritual is maintained as a recognizable pattern with variations. Changes in interaction rituals or themes require the active collaboration of all partners whose combined efforts re-establish a stable co-regulated pattern following the introduction of an innovation into the system.

---

pain, compliance or rebellion, as if the children themselves or the environment of the parent and family had nothing to do with developmental outcome.

Although I cannot promise to disprove these imperial metaphors, I do intend to offer in this book an alternative metaphor based on dynamic systems thinking. I try to translate this systems metaphor into some of its implications for our understanding of human communication and how infants become communicating individuals and members of a culture. The hypotheses about development and the formation of individual differences suggested by this systems metaphor are very different from those derived from metaphors based on central controlling influences. The practical implications for parents, educators and clinicians differ substantially from other views of human development.

Metaphors in social and developmental psychology

The individual–environment relationship is discussed in psychology in terms of metaphors. *Metaphors* (or similes) are frequently used in science as a useful way of describing phenomena. They enhance understanding by relating complex concepts to everyday examples: society is like the body, interdependent and whole; human rituals and games are like self-organizing systems, dynamic and emergent.

Metaphors are not only used for description, they are used as models to generate new hypotheses and suggest applications. A *model* is a description of the workings of a system,

> an abstractive representation of some object or state of affairs . . . it exhibits only certain properties – the ones relevant to one's needs and interests in using the model – of the object modelled. Thus a model of the solar system hanging from the ceiling of the Planetarium, or diagrammed two-dimensionally on a piece of paper, or described in the utterances of some speaker, represents a state of affairs in some abstractive version: Some properties of the model resemble, or are like, or image, or mirror, or stand in for some properties of the solar system.[23]

A model is similar to the real thing, but does not share all of its features. A model airplane that duplicates the exact scale and shape of a real airplane cannot actually fly, since as one reduces the scale the proportions must change to provide the same amount of lift. Thus, in building a model, one has to think carefully about the aspects of the system one wishes to capture – for example, its external features or its actual functioning – because the model should suit the purposes of the user of the model.

Models are more specific and detailed than metaphors, and therefore preferable, but it is often not possible to develop a model, especially in the newer sciences like psychology. 'Metaphor is used to represent the state of affairs because no more literal description of its properties can be given.'[24] Thus a metaphor is often the only kind of model we can construct.

The problem with a metaphor is that it is difficult to tell which of its various connotations is most like the phenomenon that is being explained. Yes, society is like the body in its general systemic processes, but societies are not governed by the same processes that unite the organs into a living creature. Societies are alive, but the patterns of their organization and the dynamics that create it are totally unlike the flow of blood and the movement of muscle.

Metaphors suggest interesting ideas, but they can also cause trouble. If we use the metaphor of a discrete state communication system (senders, receivers and signals) it describes some features of real human interaction, but fails to capture the co-regulated nature of that interaction.

The most commonly used metaphors in developmental and social psychology have been reviewed in some detail by Arnold Sameroff and also by Irwin Altman and Barbara Rogoff.[25] They base their reviews on ideas from general systems theory, and on the work of philosophers John Dewey and S. C. Pepper, both writing in the first half of the twentieth century.

Basically, there are two main metaphors that apply to the relationship between individual and environment: mechanism and organism. The mechanistic metaphor suggests that individuals and environments can be described in their own terms, and relationships between them are similar to material interactions. Thus, the environment may push an individual in one direction or another, or an individual may change part of the environment. Each exerts a unidirectional mechanical force on the other. This metaphor directs one to formulate laws of individual behavior based on constructs that are wholly within the individual.

The organic metaphor regards the individual's relationship to the environment as an organized living system. As in systems thinking, individuals are parts of larger systems; they can affect other parts of this system and at the same time, be affected by them. The environment becomes part of the system. This metaphor directs one to formulate principles of behavior for the organization as a whole. The focus of research is on the process of transaction between the elements of the system, rather than on the products of change within the individuals that compose the system.

For example, a mechanistic view of the development of human communication would focus on the acquisition of communicative behaviors within the individual. The researcher would want to chart the developmental changes in infant vocalizations from crying to babbling to speech, and show how these products were formed either by genetically based maturation or by speech input from the social environment, or some combination of both. Indeed, we have learned a great deal about normal development from work in this genre, and it is especially suitable to research on communication deficits, such as disorders of speech and hearing.

An organic view of the development of communication suggests that one should study communication as part of the social system in which individuals are acting.[26] Thus, a communicative behavior such as a smile is not merely an expression of an inner state, but also relates to the ongoing transaction in the social system. How a smile is used to affect another person, the sequence of events in which a smile is embedded and the relationship between smiles and other social behaviors would all be open to investigation.[27]

Mechanistic models have a useful purpose because for some forms of communication people do act as if their behaviors are discrete, and as if the behavior of one person directly affects the behavior of another. Moreover, some communication deficits and pathologies may be better modeled as discrete state, mechanistic systems.

Relationship of co-regulation to other organismic concepts of communication

The co-regulation metaphor captures the dynamics of the communication process, its continuously variable features and the fluidity of individual actions when in the company of others. It is a metaphor that falls clearly within the organismic root metaphor. There are a large number of other metaphors that have been employed to express the organic nature of communication, but none of them completely encompasses the co-regulation process.

One of the most frequently used terms in the literature of social and developmental psychology is *interactional synchrony*. This term has various definitions and usages. A strict construal of the term implies that there is an exact and precise temporal simultaneity of the beginnings and endings of actions between partners.[28]

Work by William Condon and colleagues reported finding that newborn infants moved in exact synchrony with the speech of adults.[29] They segmented the speech into phonemes, the basic elements of speech sounds, and suggested that infants made subtle changes in the speed and direction of their body movements that seemed to correspond with the phonemic changes.

Later careful analysis of this paper revealed a number of problems. One was that since the infant's actions were continuous, the researcher's segmentation of these actions into discrete bits of movement seemed arbitrary. Furthermore, the onset of these infant action segments occurring at any time during an adult phoneme, not just at the onset of the phoneme, was counted as an instance of synchrony. In other words, the actions of the infant and the sounds of the adults are continuously changing but precise synchronization cannot be concluded. Additional technical and statistical problems flawed Condon's research conclusions, and the work has never been replicated for any form of animal or human communication.[30]

More recent definitions of interaction synchrony do not require precise temporal simultaneity. Glyn Collis defined interaction synchrony in terms of one partner anticipating the actions of the other. For example, in mother–infant interaction, mothers appear to use infant and environmental cues to determine what the infant is likely to do next. An infant might be expected to look in the direction of a particular preferred toy. Once the infant looks in that direction, the mother synchronizes her behavior with his by naming the toy, talking about it or gesturing toward it.[31]

Also, when mothers are synchronized in this fashion, their behavior is not precisely simultaneous with the infants. Frame-by-frame analysis of video and film records of mother–infant interaction shows that there is an average lag between onsets of infant's and mother's behavior of about 0.05 seconds.[32]

This definition, while capturing the anticipatory aspect of co-regulation, does not mention the continuously variable nature of interaction, nor does it assume that mother and infant must regulate *each other*. The mutual and continuous nature of anticipatory action is better reflected in the concept of mutual coordination used by Beatrice Beebe and Joseph Jaffee.[33] It is enough, in both Condon's view, and in Collis's view, for regulation (or synchronization) to be unilateral. Unilateral regulation does indeed occur, especially when mothers monitor and respond to their infant's actions without the infant being much aware of the mother's continued presence.

A more recent usage of the term interactional synchrony comes from the mother–infant interaction research of Russell Isabella and Jay Belsky. According to these investigators, interactional synchrony refers to the reciprocal and mutually rewarding behavioral exchanges including those in which both members contribute, when there is an exchange of behaviors in which each partner is responsive to the other. They contrast this with the notion of asynchrony, in which exchanges are one-sided, unresponsive or intrusive.[34]

This usage of the term captures the mutual influence aspect of co-regulation. Co-regulation, however, does not require that the exchanges be 'mutually rewarding.' In my view, arguments, fights and disagreements can be co-regulated as long as each partner adapts to the other and information is created between them. Isabella and Belsky also speak of 'behavioral exchanges' in a way that suggests a discrete state concept of communication, as if it were possible to define senders, receivers and signals. Their definition is also insensitive to varieties of temporal matching between adult and infant.

During co-regulation, behaviors and actions are not exchanged since action is always occurring for both partners. In some circumstances, researchers may artificially break a continuous interaction into discrete units for the purpose of analysis. Researchers often unitize interactions into divisions marked by salient behaviors, such as speech or gesture, or into equally spaced units of elapsed time.[35] In spite of the utility of such methods for specific research purposes, a precise description of communication is significantly blunted by this convenience.

In co-regulated communication information is created, behavior is not exchanged. Information, a concept that we will explore in some detail in the next chapter, is fundamental to an understanding of how communication exerts its mutual effects on partners. How can the behavior of one person affect another? Surely behaviors do not collide like billiard balls. Nor are behaviors actually exchanged between people, like gifts are exchanged, because the behavior of a person does not transfer itself physically to another person. We can speak about *exchanging* smiles, *trading* insults or *throwing* punches, but these are only metaphors, however apt or eloquent.

In order for your smile to have an effect on me, in order for it to make me smile in return (another metaphor, since I didn't actually take your smile and give it back to you), I have to perceive the light reflected from the changes in the surface of your face as informative to me. That information may translate into a feeling, and/or another action, like a smile in response.

Information is what my body needs to create its own smile out of its perception of yours. My smile is created from the muscles and skin surfaces of my own body from information that I acquire while interacting with your body. In the case of a smiling exchange, your body is across a distance and perception is in the visual channel. The same logic applies even when we are in physical contact. I must still move my own body on the basis of information I create from yours through my own tactile perception. The information is not 'in' your body, nor is it 'in' my body. The information is what happens to me when I perceive your smile. That information may be translated into action, but because it is embodied and relational, I experience it as feeling, imagery or compulsion. In this view information is not a cognitive content, a rational and detached quantity: it is the meaning of the situation as experienced in my entire body.

If I watch two other people having a fist fight I might say they are *trading* punches. I am less likely to think or to talk that way if I am one of the participants. When my opponent lands a punch it is going to sting and that perceptual information will be translated – via anger and indignation, distress and fear – into the punch that I shall attempt to land. In this fight we're not trading anything. We are involved, we are participants, we are aroused, we are co-regulated.[36]

A definition of interactional synchrony that comes the closest to my definition of co-regulation was worked out by Frank Bernieri and his colleagues. According to them, interaction synchrony is

> the apparent unification of two behavioral elements into a meaningfully described whole, synchronous event. The elements of this event may be simultaneous, identical, and in phase or alternating, mirrored, and out of phase. The essential feature is that when the elements are put together, they create a 'whole,' or perceptual unit ... Synchrony, therefore, is operationalized here . . . as the extent of gestaltlike harmoniousness or meshing of interpersonal behaviors.[37]

Using this definition, observers were particularly good at deciding when interactions were synchronized. The definition captures the creative, continuous and emergent aspects of co-regulation. It focuses, however, on behavior of the individual as the unit of analysis: behaviors mesh and become synchronized.

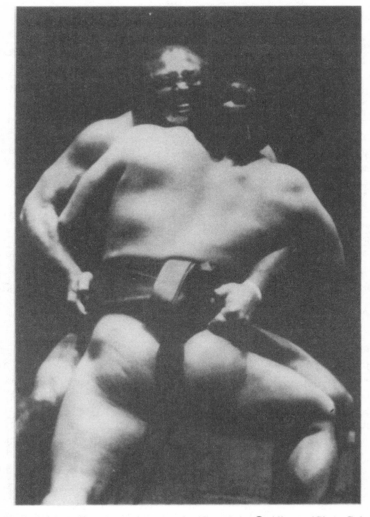

Figure 4.1 A Sumo wrestling match. (Copyright © Allsport/Chris Cole.)

In my view, individual behavior takes its characteristic form by virtue of its engagement with others; behavior is created in the process of co-regulation. The concept of synchrony suggests the opposite, that synchrony is created by combining each individual's behavior.

Other constructs have also been used in the literature. For example, the *mutual regulation model* of Edward Tronick and his colleagues is defined as the goal to achieve a joint regulation of the interaction with interactive behaviors, or the goal of achieving a joint state of reciprocity. This idea has problems similar to the foregoing, because it assumes that behaviors are exchanged rather than that information is derived from behavior. Another difficulty is the notion that partners need to have an explicit goal of achieving mutual regulation.

Goal is one of those useful metaphors that describes regularity in action from the observer's point of view, but that may not be the way in which the participants are organizing their own actions. One observes an interaction that seems to proceed toward a regularized pattern, such as a peek-a-boo game. To the extent that peek-a-boo and other games are spontaneous, creative, emergent achievements of a co-regulated process, why is it necessary to assume that the participants want to become co-regulated? Each may have had some initial intention: to play, to have fun, to get attention, to get their way. Mother may engage in peek-a-boo to assuage a baby's anger or to move it from one activity into another, such as from playing with toys to going to bed.

It is not necessary to assume that participants share the same goal in order to achieve co-regulated discourse. Nor is it necessary to assume that participants, in spite of their private goals, share the goal of achieving joint coordination. I don't think infants have the goal of achieving mutual regulation any more than circling wolves, or any more than I would like to get into a fist fight for the sake of establishing my ability to co-regulate on these terms with an opponent.[38]

Now, there certainly are instances of interpersonal communication where both partners share the same goal, such as when two or more people have to achieve a task that can only be done jointly. In some instances it might also be true that in addition to sharing the task goal, the individuals also really care about doing it with each other, they want to enter into co-regulated interactions with these particular partners. When this happens, and when we can enter into the desired form of discourse with our chosen partners, it affects our emotional experience and commitment to the relationship.

There are also situations in which only one partner may have the goal of participation in the relationship. As a result of extended discourse, the other partner may come to share that goal. In Chapter 6, I discuss how such relationships of mutual commitment between parents and infants grow and maintain themselves. Even in these cases, however, goals are not enough: they are only one aspect of a complex and dynamic communication system.

The remarkable and wonderful consequence of the way our brains and bodies are put together is that it is extremely easy for us to enter into communicative exchanges even in the absence of goals to do so, and to profit greatly by them. Focusing on goals and rules as the primary cause of such coordinations misses the essence of the process.

One other construct that deserves some mention in this context is that of matching. *Matching occurs when one individual makes his or her actions more similar to those of another individual.* One form of matching is *imitation*, where one copies what another person is doing. Imitation can immediately follow the model, or it can be delayed. *Co-action* is when partners each do something at the same time. What they do may be the same (as in singing in unison) or it may be different (as in interrupting while another person is talking, or clapping while another person sings). Unlike adult conversation in which co-active vocalizations are rare, adults with infants do it rather frequently.[39]

Attunement is a form of matching in which the referent for the match is not the external action, but the presumed feeling state of the partner.[40] Daniel Stern and his colleagues have defined and described attunement processes of which there is a wide variety. Matches can be in any behavioral modality, such as vocal, respiratory (heavy breathing, sighing), facial, gestural or movement. One can also match intensity contours within the same modality or when using a different modality. For example, an infant may suddenly jerk out his arms to which the mother responds with a sharp 'Oh!' that has the same temporal and intensity contour as the infant's arm movement. Timing matches can also occur according to beat, rhythm and/or duration. Clapping to the same beat of someone singing is a good example. Finally, there can be matches according to the spatial shape of the action, for example moving the hand up and down can be matched by another person moving the head up and down.

Attunement reflects some underlying dimension of the action that is believed to correspond to the feeling that accompanied the action. Attunement can have the following social functions: to be with another or share feelings with another, to empathize, to mock, to respond contingently, to change the other's arousal level or emotion, to change the other's goal, to teach or to play. The specific forms and functions of attunement are culturally regulated.

One problem is that all the above concepts of matching are defined as unilateral actions and do not necessarily embody a notion of co-regulation. The task of matching someone unilaterally is different from mutual matching. If mutual matching is co-regulated it would mean that the person you are trying to match is also trying to match you, and since this happens in a continuous way, you end up trying to match action that is partly the partner's and partly your own action reflected back to you.

While this seems harder, it turns out to be easier because as you attempt to match another, that person is already changing their behavior to make it more similar to yours. The 'stretch' between your behavior and the model's is reduced allowing the communication to converge toward a consensual frame. Indeed, this is the fundamental basis by which infants become communicative partners. Left to their own devices they are not very good at matching. But when partners alter their actions to fit better with the infant's abilities, the infant can become a creative co-participant.

Although I don't like the proliferation of scientific terminology for its own sake, existing metaphors describing communication processes all seem to lack an essential ingredient. Either they focus on the actions of one partner, or in focusing on both they lack the precision necessary to understand what actually goes on during a communication episode; they partly illuminate and partly obscure the process. Finally, some terms have been used in a number of different ways and so promote confusion. The co-regulation metaphor was chosen partly for such reasons.

The fundamental problem of being-in-relation

The systems metaphor of co-regulation leads to an apparent contradiction with respect to traditional Western psychological constructs of the individual. If we are always in the thrall of relationships to one or another thing or person, why is it that we develop as individual persons within those relationships? In philosophy, psychology and sociology, there are many theoretical and empirical attempts to address the mystery of the relationship of the personal to the social.

The traditional subject matter of Western psychology and philosophy is the individual.[41] It is no wonder that we tend to reason from individual capacities to construct theories of how people enter into social discourse. The Chomskian view of language as an innate faculty of the mind is similar to a host of psychological reasoning about thought, social skill, and morality. In the individualistic perspective, these faculties may be shaped and elaborated by the social environment, but they are essentially self-contained boxes within the person that are presumed to be receptive to particular forms of input from the environment and possess certain types of routines for processing that information. If one's focal attention is on individuals, relationships matter only as inputs and outputs of the individual psyche.

I take the opposite view. The essential fact about organisms is not their organic integrity but their connectedness to the environment. Evolution could not have made a creature that is first an isolate and later a participant since the primordial organism coalesced out of a primordial environmental soup simmered in a rock cauldron in the sunshine and atmosphere of a primordial earth. The first life form was life-in-the-world, and its identity was its particular relationship to the world. The living cell today is not a copy of the original cell. All cells living today have evolved, have become more complex over an eon of test trials. Cells have got better at one essential task that has not changed over time: relating to their environment. Cell walls are permeable in that the interior structure of the cell is incomprehensible without a knowledge of the relationships between the interior and the exterior. No less is true for the organism as a whole.

The primacy of the relationship over the individual is expressed by twentieth-century philosopher John MacMurray,

> human behavior is comprehensible only in terms of dynamic social references; the isolated, purely individual self is a fiction ... [This idea] compels us to

abandon the traditional individualism or egocentricity of our philosophy. We must introduce the second person as the necessary correlative of the first, and do our thinking not from the standpoint of the 'I' alone, but of the 'you and I.'[42]

My own approach is similar in spirit. I use the metaphor of the co-regulated communication process as the starting point from which I try to explain the individual. The design, function and development of individuals is centered around the nature of the communication process, whether we are communicating with animate or with inanimate objects.

Many scholars who are trying to understand the individual often take refuge in simpler conceptual frames. Buoyed by the idealism of nineteenth-century scientific objectivity they pursue a quest for better measures of individual functioning, for tracking individual change, for predicting risk and outcome. We assess people in terms of their presumed faculties and we evaluate relationships as input to those faculties. It is common practice, for example, to speak about particular types of parental behavior as contributing either to healthy or pathological outcomes for children, even when it is acknowledged that children can affect their parents. It is as if we were speaking about billiard balls whose collisions impact in predictable ways directly on the future behavior of each ball.

Co-regulation, at least as I define it, is not a conceptual commodity that one typically finds in the Western behavioral scientist's pantry. And why should this be so? The concept of co-regulation emphasizes the dynamically changing individual at the very moment of transaction with others: an individual whose behavior and goals are not entirely planned in advance but emerge creatively out of social discourse. If science is the study of objective entities, if it requires those objects to remain identifiable and invariant through the measurement process, then co-regulated individuals are not amenable to this kind of scientific study. It is my belief, however, that co-regulated systems are scientifically understandable. The science, however, will not be based on the logical manipulation of objective entities.

We forget the insights of the early twentieth-century because the tools of our trade are not up to the task of a relational science. Without tools, there is an impoverished culture, and without a culture individuals can't affirm themselves as members. To be a behavioral scientist of beings-in-relation is to stand outside the mainstream of that culture. Those who take seriously the power of relational concepts are still struggling at century's end to elaborate the insights of its beginning.

Notes

1. Ekstein (1989, pp. 10–11).
2. Ekstein (1989, p. 16).

3. The American, French, Russian and Chinese communist revolutions, to name a few, although such revolutions and empire dissolutions occurred also in the British, Dutch, Spanish, and Portuguese empires and monarchies in the Southern Hemisphere.

4. Dictators and some religious groups still cultivate the primacy of the citizen–leader relationship, which to most Europeans and North Americans seems anachronistic: a breakdown of relationships between individuals at the grassroots.

5. The works of William James, Sigmund Freud, Ludwig Wittgenstein, and the existentialists, for example.

6. Modern art became disconnected from its pictorial roots to explore the properties of form and color.

7. Ekstein (1989).

8. Indeed, the West is late coming to the concept of interdependence, an idea that is present in oriental cultures and in some primitive cultures. These cultures, however, did not evolve a science of human behavior. Since this scientific approach arose in the West, the focus here is on Western history and culture.

9. Ford (1987); Mason (1953); Worster (1977).

10. Mason (1953).

11. Often, the scientists were mere window-dressing. In order to get their expeditions funded, explorers used scientific reasons for justification.

12. Goetzmann (1987); Mason (1953); Stegner (1982).

13. Aries (1962); Gould (1981); Somerville (1983).

14. Mason (1953).

15. Ashby (1952); Bertalanffy (1968); Ford (1987); Sameroff (1984); Weiss (1969).

16. Weiss (1969, pp. 8–9).

17. Lilienfeld (1978).

18. Markova (1990); Rommetveit (1990).

19. Ideas presented in this Table and echoed throughout this volume are about the applications of systems ideas to developmental biology and developmental psychology. These ideas are my own synthesis based on many sources, but in particular: Fentress (1976; 1989); Fogel & Thelen (1987); Kugler, Kelso & Turvey (1982); Lilienfeld (1978); Oyama (1985; 1989); Sameroff (1984); Skarda & Freeman (1987); Thelen (1988; 1989); Thelen, Kelso & Fogel (1987); Weiss (1969).

20. Oyama (1985); Sameroff (1984); Weiss (1969). Susan Oyama's (1985) appeal for understanding heredity as a developmental process is eloquent and meticulously documented. Her book examines the hidden assumptions of genetic causality in both biology and psychology, assumptions that sometimes lurk in the corners of what may, on the surface, seem like a systems perspective.

21. Bronfenbrenner (1979); Fogel, Nwokah & Karns (in press); Rogoff (1990); Thelen & Fogel (1989).

22. BS in Physics, minors in Mathematics and Chemistry, from the University of Miami, an MA in Physics from Columbia University, a PhD in Educational Psychology, University of Chicago.

23. Wartofsky (1979, p. 4).
24. Haroutunian (1983, p. 35).
25. Altman & Rogoff (1987); Sameroff (1984).
26. Bruner (1983); Kaye (1982).
27. Fogel *et al.* (1992).
28. Capella (1981); Condon & Sander (1974); Kendon (1970); McDowall (1978).
29. Condon (1982); Condon & Sander (1974).
30. McDowall (1978).
31. Collis (1979).
32. Kato *et al.*, 1983; Stern, 1974.
33. Beebe & Jaffee (1992).
34. Isabella & Belsky (1991).
35. Bakeman & Gottman (1986); Duncan & Fiske (1977).
36. See quote by Birdwhistell, Note 3, Chapter 3.
37. Bernieri, Reznick & Rosenthal (1988, p. 244).
38. See discussion of shared activity vs. consensual framing in Chapter 3.
39. Anderson, Vietze & Dokecki (1977); Ginsburg & Kilbourne (1988); Papousek, Papousek & Bornstein (1985); Stern *et al.* (1977).
40. Stern *et al.* (1985).
41. There are a number of examples of non-Western psychologies, based principally on the Eastern concepts of interdependence (Azuma, 1986; Befu, 1985; Ching, 1984; Cushman, 1991; Diaz-Guerrero, 1977; Doi, 1973; Ho, 1982; Kojima, 1985; Lagmay, 1984; Prothro & Melikian, 1955; Sexton & Misiak, 1984). Unfortunately, many of these world views have been hindered by inadequate research support or the importation of Western research methods. I will return to the theme of cultural differences in development and in metaphors about development in Chapter 10.
42. MacMurray (1958, p. 38). See also any of the phenomenological philosophers such as Buber, Husserl, Sartre, or Merleau-Ponty, and more recently McGeer and Braybrooke (1992).

Chapter 5

A model of communication: meaning and information

In the early part of the twentieth century, physicists discovered that ordinary light, and other electromagnetic radiation, could be mathematically modeled as a particle (the quantum mechanical model). The particle model of light had been around in some form since it was first proposed by Sir Isaac Newton in the late seventeenth century. The particle model did not receive much attention for the next 250 years, in part because it was not as well articulated as the wave model of light, first proposed in 1690 by the Dutch physicist, Christiaan Huygens in his *Traite de la lumière*.[1] Both the wave model and particle model are used today, depending upon one's applied and theoretical perspective. Models are not true or false. Each model captures a particular feature of the phenomenon and no model expresses all of its properties.

If something physical like light can be described legitimately from different and apparently contradictory points of view, something complex and biological like communication must also be accorded a wide field of interpretation. Natural phenomena are understood using models as interpretive tools, and those tools should match our world views and purposes. Thus, in what follows, I shall favor a model of continuous process communication, while also suggesting that discrete state models continue to play a role in our understanding of communication.

Discrete and continuous models of communicative information

When people communicate, information links the actions of one individual with those of another. According to a number of theoretical analyses of information,[2] how one defines information is related to how one conceptualizes the communication process: the mechanistic discrete state model and the organismic continuous process model each have different concepts of information. In the following discussion, communication is used in a generic sense that can apply to the communication between genes and proteins, between brain and body, or socially between individuals.

Information in discrete state systems

In discrete state models, there are senders and receivers. The purpose of communication is for the sender to alter the behavior of the receiver by transmitting informative messages. In such a model, the role of information is *to cause* a change in the receiver. One can speak of the 'message' of the sender, or one can talk about genetic 'messages,' or information coming from the brain that 'tells' the body how to perform.[3]

This model of information moving from one location to another is based on John von Neumann's theory of information processing using the computer as metaphor.[4] In the digital computer, information is transmitted from one processing unit to another. This information can be defined and measured in units called bits that can take on one of two values: on or off.

Although messages in a computer are always transmitted faithfully, in real physical systems messages don't always have their intended effect. Communication systems, because of their complexity, are inherently *noisy*, obscuring the message and reducing the likelihood that it will be read by the receiver as intended by the sender. A message with a high *signal-to-noise* ratio is read more clearly, is transmitted with less ambiguity. In a model developed by Claude Shannon, information is measured as the probability that the message will cause the presumed change, or the correlation between the input and the output.[5] In discrete state systems, information is synonymous with *reliability*, the extent to which the transmission process preserves the content of the sender's message.

Because noise in the discrete state model is presumed to be an inevitable part of any communication process, communication systems need to include redundancy in order to increase the likelihood of a message getting correctly transmitted. Redundancy can be built into communication systems by using repetition, and by using multiple channels of information. Receivers are also designed to detect the signal within the noise and to amplify and enhance the signal. This discrete state model of information works remarkably well for all types of electronic communication media, such as the transmission of radio and television information between the broadcasting station and the home receiver sets. Such models have also been applied to the functioning of the brain and to social communication with varying degrees of success.

Information in continuous process systems

The concept of information in discrete state systems is appealing because it is concrete and intuitive. We users and perceivers of social information are comfortable thinking about it as messages, and in terms of clarity and distortion of those messages. The concept of information in continuous process systems is considerably less intuitive because of the difficulty in grappling with the fundamental interconnectedness of constituents in dynamic systems: that nothing – quite literally, nothing at all – exists or can be defined by itself without reference to its relationships with other constituents. Information as 'message' or 'signal' is concrete, bounded, a thing-in-itself. Information in continuous systems is relational, open, not observable except in its effects on action.

We need a model of information that takes account of the complexities of a continuous communication process. The most fully developed models of information as a continuous process come from research in the area of perception–action systems, which are essentially information-mediated correspondences between an individual's action and the environment.

According to the theory of ecological perception formulated by James J. Gibson,[6] there is information available in the environment but only with respect to biological organisms that have the sensory systems to perceive that information in relation to their action. Information, therefore, is created as the linkage between the environment and the involvement of one's body with the environment.[7] Perception, therefore, involves action. The body is not passive when perceiving, it is walk*ing*, chew*ing*, see*ing*. One sees not by passively letting light hit the retina, but by turning one's head, moving the eyes, scanning the surface, walking around something, etc. I can perceive only when either myself or the object of perception, or both, are in motion or have moved. The fact that perception and action are coordinated implies that they inform each other.

The case of visual perception is easiest to illustrate. As one looks out on the world, light enters the eyes. As humans, we can see primarily what is in front of us, with light entering the eyes in the shape of a spherical cone whose point is at each retina, and whose base is along the surface from which the light is reflected. Surfaces reflect more complex patterns of light if they have more texture: folds, bumps, dimples, waves and the like. What our eyes pick up is all the bits and pieces of reflected light from the differently textured surfaces in our field of vision. This set of light patterns is called the *optic array*. When the individual moves, even a little bit, such as when the eyes move or the head turns, or when I move forward (locomote) into the environment, this optic array appears to move. As soon as I move my head or eyes just a little bit, the pattern of light falling on my retina changes.

Instead of a stationary optic array, I now see a *perceptual flow field*. Suppose I move straight ahead and parallel to the ground, as in driving a car down a highway, I would see the optical flow field shown in Figure 5.1. The lines in the field represent the movements within the flow field of the textured elements in the environment. If I move forward, parallel to the ground, and turning to the right I would see a flow field like that shown in Figure 5.2.

Figure 5.1 Optical flow field for moving parallel to a surface without turning. The direction of flow is toward the viewer. (*Source*: Bloch, H. and Bertenthal, B. *Sensory-Motor Organizations and Development in Infancy and Early Childhood*, 1990, reprinted by permission of Kluwer Academic Publishers.)

Figure 5.2. Optical flow field for moving parallel to a surface while turning to the right. (*Source*: Bloch, H. and Bertenthal, B. *Sensory-Motor Organizations and Development in Infancy and Early Childhood*, 1990, reprinted by permission of Kluwer Academic Publishers.)

Experiments have shown that individuals perceive their direction of movement from information obtained across the entire flow field. Even though the lines in the flow fields shown in the figures all seem to emanate from a distant point in the field, the point of convergence is not enough information to tell someone that they are going straight or turning. As the number of textured points in the surface is reduced, using computer simulations of flow fields that vary in density and heading, subjects become less accurate in judging the direction of movement.[8]

What is informative about the optic array that allows subjects to judge their direction of movement? According to Gibson, individuals have the ability to look at a complex optical flow and detect what is the same and what is different in the optic array as it changes over time. In Figures 5.1 and 5.2, the array changes since the individual points of texture appear to move and they also appear to get farther apart (the direction of travel of each point is toward the viewer). On the other hand, there is a constancy in the array since the lines of movement maintain a constant angle with respect to each other and also a constant curvature. These constancies across changes in the optic array (or in any perceptual flow field) are called *invariants*.

Thus, according to Gibson's theory, information is created in a perceptual flow field in the form of *the perceived relationship between the variants and the invariants*.[9] In another example, how do individuals know when they will make contact with a surface that they are approaching? In this case, optical texture appears to flow outward from the center of the surface, and the textural details of the surface get larger as one approaches, that is, there is a progressive magnification of details that appear to emerge from the center of the surface being approached. From the rate of change of the magnification (how big the image gets as a function of time), the observer can estimate the time until contact is made.[10]

The approach to a solid surface, or the approach to the edge of a surface (as in coming up to the edge of a cliff), is one example in which the relationship between perception and action has been studied in some detail. In the example of the ski-jumper shown in Figure 5.3, note that the jumper begins to emerge from the tuck posture and changes the position of his arms before actually arriving at the lip of the jump. Somehow, the jumper uses the invariants in the optical flow field in order to inform his actions to be appropriate for making the jump.

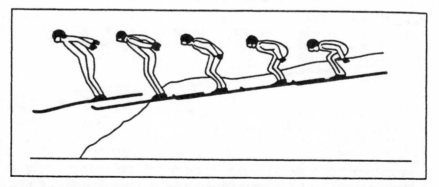

Figure 5.3 The relationship between perception and action as a skier approaches a jump. The changes in the skier's posture depend on information detected from the edge of the drop-off regarding the time to contact. (*Source*: Lee, D. 'Getting around with light or sound', in Warren, R. and Wertheim, A.H., eds. *Perception and Control of Self-Motion*, 1990, reprinted by permission of Lawrence Erlbaum Associates and the author.)

Research has shown that jumpers begin to change their posture at a time interval before the jump that is proportional to their speed, which is related to the time remaining until they reach the edge. Information about time-to-contact is available from the changes and invariants in the optical flow field, and this information is converted into the forces applied by the body to change one's posture and the position of the skis. Birds about to land use the same time-to-contact visual information, and bats use time-to-contact information perceived from auditory echoes.[11]

In a *perception–action system*, therefore, information links kinematics (the motion of the flow field) to dynamics (the application of forces). At the same time, the dynamics are causing one to move and therefore contributing to the changes in the optical array that produce the information regulating the action. This interdependence of perception and action, mediated by information, is shown in Figure 5.4.

From these examples, one can see that information is *created* out of the dynamics of action in an environment. Information is *in formation*, always being created out of itself and always changing with respect to action.[12] Information is specific to the particular individual–environment transaction. If one's intention is not to ski off the edge, but to ski along the edge, time-to-contact would be adjusted to a visual point before the edge of the cliff, and the action dynamics would be related to turning rather than jumping. As the turn was being executed, the optical array would change and the information needed to regulate actions related to turning would change correspondingly (as shown in Figure 5.3). And finally, information is specific to the type of body one has, its possibilities for perception and action.

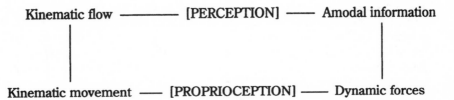

EVENT

Kinematic flow ————— [PERCEPTION] ——— Amodal information

Kinematic movement —— [PROPRIOCEPTION] —— Dynamic forces

ACTION

Figure 5.4 Basic model of a perception–action system. *Actions* and *events* are more than just movements and objects. Actions and events are movements and objects that are meaningful with respect to each other as part of a dynamic perception–action system. Events possess information relative to the individual's actions. As movements change, it changes the perceptual flow, which changes the information, which changes the forces and the resulting movements. There is no starting or ending point in this loop. Action can only be understood as an entire process, as a self-organizing system.

Perception–action systems in early infancy

As early as the first month of life there is evidence that human infants participate in perception–action systems. Auditory and tactile sensations are perceived in relation to action from birth. Awake and alert infants only 3 minutes old can turn their eyes and head in the direction of a pleasing sound. If the sound is intense, infants turn their head in the opposite direction. These are not mere reflexive actions since infants will visually scan around the area of the room in which the sound source is located.[13] Even though newborn reaction times to the sound are rather slow compared to later in infancy, and even though the sound must be played for at least twenty seconds and in the middle range of audible frequencies,[14] when newborns respond their actions are coordinated with their perceptions.

Infants only a few days old will turn their heads and make appropriate facial expressions according to the pleasantness or unpleasantness of the odor or taste. When given sweet solutions newborn infants will slow down their sucking rate in order to hold the liquid in their mouth for longer periods as if savoring the taste, and they will consume more of sweet liquids. They become restless and stop sucking when the solution is bitter or very salty.[15]

The hand and mouth of a newborn are especially sensitive. Infants will suck as if trying to get nutrition from a normally shaped nipple, but they will perform more exploratory movements of the tongue and lips when nipples have unusual shapes. They suck and touch differently depending on whether objects are hard or soft.[16] Newborns will recoil from pain and curl snugly into the arms of a warm adult.

Thus, for some sensory and motor systems, newborn behavior is related to information created by a perception–action system. This is not true for all aspects of the newborn's behavior or for all aspects of the environment. Babies of this age are relatively insensitive to changes in the saltiness of solutions and will often suck on water so salty it would choke an adult. They are not capable of perceiving a great deal of what happens around them. Nevertheless, when they do act it seems to be in relation to what is informative for them in the environment and their actions are created with respect to the discovery of that information.

One way to conceptualize the development of infant action is in terms of an increasing sophistication of the kinds of information the infant can create in relation to the environment. This sensitivity depends on their ability to perform actions that are coordinated with their senses. In this way, neither action nor perception is the primary cause of development. Rather, action refines perception at the same time that perceptual discoveries spur new actions.

By the time infants are 6 months, for example, they possess a remarkable range of manual actions that are specifically related to differences in environmental invariants. They can adjust their reaching to an object's speed, shape, size and distance.[17] When given objects of the same shape but varying in texture, 6-month-olds move their hands or fingers from side-to-side across the surface of the object. When given similarly shaped objects varying in hardness/softness, they will apply pressure by squeezing. They will bang hard objects on a table but not soft objects.[18]

These infants are using properties of the environment to inform them about the types of action that are most appropriate with respect to creating that information. The distinction between information as a created psychological construct and the physical properties of events and objects is crucial. The same objects or events do not affect different individuals in the same way. The edge of the cliff means something entirely different to an expert compared to a novice skier. A textured rattle would have considerably more significance to a 6-month-old infant compared to a 6-day-old infant. The analysis of action must take account of what is informative for the individual, and not what is 'out there' concretely defined. With babies it is especially clear that changes in their sensorimotor systems lead to changes in the availability of information: the body is central to an understanding of information and its development.

Although we know that animals have the capacity to use the variants and invariants of kinematic perceptual flow fields as informative for the dynamics of their own action, it is a mystery how this is actually accomplished. Clearly neural circuits, muscles, bones and joints, and the connections between various body tissues play a role. So do the types of culturally available tools (such as whether one is wearing racing skis, touring skis or snow shoes).[19] In this book, I accept as a given that perception–action systems exist, and I explore how they function in communication and its development.[20] I will not attempt to probe the details of the neurophysiological and neuromuscular processes that are at the heart of the perception–action linkages.[21]

Information in continuous process communication systems

Cross-modal perception

In order to move from the theory of ecological perception and perception–action systems to a theoretical model of social communication, we have to examine the kinds of perceptual information that are available to participants in social discourse. The discussion here focuses on human communication, but it could be generalized to all forms of animal communication, and to animal–human communication.

Participants in social interactions perceive each other across a number of different sensory modalities – including vision, audition, olfaction, taste and touch – depending on the type of relationship between the partners. Although some perceptual information is specific to modalities, like color to vision, or timbre to audition, some perceptual information may be cross-modal: *Cross-modal perception occurs when information perceived in one modality is translated into perception or action in another modality.* An example is clapping to the beat of music. One translates the rhythm and intensity information invariants from the auditory perception into the tactile–motor action of clapping.

Even though infants cannot clap to the beat of music, they are able to perceive when events in different perceptual modalities have the same temporal pattern. A number of studies have been done on the infant's perception of a relationship between sight and sound. For example, infants are shown two animated cartoon films side-by-side. A sound track, matched to only one of the films, is played from a speaker mounted between the film screens opposite the mid-line of the infant's body. Infants as young as 4 months prefer to look at the film matching the sound track.[22] If infants of the same age are exposed to an auditory rhythm and later shown two visual images – one with the same rhythm and one with a slightly altered rhythm – they prefer to look at the image with the matched rhythm.[23]

In another experimental design, the infant's mother and father are seated across from the infant, one on the right and one on the left. A speaker in the center plays the mother's voice and then the father's voice eight different times in a random sequence. It is highly likely that 4-month-olds will look in the direction of the parent whose voice is heard from the speaker.[24] We know less about younger infant's cross-modal abilities because fewer studies have been done. The fact that newborns will turn toward the source of a sound suggests a rudimentary cross-modal relationship between auditory perception and head movement. Certainly by 3 months infants can reach for objects that they can see, and recognize objects visually that they had been exposed to in the dark by touch alone.[25]

It seems quite likely, therefore, that from the beginning of postnatal life, human infants do not behave like reflexive automatons. Their perceptions are continuously linked to their actions and these linkages can be cross-modal across both perceptual and action modalities. Thus, infants are especially suited to enter into continuous process communication systems that are based on perception–action linkages.

Perceptual information available in social systems

What kinds of information mediate the social interaction between individuals? Based principally on the work of James Gibson (who catalogued the general forms of invariants related to perceptual events that occur in the natural world), Daniel Stern (who described the detection of perceptual invariants during social communication with infants) and Klaus Scherer (who elaborated the invariants of vocal communicative patterns),[26] Table 5.1 presents a listing of the common forms of perceptual invariants and elaborates their application to information during social communication systems.

Table 5.1 Varieties of perceptual information based on the relationship between variants and invariants in a kinematic flow field (created by motion of the field and/or the subject). Also listed are some communicative actions whose dynamics typically connected with each form of information

Invariant	Information	Action
Distance displacement, expansion and contraction, increasing and decreasing intensity	1. Expansion from a point and magnification or increasing of intensity	1. Approaching a partner, becoming louder, surging, crescendo, explosive
	2. Contraction toward a point and minification, or diminishing of intensity	2. Avoiding, leaving or withdrawing, fading away, trailing off, becoming softer
	3. Maintaining constancy in size of elements or intensity	3. Maintaining a constant distance, leveling off, framing
Lateral displacement and rotation, movement against a background	1. Deletion of background texture on one side of an object, and addition of texture on the other side	1. Partner's body moves across perceptual field, hiding and revealing, masking and deceit, stroking, clothing and make-up
	2. Shearing of texture against a constant background	2. Turning toward or away, rubbing, role change and taking the perspective of the other
Elasticity and rigidity, shape and surface deformation	1. Deformation of shape	1. Changes in body posture, stance, gait, effects of clothing, sensitivity, pliability, suggestibility
	2. Deformation of surface	2. Changes in facial expression, dimpling, wounds, swelling, muscle contractions and flexions, changes in flow (tears from eyes, mucus from nose, saliva, genital secretions, blood, perspiration), hair or beard style
	3. Rigidity of form	3. Immobility, stiffness, insensitivity, impassivity
Dissolution and emergence of form	1. Dissolution of perceptual texture	1. Disappearance, silence, pausing, leave taking, ending a topic
	2. Emergence of perceptual texture	2. Appearance, action following pause, greeting, growth, eruption, aggregation, beginning a new topic
Color and texture	1. Changes in color	1. Blushing, tanning, becoming pale, reddening (anger, exertion, engorgement of sexual

Table 5.1 (cont.)

Invariant	Information	Action
		organs), clothing and hair color changes; timbre of voice
	2. Changes in texture	2. Wrinkles, pimples, creasing of skin or clothes, goose bumps, moistening or drying
Frequency and regularity	1. Changes in spatial density or temporal frequency	1. Number of textural elements, beats (claps, head nods, vocal sounds), pitch of voice, synchrony in time
	2. Changes in regularity of time or space between events	2. Rhythms, regularity vs. irregularity of time between beats or points, uniform vs. non-uniform distribution of spatial elements

The point of this table is to show that a small number of invariants create information that underlies a great variety of communicative actions. In addition to those actions listed in the Table, one can imagine an even larger catalogue of actions that represent combinations and variants of these information types.

Take, for example, the invariants of intensity and of temporal frequency and regularity. The intensity invariant allows one to perceive a change of intensity, say changes in stress within a word or sentence. The temporal pattern invariant allows one to perceive differences between stress change patterns that have different temporal properties. For example, the word 'hello' can be spoken with an abrupt stress increase on the first syllable (hel – o), or with a more gradual stress increase on the second syllable (he – lo), or with a gradual increase and maintenance of high stress on the second syllable and the artificial addition of a lowered-stress third syllable (he – lo – o). The resultant differences in information from these three readings of 'hello' come from the listener's and speaker's perceptual detection of the invariant and variant properties of intensity changes over time, the *intensity contour* of the speech. Intensity contour is one of many possible combinations of informational modes used in social communication.

Although the research is a bit sketchy, there is evidence that infants may perceive all of the invariants listed in Table 5.1.[27] Sensitivity to each invariant may emerge at a different age and may be more acute in some perceptual modalities compared to others. In any case, infants are capable of using perception to derive meaningful information in social interaction well before the onset of language and gesture: merely by being a participant in a mutually coordinated action system with another person.

This model of continuous information creation provides a link to the continuous creation of mutual action during co-regulation. In one example (Figure 3.2), a speaker stretched out a word (herrrr) and shifted his posture with the result that the listener, who had momentarily looked away, resumed looking at the speaker.

How can we describe this in informational terms? The speaker perceived a shearing in the visual flow field around the listener's head (rotation, turning away) that had meaning with respect to the speaker's actions (this information means to the speaker that the listener may be inattentive). The listener perceived a change in the intensity contour of the speech (drawing out the word with falling stress and pitch), a dissolution of the speech sounds (silent pause), and perhaps caught in peripheral vision a deformation of the speaker's form (posture shift). Each of these perceptual flow fields become informative to the listener (information meaning that the speaker is requesting the listener's visual attention), whose head turn and gaze back at the speaker was perceived as a form of rotation signifying that the talk could resume.

Similarly, very young infants will alter their behavior when adults turn away, leave, interrupt their activities with the infant, drastically change their intensity of touch or speech, or change their posture.[28] I suggest that infants perceive these changes in action according to similar invariant dimensions as adults. Infants, however, may have less elaborate cross-modal linkages to actions than adults.

In a study I did in collaboration with Sueko Toda,[29] we observed infants at 3 and again at 6 months interacting with their mothers. Following a 3-minute spontaneous face-to-face interaction, the mothers were asked to cease talking and moving and just sit quietly and watch the infant. Previous work[30] using a similar procedure at 3 months showed that when mother displayed the 'still-face,' the infants reduced their smiling and looked away from her more than during the spontaneous play. Toda and I found that in addition to merely looking away, 6-month-olds, compared to 3-month-olds, were more likely to look at something they were doing with their hands, such as touching their clothing or the chair, or their own hands. In other words, the creation of information related to maternal interruption was disruptive of the infant's social activity at both ages, but the older infants were able to link the perception of interruption to a wider array of action modalities.

The concept of information used here is similar to the concept of *meaning* used by others. According to the theory of activity (see Chapter 8 for a fuller discussion), the meaning of an event is related to the individual's purpose or goal. Jerome Bruner[31] views meaning as initially functional and as related to the context of events in which the individual is acting. Proponents of this perspective typically view meaning as constructed through action, not as a representation of some objective reality 'out there.' I shall use the terms meaning and information as synonymous, with the assumption that meaning is not taken as pre-existing, nor as categorical, nor as objectively inherent in actions and objects, but rather as continuous and created through action.

Information is created at the interface between perception and action. Events that one can perceive (including physical objects and the actions of others) are informative only to the extent that they are meaningfully related to one's current actions: different actions with respect to the same events will yield different information. The information is therefore not 'in' the situation nor 'in' the perceiver, but is created when the perceiver engages in an active discourse with the event. Information is cross-modal in the sense that it can be perceived through different sensory systems and translated into different forms of action in any part of the body.

Information is also meaningful with respect to the *experience of one's own body*. It is not just that I can perform an action to achieve a purpose that is meaningful, but it is what I discover about *how* I perform the action: what my arms and legs can do, my cardiovascular tolerance, my trust in my ears and eyes to assist me. It is this last point, the saliency of the body – the artistry of the performance and the simple pleasure of perceiving – that is missing in many theories of meaning.[32]

In ordinary social communication, participants do not always detect the same information. Although information is, in theory, available in both social and non-social situations, those situations will be informative in different ways for different people, and at different times for the same person. In general, because co-regulation moves individuals toward consensual frames, this enhances the probability that partners will create particular forms of information. When interacting in non-social situations, the individual must do all the work of accommodation. According to Gibson,

> The information for perception is not transmitted, does not consist of signals, and does not entail a sender and a receiver. The environment does not communicate with the observers who inhabit it. Why should the world speak to us? The world is *specified* in the structure of the light that reaches us, but it is entirely up to us to perceive it.[33]

The unique feature of the social world is that it increases the likelihood that we will perceive certain features of the environment, of ourselves or of the social partner.

G. H. Mead captures the dynamic nature of information creation in social communication. He states that 'the act or adjustive response of the second organism gives to the gesture of the first organism the meaning which it has.'[34] Co-regulation enhances the creation of information because the events to be perceived are the actions of another person, actions that are fitting more closely over time with one's own. Although it may seem more difficult to create meaningful information with respect to a complex, dynamic social partner compared to an inanimate object, the 'adjustive' response of the social partner that is becoming coordinated into a consensual frame with one's own makes one's action more readily perceived as meaningful by the partner.

Information in infant–adult communication

Consider the following examples[35] in which an infant's mother holds out her hand in an offer to pick up an infant.

> *Successful offer to pick up.* Laura (age 12 months, 15 days) is seated in the highchair. Her mother is kneeling in front of her and talking to her. Both are looking at each other. Mother points to 'Woodstock' (a toy bird suspended from the ceiling) and comments, 'Look at Woodstock.' Laura follows the directive and then vocalizes. She then looks back to her mother and grins. Her mother forms a pick-up offer and asks, 'Are you coming?' Laura immediately forms a reply. As her mother places her hands in position, Laura leans forward into her arms and her mother starts to lift.

> *Unsuccessful offer to pick up.* Stuart (age 9 months, 18 days) is strapped in the highchair. His mother stands to the side by the mobile, approximately 3 meters away. She is touching the animals on the mobile and asking Stuart if he can see the tiger. Stuart's attention is focused on the rattle in his hand, but he occasionally glances toward his mother and the mobile. Stuart looks toward his mother, who forms an offer to pick up, 'Want to come?' Before she has completed the offer, Stuart looks back to the rattle. 'Do you want to come and see?' He briefly looks at his mother and then continues to play with the rattle. His mother drops her offer.

In a discrete state model of information in communication we would view these examples in terms of individual states and signals related to those states. In the first instance, mother signals an offer to pick up and Laura signals her willingness to accept the offer. In the second instance, mother's offer signal is met with a signal of rejection from Stuart. From a discrete state perspective, we might infer – reading backward from action to intention – that Laura is willing, cooperative and friendly while Stuart is uninterested, uncooperative or unfriendly at that moment.

From the perspective of a continuous process model of communication, however, this reasoning about inner states and communication signals often leads to erroneous assumptions about the participants and their motives. The logic and language I am trying to develop here, however, may seem to exclude the possibility that individuals have internal states. That is definitely *not* my view. Rather, because of co-regulation, cognitions and emotions are created as part of the communication and are not fixed in advance.

After studying many instances of pick-up offers, Valerie Service, Andrew Lock and Penelope Chandler[36] were able to distinguish successful and unsuccessful offers on the basis of differences in the ongoing communicative process and not on the basis of each individual's presumed internal state or intention. Successful offers occurred when mother and infant's actions were both visually focused on the pick-up offer, and when the infant was not otherwise occupied. Thus offers were more likely to be informative for the infant's actions when there was already a frame for consensual attention, and when mother's position was such that it captured the infant's attention (Stuart's mother stood off to the side and above the infant; Laura's mother was directly in front of and at eye level with the infant). Because the infant was not holding or sucking on anything there was an opportunity to create a consensual frame for picking up and accepting the offer. If the child is not ready and able to be picked up, the offer is not informative for the child's next action. The child can clearly see the offer: it is not enshrouded in a haze of noise. It is simply uninteresting, not apparently relevant to the ongoing action. Thus, offering as a discrete and bounded action is not by itself informative even to an infant who might respond on another occasion.

Many investigators have found that infants appear to be more compliant, friendly and cooperative – that is, they take adult actions seriously as meaningful – when adults time their requests to the infant's readiness to respond, and when the adults set up a sequence of continuous interaction that ultimately may lead to such readiness.[37] In work currently in progress in my laboratory, Daniel Messinger and I[38] have analyzed successes and failures in both the mother's and the year-old infant's offers of objects to each other. Offers to give or to take an object are most successful when framed by mutual attention. Although infants at 1 year are not as skilled as their mothers in setting up a prior sequence of actions that heighten the probability of informative offers, infant offers are often accompanied by an infant smile at the mother at the time of the offer. By smiling and looking at mother at the same time, and often by exaggerated extensions of the arm, infants of this age seem to recognize the need for communicative strategies that make their offers more informative for their partners.[39]

If mother fails to respond to infant offers or to other types of communicative bids, infants as young as 6 months of age have been observed to try alternative strategies to capture the adult's attention. Depending on their age, infants will vocalize repeatedly, use alternative forms of gesturing, grab an adult's arm or clothing, reject adult's alternatives, and otherwise persist until the adult responds in an acceptable manner. Adults do the same.[40] This phenomenon, called a communicative *repair*, suggests that from a very early age infants act as if they view communication as a process over time and not as a set of discrete signals, and they act as if the information for the partner related to their offer is based upon how it is framed and co-regulated.

A final example of information in continuous communication systems comes from my research on postural communication during face-to-face interaction with 3-month-old infants.[41] In the series of photos shown at the top of Figure 5.5, mother holds infant Linda in a semi-upright position and facing mother in frames 1–3. In frame 4, mother tips Linda to one side and leans her back to a semi-supine position (frame 6) while supporting her head (frame 7). During the position shift Linda opens her mouth wide (frame 5) and initiates a bout of smiling while looking at the mother (frames 6–8). What we see in this series of photographs is a smooth shift in infant posture toward a more supine position in which both mother and infant are moving together.

The fact that the position change is achieved by a process of continuous communication is revealed by an unsuccessful attempt to move the infant's body seen in the bottom half of Figure 5.5. Linda's mother tries to attract the infant's attention to her face by turning Linda's head, which the mother supports with her left hand. Mother succeeds in capturing Linda's gaze in frames 2–5. In frame 6, however, Linda looks down then puts her hand to her mouth and turns away again, which is accomplished as her mother gently relaxes her grip on Linda's neck.

Thus, mother does not force Linda to look at her by applying more pressure to turn her head. Getting the infant's attention seems to work best

(a) Successful posture change

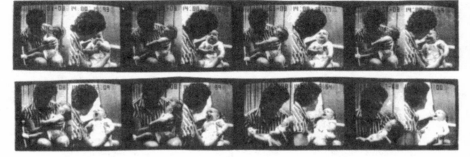

(b) Unsuccessful posture change

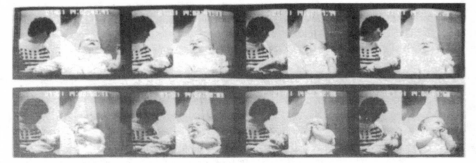

Figure 5.5 An example of a successful and an unsuccessful attempt to change an infant's position. In each case, co-regulation creates information that is meaningful in guiding each partner's actions with respect to each other. (*Source*: Fogel, A. 'Movement and communication in human infancy: the social dynamics of development', in *Human Movement Science II*, 1992, reprinted by permission of Elsevier Science Publishers.)

if the mother's attempt to turn the infant's head or move her body is timed to when the infant is already turning toward her and relatively relaxed. Linda's smile in the top half of Figure 5.5 may not have occurred if the infant was not ready for the position change, and Linda's face in the bottom half of the figure shows how infant facial expressions become informative for the adult during the co-regulation process.

Information in this system is continuously updated and mutually negotiated. It is not in the form of a signal and a response but is part of the process of how the interaction unfolds over time. Because information in continuous systems is broadly defined as anything created by co-regulation, infants of any age can be participants in the creation of information that is meaningful to them.

Notes

1. Huygens' investigations of the physics of light occurred at a time when Dutch painters were making stunning artistic innovations in the use of light in paintings. Rembrandt, Hals and Vermeer were contemporaries of Huygens. The Netherlands today is one of the centers of research on the relationship between visual perception and action.
2. Although there are many sources, I have relied primarily on the following. James Gibson (1979) discusses information between the environment and a perceiver. J. A. S. Kelso and B. Kay (1987) and David Lee (1990) define information in the control of action in relation to the environment. Susan Oyama (1985) and Howard Pattee (1987) discuss information in developing systems at all levels from genetic information to socially communicated information. Daniel Stern (1985) elaborates the nature of information in the relationship of the environment to self-experience in infancy. The concepts of information used here, therefore, apply widely to a range of biological phenomena. My own contribution is to make these ideas explicit in their application to social communicative systems, and in particular, to the development of communication in infants.
3. Ford (1987); Wertsch (1991).
4. von Neumann (1958).
5. Shannon (1963). Shannon's measure is actually for the entropy of a system, the amount of information that is missing after a transmission occurs.
6. Gibson (1966; 1979).
7. Here, we have the essence of the origins of the sense of self, to be elaborated in Chapter 8.
8. Warren, Morris & Kalish (1988).
9. This is a fundamental point. Some interpreters of Gibson's view focus primarily on the detection of the invariants in perceptual arrays. Gibson himself, however, was quite clear that information is the relationship between the variants and invariants. It is essential to know what is changing and also what remains the same.
10. Gibson (1979); Lee & Young (1985).

11. Lee (1990).
12. Varela (1983).
13. Butterworth (1981).
14. Clarkson *et al.* (1989); Kessen, Haith & Salapatek (1970); Muir & Field (1979).
15. Crook (1978); Desor, Miller & Turner (1973); Lipsitt (1979); Steiner (1973).
16. Rochat (1987).
17. Field (1976); Mathew & Cook (1990); von Hofsten (1984).
18. Bushnell & Boudreau (in press); Lockman & McHale (1989); Ruff (1980); Steele & Pederson (1977).
19. I shall return to this idea in Chapter 10. As cultural events (for example, language and gesture) or tools (chairs, writing implements) become part of the perception–action system, culture becomes informative for the individual.
20. Social psychology also has a tradition of applying Gibsonian constructs to the study of social action (Ginsburg, 1985; Harre, 1981).
21. These processes operate at a different hierarchical level of the same perception–action system. Each level can be studied as a system in its own right, and there is no reason to assume that the neural level is any more important than the action level or vice versa. Neither could exist without the other.
22. Spelke (1976). In studies such as these, researchers present the films and the sound to the same infant many times. Different films may be used, sometimes the matching film is shown on the right, sometimes on the left, in random order. This strategy is used to eliminate the possibility that infants look to one side or the other merely by chance. If they can perceive the temporal match for any film in any position, the evidence is stronger that they possess such cross-modal skills.
23. Mendelson & Ferland (1982).
24. Spelke & Owsley (1979).
25. Bushnell (1981); Butterworth (1981).
26. Gibson (1979); Scherer (1982); Stern (1985)
27. Butterworth (1981); Fogel (1991); Stern (1985).
28. cf. Fogel (1991), for a review; Walker *et al.* (1992).
29. Toda & Fogel (in press).
30. Fogel *et al.* (1982); Mayes & Carter (1990); Tronick *et al.* (1978).
31. Bruner (1990).
32. I will return to the theme of the embodiment of cognition in Chapter 8.
33. Gibson (1979, p. 63).
34. Mead (1934, pp. 77–8).
35. Both examples are from Service, Lock & Chandler (1989, pp. 30–1).
36. Service, Lock & Chandler (1989).
37. See Schaffer (1984) for a review.
38. Messinger & Fogel (1991).
39. cf. Kaye's (1980) notion of shared intentions.
40. Giannino & Tronick (1989); Golinkoff (1983); Robinson (1987); Rogoff (1990).
41. Fogel (1992).

Part II

The relationship processes

Chapter 6

The formation of relationships: creating new meaning

Relationships form when communication between the same individuals occurs over repeated occasions. For most of us, communication takes place within the context of ongoing relationships and it is within the sanctuary of relationships that we develop as individuals: with parents, with children, with friends and lovers, with opponents and enemies. We come to know ourselves first from moorage in the harbor of family relationships, hopefully, before we drift or sail under full steam to unknown protected waters.

In this chapter, I examine some of the existing theories of individual development in relationships and the development of relationships. I compare discrete vs. continuous models of relationship formation. I propose that babies are participants in relationships from the beginning and that they share with their parents in the creation of meaning.

Models of relationship formation

The discrete model of relationship formation

One model of development suggests that a relationship is organized into discretely different time periods in such a way that the characteristics of the relationship at prior time periods are necessary precursors to the current and future characteristics. This model of relationship formation is called a *stage model*. In a stage model, development is viewed as an invariant sequence of discretely different stages, each of which contains the seeds for the next. One problem with such models is that stages often take on a life of their own, as if they occur by design.

A continuous process model of relationship history assumes that new consensual frames in a relationship emerge via continuously changing and co-regulating processes. The relationship system has a history because each new encounter creates new information that then becomes part of the consensual

85

frame between the partners. Consensual frames emerge and stabilize as part of the active process of re-creation and not because of the organizing influence of some generalized stage representation inside each individual.

I don't want to resurrect the lengthy, ongoing and important debate within developmental psychology about the strengths and limitations of stage vs. continuous process models of development.[1] A brief critique of stage models is useful, however, within the general theme of this book. The critique is based on theoretical approaches to development that rely on dynamic transactions and continuous process models of development.[2]

It often happens that stage concepts are developed as heuristic tools for talking about different periods of development, but later become reified as discrete units: stored in some dedicated area of the brain and presumed to be causes for the emergence of later discrete stages. There are models of infant development that are based on representations of relationship stages and therefore on the individual's use of such representations to guide their progress through the relationship.[3] The only way to defend such models in early infancy, for babies participating in their first social relationship outside the womb, is by an appeal to an innate representation of relationships and their changing frames.

Table 6.1 shows the rather well-known sequence of stages in the development of parent–infant attachment proposed by John Bowlby. At all stages the child has a 'working model' of the relationship, a representation in memory for the accessibility of the parent to intimate encounters.

The reductionism to a discrete state representation within the individual of developmental stages of increasing intimacy reflects an objectivist, that is non-relational, core hidden in many developmental theories that on the surface at least, appear to be interactional in focus. John Fentress,[4] Susan Oyama,[5] and Peter Wolff[6] have written excellent essays on the meta-theoretical error of this sort of reductionism in developmental thinking.[7] The ultimate question – for adults and for infants – is, if there are representations of stages, where are they stored and where did they come from? Since infants don't become attached to all their acquaintances, it can't be the case that infants automatically invoke an attachment and intimacy development plan or a shared meaning progression with everyone they meet.

The danger of stage models is that individuals take the stage notion that is created purely as a descriptive metaphor and reify it into a determinism of inevitable succession.[8] Once stages are reified, people are compelled to search for where and how they are stored in the individual (in the genes or in a genetic predisposition for the brain to develop in such invariant sequences) or in the environment (in the parent's model of the infant and of infant development).

In my view, stage models can be useful in the following ways. They provide a set of cultural metaphors for talking about changes in what happens between parents and infants over time. They offer some guidance for parents,

Table 6.1. John Bowlby's model of the development of parent–infant relationship stages during the first years of life

Approximate age (months)	Stage	Description
0 to 2 and over	Orientation to signals without discrimination of a figure	The infant shows orientation to social stimuli – grasping, reaching, smiling and babbling. The baby will cease to cry when picked up or when seeing a face. These behaviors increase when the baby is in proximity to a companion, although the baby cannot distinguish one person from another.
1 to 6 and over	Orientation to signals directed toward one or more discriminated figures	Similar orientation behaviors as in Stage I appear, but they are markedly directed to the primary caregiver. Evidence of discrimination begins at 1 month for auditory and at $2\frac{1}{2}$ months for visual stimuli.
6 to 30 and over	Maintenance of proximity to a discriminated figure by means of locomotion as well as signals	The repertoire of responses to people increases to include following a departed mother, greeting her on return and using her as a base for exploration. Strangers are treated with caution and may evoke alarm and withdrawal, others may be selected as additional attachment figures (for example, fathers).
24 to 48 and over	Formation of a goal-corrected partnership	The child begins to acquire insight into the mother's feelings and goals, which leads to cooperative interaction and partnership.

(*Source*: Bowlby J. *Attachment*, 1973, copyright © 1969 Tavistock Institute of Human Relations and © 1973 Random House UK Ltd., reprinted by permission of HarperCollins Publishers and The Hogarth Press.)

caregivers and clinicians for patterns of interaction that are normative or expectable at particular ages and they can be useful tools in the hands of a skilled diagnostician. Finally, stage descriptions are concise narrative models for what a theory of relationship must explain as an outcome of a more fundamental process. Stages are, in a word, metaphors for development and not models of the developmental process.[9]

The continuous process model of relationship formation

Assuming that relationships do progress toward an increasing consensus about intimacy or about shared meaning, how can we explain this process without resorting to discrete stages or innate pre-knowledge as the explanation of this progression? Social psychologist Steve Duck[10] describes relationships as moving through stages of increasing intimacy, but his view of relationship formation is a continuous process model. For Duck, the stages of intimacy are continuously created by the participants: intimacy emerges from the process of mutual interaction. After an initial mutual attraction is established, a discrete state model would suggest that each individual must assess for himself or herself the risks and benefits of moving to the next stage of intimacy as if both partners knew what was coming and could make the decision independently of each other.[11] In Duck's continuous process model, moves to new consensual frames for increased intimacy are the result of mutual negotiation.

> The wish to become closer can be shown by indicating greater interest in the person, by showing that you enjoy his or her company, by confiding, by asking for personal advice and seeking opinions, or by generally creating more opportunities for further meetings in a wider variety of circumstances. When the invitation is thus indicated obliquely, indirectly and ambiguously, it may be acknowledged or ignored without offence ... Such changes in the patterns and diversity of their activities, the frequency of their meetings and their communication styles, are all ways of indicating, cementing and establishing increases in intimacy and commitment.[12]

It is notable that this observation on relationship formation is similar to the examples I cited in earlier chapters on the establishment of consensual frames during a single interaction. In other words, in the same way that the agreement about the type and topic of discourse must be mutually negotiated via co-regulation, the developmental changes in the frame must also be negotiated. As individuals spend more time together – a mutually co-regulated change in their relationship – they have more opportunities to know each other better and thus more intimate frames arise spontaneously.

According to Duck, couples do not start out talking about intimacy but as they become increasingly intimate they turn their discussions toward the topic of intimacy itself. They discuss their mutual commitments in such a way that the decision-making in the couple is not individualistic, based entirely on personal judgements of reward and cost, but rather socially co-regulated. It may actually be impossible to say whether a commitment to marriage, for example, is based on one's independent evaluations of the other person, or on one's sense of the other's commitment, or on a mutual agreement to be committed to each other.

Couples also begin to recognize the concreteness of the relationship by increasing communication about their shared past and less about their individual experiences prior to their meeting. According to Duck, this 'has the consequence of making them focus on the relationship itself and their feelings about it. It thus promotes an agreed definition of the relationship and its form, which is essential for its growth.'[13] People mutually create stories about their relationship. Duck makes a remarkable statement about stories that captures what I believe is the essence of the relationship formation process: 'I would go so far as to say that the creation of such stories is a part of the creation of the relationship itself.'[14]

Cultural and individual factors clearly play a role in relationship formation. Relationships are constrained to develop by cultural norms, as illustrated by culturally imposed restrictions on dating, and also by moral and ethical restrictions on sexual intimacy between, for example, siblings, parents and children, clients and therapists. Relationships are also constrained by the individual's tolerance for intimacy and willingness to enter into co-regulated discourse with a particular partner.

Nevertheless, a continuous process model of relationship formation suggests that relationships create themselves in the context of these cultural and individual constraints, but without following the constraints slavishly as if they were rules. Indeed, those cultural and individual constraints may become more or less important as the co-regulation creates new frames over repeated encounters. Relationships, therefore, are dynamic systems. They are created out of repeated interactions between the same two individuals, they develop stable and consensual frames over time, they change via creativity and variability.

When we examine the ways in which relationships change over time, it becomes apparent that the same kind of consensual frame may persist nearly unchanged for weeks until something unexpected happens and the dyad shifts dramatically to an entirely different frame of discourse. This patterning of stability and relatively sudden change has a stage-like quality. As we will discuss in the next section, this pattern of developmental change can be explained with respect to the creativity of co-regulation without appealing to pre-planning or to discrete state concepts.

Creativity in relationships

Meaning and information creation

Co-regulation is creative because information is not entirely fixed in advance, not entirely 'in' the self or 'in' the other. Information becomes available only through active engagement. I propose that the creation of meaning is the motivation for communication and for the persistence of relationships over time, not the mere meeting of needs through other people.[15] Ernest Schachtel, a psychoanalyst who has written about normal development, captures this idea in the following way.

> A painter may spend many days, weeks or months, or even years, in looking at the same mountain, as Cezanne did, or at blades of grass or bamboo leaves or branches of a tree, as many of the Chinese and Japanese masters did, without tiring of it and without ceasing to discover something new in it. The same is true of the poet's or writer's devoted love for his object ... of the true naturalist's perception of the plant or animal with which he has to live for long periods of time in order to acquire that intimate knowledge from which eventually new meaning and understanding will be born.[16]

The same is true, he goes on to write, of getting to know another person 'truly and deeply.'

The continuous process model of information provides an understanding

of how repeated encounters with the same object or person can continue
to create new meaning. When relationships evolve into patterns in which
participants perceive them as sequences of discrete exchanges of reward and
cost it is quite likely that the creativity has gone out of them. They are no
longer dynamic systems in which individuals grow, they have become prisons
of the soul. Repeated encounters, therefore, can sometimes dull the senses
and produce hatred, anger and boredom. It is not mere repetition that leads
to creative elaboration, it is one's stance toward the other, one's openness to
change and desire to create new meaning through the relationship.

Relationships must have a mystique: there must be something not quite
known, something that may never be understood or even articulated, something that entices the mind and body and that renews the meaning in the
relationship.

I am using the concept of continuously created information in co-regulated
systems to explain their persistence over time; the desire and the thrill of
that information creation is the principal motive for staying involved. By this
definition, I am not suggesting that relationships are primarily cognitive, for
that would be taking the term information in its discrete mentalistic sense.
As explained in Chapter 5, information in a continuous process model can
be anything that is perceived and created through co-regulated interactions
with objects and people: information can be in the form of body movement,
emotion, thought, memory, or sensation.

Equally, I am not suggesting that there is a motivation to become intimate
with another person as the primary cause of relationship development. Earlier,
I rejected this type of prior representation of the progress of a relationship.
I may begin a relationship with an individualistic need or wish to become
intimate, but the process of information creation about that need with the
other person should eventually replace it. If my body needs or wants to
gain information about something in particular, this is what organizes my
action and makes the information meaningful to me, but it is always in
relation to the object of my encounters. The same relationship can mean
different things to each participant. Having a shared goal is not required
initially for relationships to form and develop, although at later stages of a
relationship it may become an explicit goal for the continued growth of the
relationship.

Innovations in the formation of parent–infant relationships

I will illustrate how the creation of information across repeated encounters
leads to the development of the parent–infant relationship by using examples
from my own longitudinal research. The first example comes from research
on infant transactions with objects in the company of their mothers near the
end of the first year of life.

Around this time infants acquire the ability to release objects voluntarily into an adult's outstretched hand, that is, to offer objects to the adult. A case study on the development of offering done by Mark Reinecke and me[17] shows the progressive co-regulation of the consensual frame for offering.

Infant Hannah had become comfortable grasping and examining objects on her own. At 40 weeks of age (about 9.5 months), Hannah's mother began to take the objects gently from Hannah's hand, which Hannah immediately demanded back. Mother waited until this request was made before returning the object. Several weeks passed in which mother took the object, waited for Hannah to reach for it and then gave it back to her.

A delicate period of negotiation ensued in which Hannah's mother grasped the object Hannah was holding as if to take the object, but stopped short of taking it out of Hannah's hand. She waited with gentle pressure until Hannah released the object. This barely noticeable tug-of-war became a barely noticeable little game in which, for the moment, everything depended upon who held and who released. It is identical to the balance of forces exchanged in the pull-to-sit example of Figure 2.1.[18]

Perhaps a moment occurred between Hannah and her mother that was like the moment I showed between Andrew and his mother in Figure 2.3: a moment in which the infant's releasing the object and the mother's taking of it were entirely co-regulated, a jointly created activity in which no one actually took or actually offered the object. Unfortunately, we didn't capture this on tape for Hannah.

I believe that the genuinely decisive episodes in development are just such moments. These epiphanies of innovation are brief in elapsed time, mostly occurring in private, and therefore rarely observable by developmental scientists or clinicians.[19] Innovations emerge out of the fabric of the ongoing relationship process, and then become integrated into that process often leading to new consensual frames for co-regulation.

Regardless of the specifics of the process, only after genuine negotiation about how to manage object possession did Hannah begin to release the object voluntarily into the mother's hand. Hannah watched the object intently as it travelled away from her, carried by the mother's hand. As mother held it, waiting for a request, Hannah pre-emptively crawled over to her mother and took the object back. New negotiations emerged, this time framed by Hannah as the grabber and mother doing the holding and releasing. We could say that this constitutes a new 'stage' in the relationship, but we also see how it evolves in a continuous way, via innovation and transformation, from the prior pattern of co-activity.

One of Hannah's favorite toys was a bright red telephone that made a ringing noise. As with other objects, she would hand it to her mother to whom the telephone meant a game of pretend conversation with grandma or daddy. Hannah typically became impatient with what she perceived as a meaningless delay and climbed into mother's lap to get the phone back.

All of this changes at 44 weeks, when we recorded the following observation.

Hannah picks up the phone and looks at it, then at her mother. She offers the phone to her mother in the same manner that she had done in previous weeks. Mother takes the phone, puts it to her ear as in previous instances and says, 'Hi, grandma!' At that point, Hannah looks and smiles at mother and reaches out to request the phone. Her mother offers the phone to Hannah, who puts it to her ear and says, 'Ha–o.' Hannah again looks at mother then offers the phone to mother.

Hannah's explicit offer of the phone in this example shows an important difference because the offer now incorporates looks to the mother's face, an actual request rather than a grab, a smile and a word indicating that the offer is framed as 'I want to play the phone game.' These changes in the meaning of the offer and request for the infant occur over repeated negotiated encounters with the mother. In the early instances, Hannah and her mother perceived different information about the telephone. In the last instance, the information about the phone was consensual.

This research illustrates how consensual frames are transformed and how information is elaborated over the course of relationship change. One could say, as Kaye has done, that the change here can be described as a movement from shared rhythms (the turn-taking rhythm of give and take) to shared intentions (the agreement about jointly engaging in a game with a single purpose).[20] There is also evidence here of a shared memory and a shared language. This is as effective a way to describe this change as any that I know of.

From my perspective, however, all of the phases in the development of offering described here were based on co-regulated communication within an established consensual frame. In the early instances, information was created about issues like possession, holding on and letting go. In the latter instance the information was about how to create a pretend conversation. Each communication episode involved consensus and each involved negotiation around aspects where consensus was absent. I prefer, therefore, to speak about cognitions that arise as part of the communication process rather than about communication as exchanging messages about one's cognitions.

Another essential aspect of the development of the telephone game is that a small innovation in the communication system leads to a major change in the types of consensual frames for co-regulated discourse: from merely giving and taking routines to games with symbolic elements of pretend and imagination. These innovations are not pre-planned, and they only make sense in terms of the spontaneous discovery of new meaning. One is left to conclude that developmental change in a relationship arises spontaneously from the creative elaboration of information within ongoing stable consensual frames. Thus, the same information creation process that is responsible for the maintenance of consensual frames linking perception and action is also responsible for the creation of entirely new information that leads the communication system to evolve into a new consensual frame.

A final aspect of this developmental process is what Jerome Bruner calls *conventionalization* and what Maria Lyra refers to as the *abbreviation* of joint action.[21] They are referring to what happens in the developmental transition from negotiation to consensus, from co-regulation to framing. Initially, there is no frame for giving and taking objects and it takes weeks of mutual negotiation to establish the frame. A single act of giving or taking may take a long period of time as the infant wants to hold on to the object or to chase it down after giving it away. Once this procedure is worked out, it becomes stabilized, repeatable and patterned into a mutually created frame in which giving and taking occur rapidly and automatically and begin to serve as the launching pad for more elaborate forms of discourse in which the give–take frame plays a small but necessary part. The abbreviation metaphor captures the fact that frames form out of earlier co-regulated dialogue by a process of shrinking the action in time and smoothing out the performance.

Thus, relationships change by the dual process of innovation/negotiation and consensual framing/abbreviation. There is no single developmental trajectory. Different features of the communication are at different phases in this process. At any given point in time there is always some consensual frame and always something being negotiated within the frame.

What is the role of the adult guide?

In the study of the relationships between infants and their parents, a comparison between their relative knowledge and abilities inevitably arises. Adults, clearly, are more skilled and considerably more knowledgeable about the culture, about infants, and about relationships than their infant partners. Adults also act in certain recognizable ways when in the company of infants.

As noted by a number of investigators of the parent–infant relationship, parents and other more capable partners provide supportive frames in which infants can act with higher levels of performance than when alone. The Russian psychologist Lev Vygotsky was among the first to point this out with his concept of the *zone of proximal development*, defined as 'the distance between the actual developmental level as determined by independent problem solving and the level of potential development as determined through problem solving under adult guidance or in collaboration with more capable peers.'[22] There is a considerable amount of recent research to support the idea of 'distance' between the child's skills when alone or even with a similarly competent peer and the child's more advanced skills when with an adult.[23]

The difference in the child's performance during interactions with adults is believed to be due to the structuring, the guidance given by adults to the infant's activities. Kenneth Kaye talks about what he calls 'parental frames' in this way:

infants learn to play the role of system members because adults place them in
situations where the skills they lack are performed for them . . . By taking his role
for him, they [the parents] also demonstrate that role. Gradually, they relinquish
it to him as he shows signs of being able to take it on.[24]

Jerome Bruner describes the 'language acquisition support system' that
occurs over the course of development within relationships, especially during
elaborations of games like 'peek-a-boo' over several months of the infant's
life.

If the 'teacher' in such a system were to have a motto, it would surely be 'where
before there was a spectator, let there now be a participant.' One sets the
games, provides a scaffold to assure that the child's ineptitudes can be rescued
or rectified by appropriate intervention, and then removes the scaffold part by
part as the reciprocal structure can stand on its own.[25]

The adult, it is believed, by virtue of increased experience, brings prefabricated
structure to the interaction, perhaps using culturally available games, and
assists the infant in discovering the characteristics of that structure. Barbara
Rogoff also applies Vygotsky's ideas to her concept of 'guided participation.'

Shared problem solving – with an active learner participating in culturally
organized activity with a more skilled partner – is central to the process
of learning in apprenticeship. So are other features of guided participation
that I emphasize: the importance of routine activities, tacit as well as explicit
communication, supportive structuring of novice's efforts, and a transfer of
responsibility for handling skills to novices.[26]

Each of these theorists is clear about the fact that transition to the next
phase of a relationship, toward more infant responsibility for action, is partly
dependent upon the child's abilities and desires to become more responsible.
Adults decide to transfer responsibility in response to the child's widening
skill. Rogoff, for example, emphasizes the child's own initiative, creativity and
activity. It is the child's intrinsic motivation to be active that brings the child to
the adult and makes children 'active participants' in their own development.
Kaye also recognizes the importance of the adult in responding to the child's
own initiatives.

It may seem contradictory to say that mothers organize the world for their infants
and also to say . . . that interaction is a matter of the mother's adjustment to
their babies. Yet this is not a contradiction . . . When adults do allow their own
behavior to be temporally organized by the infant's, they are really assimilating
his cycles of attention and arousal to the adult world's cycles of speaking and
listening, gesturing and observing. So the adult's adjustment is in fact a form
of socialization. They construct a consistently organized social world around the
infant, teaching him to punctuate the flow of experience.[27]

Adults, therefore, participate in the creation of meaning for infants. They
provide the outlines of frames and are open to adjust their actions to achieve
co-participation.

These writers accept the idea that meaning is created in pre-verbal interactions with infants. Infants do not need to be able to describe in words the meaning of a situation in order to participate in that situation via meaningful actions. These views also suggest that infants develop toward increased skills and more responsible cultural participation – using cultural tools like language – by having their actions structured and interpreted as meaningful by adults. Because adults can interpret the infant's rudimentary actions and help the infant fill in the blanks of those actions in order to realize their goals – through support, modeling, co-participation and gradual transfer of expertise – infants become increasingly sophisticated social partners.[28]

In the guidance metaphor, the adult provides interaction formats – cultural practices, games, tools – to the relationship with the infant and becomes a participant in co-activity by actually playing the game with the baby. For some theorists the adult is also the source of innovations by pushing the child to new levels of activity with sensitively presented challenges. Like the water to which a thirsty traveller is drawn, infants are encouraged to drink in the parental culture. The infant apprentice later leaves to return to life's travels, and the surface of the water – the adult guide – returns to its expectant clarity, untroubled, waiting to be shaken into happy ripples at the traveller's next visit: the eternal mother of still waters, the mother as cultural saint.

Saints, however, do not develop; they always have the right answer and the necessary patience. Parents, though, develop by participating in co-regulated communication with an infant. The adult discovers how to negotiate and how to maintain consensual frames. Although most authors I have mentioned in this section are quite willing to apply the concept of directed action, discovery and creativity to the *infant's* action, they have only implicitly applied them to the adult.[29]

Some authors suggest that guidance is the product of a mutual interaction between adult and child, with spontaneous and *co-created* discoveries of relationship innovations.[30] Relationships can grow even when neither individual is consciously planning a guided curriculum because the very nature of co-regulated activity provides its own source of new consensual frames and information, new for both participants and available for further mutual elaboration and innovative change.

Those who favor the guidance metaphor recognize that novices have input to the extent that the expert must take account of their level of performance and motivational readiness. In many instances, however, the infant and child may see the situation in a legitimately different and potentially more useful way than the adult. The adult's action in this situation is not simply a matter of being responsive to the needs of the child on the way to competent cultural skills, but rather to let the child take the expert role.

In her work on training animals, Vicki Hearne describes moments in which trainers must abandon their own intuitions and allow themselves to trust in the dog's far superior sense of smell and be led on a tracking mission in what seems, from the human's perspective, to be an illogical direction. Trainers not only have to impart their knowledge to the dog during training, but at key moments they have to 'let their knowledge come to an end.'[31] Co-participation means that both individuals must be willing, at appropriate times, to accept expertise and guidance from the other, and to be vulnerable to being changed.[32]

The first non-human examples of adult–child co-regulation of a cultural activity have been observed recently among chimpanzee groups in the wild. Some, but not all, groups of chimps living in Africa have developed specific forms of tool use. Among those that use tools there are differences. They may use stones to crack nuts, sticks to catch termites in their nests, or leaves as drinking cups or sponges. Indeed the cultural diversity between chimp groups is considerably more than primatologists had ever expected.[33]

How do young chimpanzees learn to crack nuts with a rock? Mothers have been observed to leave hammers and nuts near the cracking anvil when the children are around the area, a rather remarkable occurrence since the mother risks the loss of her hammer and nuts to another adult. Mothers will also provide hammers that are the easiest to use, and they will give some of the nuts they collect to the infant.

> Salome (mother) was cracking nuts of the very hard *Panda* species. Sartre (infant) took 17 of the 18 nuts she opened. Then, his mother watching, he took her stone hammer and tried to crack the nuts by himself. These nuts are tricky to open as they consist of three kernels separately embedded in a hard wooden shell, and the partly opened nut has to be replaced precisely each time to gain access to the different kernels. After successfully opening a nut, Sartre replaced it haphazardly on the anvil in order to attempt access to the second kernel. Salome took it in her hand, cleaned the anvil, and replaced the piece carefully in the correct position.[34]

We cannot attribute this maternal behavior to genetically given programs for guidance, since it does not occur in all the chimp groups, nor even in all the tool-using chimp groups. It is also unlikely that the chimp mothers have the goal of acculturating the infant, and they probably have no concept of a tutorial progression. The only reasonable explanation is that this guidance is spontaneously emergent from repeated communication with a less skilled partner within a culture that provides certain tools for specific purposes; that is, guidance is a consensual frame, the outcome of co-regulation rather than a plan enacted with forethought.

I don't mean to imply by this example that human parents merely stumble upon guidance. Rather, I want to strip down the process of adult–infant interaction to its minimal constituents of mutual construction. Humans are very different from chimps. Not only is there a culture of tools and infant care practices, there is also a culture for guidance and its practices. Nevertheless, as I discuss in Chapter 10, mutual construction and creativity are at the core of putting those cultural practices into action with an infant.

Parenting can be done by almost anyone because in the company of an infant, if one is willing to enter into a co-regulated communication, parenting behavior will emerge over repeated encounters. The pattern of parental action is a creative product of a co-regulated interaction with an infant in just the same way that infant action emerges from the creative interaction with the parent figure. Parenting is the participation in a long-term relationship of mutual commitment with an infant.[35] It is a lasting relationship in which meaning is created, in which mutual understanding evolves and becomes the basis for continued involvement, and in which there is a willingness to work through the misunderstandings and mistakes. It is not to be encompassed merely as sensitivity or emotional attachment. Biological priming is not enough to make one a parent, no more than sexual attraction is a guarantee of a successful marriage.

A parental figure is someone who can provide a nurturing environment that meets the basic needs of the infant, needs for companionship and sustenance, needs for comfort and repose. Virtually anyone can serve in the parental role,[36] assuming they are motivated and capable of providing what infants need for their development: the biological mother and father, adoptive and foster parents, grandparents and other relatives, and professional infant care providers. In some cultures, older children provide infant care; in others infants are handed to any available adult in the community for tending when the immediate family is otherwise occupied. Parents are created through their participation.

Conclusions

The co-regulated creation of consensual frames is the process by which relationships develop. The specific types of relationship patterns that emerge will depend on the types of skills available to the participants, their ability to regulate attention and body position, and the presumed purpose of their activities together. Just as the pattern of wolf-circling emerges from the constraints imposed by the animal's body shape and movement potential, and by the motivation of each individual, I propose that relationship histories are similarly emergent processes to be understood from the way in which information is created for the participants.

Relationships sustain themselves when information is mutually created. The co-creation of information is inherently rewarding and leads to a continuing mutual orientation to the partner with whom it occurs. Relationships will not persist in the absence of creativity. When people come back together they don't simply follow a script or plan, they re-create frames and continue to elaborate them. The rewards of mutual creativity are not necessarily associated with positive emotions, as presumed by a number of relationship theories.

There is considerable evidence that relationships exist and grow under conditions of adversity, such as between conflicting siblings, within animal and human dominance hierarchies, in pathological parent–child conflict, aggressive and abusive relationships, and in dysfunctional family interactions.[37] The only way to explain such persistence in relationships in spite of adversity is with respect to the sustenance of the co-created information: information about how to meet needs in spite of the potential for threat, information about how to be an equal participant in the battle, or information about how to diffuse conflicts even temporarily.

Successful therapies often involve re-framing the process of relationship in order for partners to be creative with each other in less destructive formats. It may also be that successful long-term relationships have developed ways to capitalize on the creative process in order to elaborate new patterns. A long-term relationship is never static. It is constantly self-renewing and therefore self-sustaining.

Notes

1. Green (1988); Miller (1989).
2. Fentress (1989); Fogel (1989); Fogel (1992); Fogel & Thelen (1987); Thelen (1989); Thelen & Fogel (1989); Thelen, Kelso & Fogel (1987); Thelen & Ulrich (1991); Wolff (1987).
3. Bowlby (1969); Emde (1989); Mahler, Pine & Bergman (1975); Spitz (1965); Trevarthen (1979); Tronick (1980).
4. Fentress (1976; 1989).
5. Oyama (1985; 1989).
6. Wolff (1987).
7. See Fogel (1992) for a discussion of the problem with respect to relationships.
8. Stephen Jay Gould, in his book, *The mismeasure of man* (1981), makes a similar case for the reification of intelligence as a quantity based on notions of cranial size or scores in IQ tests. When individuals attribute a reality to their own metaphors in the absence of confirming evidence, it is usually due to a cultural perspective. In the case of intelligence, the reification was insidious and fostered a belief in racial and gender differences in intelligence. The reification of developmental stages has profound cultural, educational and clinical consequences. It is difficult to take stages too seriously when the theories presented here paint such remarkably different metaphorical portraits of infants. In addition to this diversity among Western psychologists, there is an enormous diversity of stage-related beliefs in folk psychology across different cultures (Fogel, 1990a).
9. Kaye (1980) makes this point clearly, although his notion of sharing invokes a discrete state model of cognition and communication.

10. Duck (1991).
11. Such a model was proposed by Altman & Taylor (1973).
12. Duck (1991, pp. 90–1).
13. Duck (1991, p. 93).
14. Duck (1991, p. 93).
15. Bruner (1975); Piaget (1954); Trevarthen (1979).
16. Schachtel (1959, p. 239).
17. Reinecke & Fogel (1988).
18. According to Hearne (1987), such simple games form the initial basis for acquiring meaning and for extending meanings into new frames for discourse during animal training work.
19. In the kind of work that I do, one must record many hours of videotaped interactions from the same dyads at frequent intervals over the first years of life, later to sift through them in the hope of finding a few bits of theoretical gold (cf. Fogel, 1989). The more standard research model is to devise a manipulation of normal circumstances, bring parent–infant pairs into the laboratory or even in their own homes, and after several minutes or hours of observation at half-yearly intervals, compute a numerical score that predicts the likelihood of positive vs. negative outcomes later in life. So long as these test scores are used as diagnostic of potential problems for the purpose of remediation, they are useful. To assume, however, that these scores and the presumed latent variables they represent are central to the developmental process is to me an act of hubris. One only has to read Gould's (1981) analysis of the misuse and misinterpretation of IQ scores to be chastened about assuming that test scores represent anything real in the dynamics of individual developmental change. Awe, it seems to me, has a role in social and behavioral science to prevent reducing ourselves to numbers and computations.
20. Kaye (1980). This type of developmental process has been described by others for the development of other gestures such as requesting (Braunwald, 1978; Bruner, Roy & Ratner, 1982; Lock, 1980).
21. Bruner (1983); Lyra & Rossetti-Ferreira (in press).
22. Vygotsky (1978, p. 86).
23. Bakeman & Adamson (1986); Camaioni *et al.* (1984); Rogoff (1990); Ross & Lollis (1987); Slade (1987).
24. Kaye (1982, pp. 70–1).
25. Bruner (1983, p. 60).
26. Rogoff (1990, p.39).
27. Kaye (1982, pp. 71–2).
28. In addition to the authors already cited, see also Heckhausen (1987); Ignjatovic-Savic *et al.* (1990); Wertch *et al.* (1980).
29. Bruner (1983) recognizes that frames (or formats, as he calls them), are jointly negotiated constructions of the dyad. Rogoff (1990) suggests that adults' adaptations to infants are 'momentary' (p. 73) compared to the changes in the infant. In another work (Rogoff, 1989), she suggests that adults develop both in their skill at the activity and in the process of guiding others in that activity as a result of their participation with the child. The real issue is the extent to which the adjustive response of the parent to the infant is merely a skilled

action requiring little effort, or the result of a creative co-participation with the infant: as much a discovery and innovation for the adult as for the baby.

30. Rogoff (1990).
31. Hearne (1987, p. 85).
32. Ochs, Smith & Taylor (1988).
33. Gibbons (1992).
34. Boesch (1991).
35. Hearne (1987) makes a similar point with respect to the long-term commitment required when entering into a training partnership with a horse or dog.
36. See my infant development textbook (Fogel, 1991), for an extensive review of the many types of relationships in which infants participate around the world. There is no concrete evidence to support the commonly held belief that women, particularly biological mothers, are the 'best' parents for infants. In experimental studies involving non-human species, foster parents can be created merely by olfactory priming even in adults who have never given birth. Across species there is not a universal pattern of maternal care, even among mammals who nurse their young. In some non-human primates cross-fostering is common and so is paternal care. My own research with Gail Melson (Melson & Fogel, 1982; Melson, Fogel & Toda, 1986) shows that there are no differences between young boys and girls in their knowledge about, interest in or willingness to engage in infant care, assuming they are in the company of a responsive adult when with the infant.
37. e.g. Dunn & Kendrick (1982); Patterson & Bank (1989).

Chapter 7

The formation of relationships: differences between dyads

In the novel, *Love in the Time of Cholera*, Nobel prize winner Gabriel Garcia Marquez tells the story of youthful love in his native city of Barranquilla, Colombia at the end of the nineteenth century. Like Romeo and Juliet, the adolescents in Marquez's novel share a secret love, forbidden by family prejudice and the cultural standards of the time in which young women were only permitted to see young men who were approved of and chaperoned by the family. Like Shakespeare's unlikely couple, the Colombian lovers met rarely. Instead, they developed a correspondence, passed between them by accomplices, lasting several years until the affair was discovered and forced to end by the girl's father.

The young woman later married another man with whom she lived for sixty years and to whom she bore several children. The young man never married, and through numerous affairs and personal trials he kept alive the dream of eventual closeness with the object of his childhood infatuation. Following the death of the husband, the estranged couple finally court openly and establish sexual intimacy in their seventies. These literary allegories illustrate the power of relationships to persist, to shape individual lives and destinies, to capture the imagination.

Most literature tells of relationships evolving and dissolving, remaining solid or breaking up through adversity. We hear stories of dogs and cats wandering for thousands of miles to find families who have re-located and of children who mourn the loss of their cherished pets. Less apocryphal are Vicki Hearne's descriptions of the faithfulness and responsibility of dogs and horses to their trainers, relationships lasting entire lifetimes and marked by mutual trust, respect and love.[1] Newspapers report emotional family reunions: of adopted children with their biological parents, of twins separated early in life, of families torn apart by war. These examples are extreme cases of what we know intuitively to be true about relationships: they last, they have a history, they ennoble and they shame, they define us and hold us in their grip.

Like individuals, no two relationships are alike. It thus becomes part of the task of understanding relationships that we explain their variety and the process by which such differences form. There are a large number of possible dimensions of difference between relationships. These include the degree of mutual commitment, the relative degree of affection vs. hostility, amount of mutual support and nurturance, and the nature of the roles and status relationships between partners.[2]

A theory of relationship formation should provide a model for how relationships preserve themselves and change over time and why human relationships develop along such dimensions of difference. Taxonomies of relationships' dimensions should not, however, be taken for a theory of relationship formation. In this book, I will not be able to address the variety of relationships found in this taxonomy. I offer instead a way to think about relationships that may generate such explanations in the future.

Processes of self-organization within relationships

Creating information by reducing degrees of freedom

Why is each relationship in which we participate different? How do relationships come to display stable consensual frames and yet maintain their creative variability? Although each encounter with the same person is somewhat different than the previous encounter, successive meetings with that partner have a degree of sameness. The ethologist Robert Hinde has written that

> to understand the stability of relationships we must understand both how they are preserved in spite of changes in the participants and the vicissitudes to which they are exposed, and we must also understand how they may change progressively and yet preserve their integrity.[3]

There are perhaps many thousands of potential patterns that might emerge when two people interact with each other at the beginning of a relationship. Thus, the theoretical problem is to discover why a particular pattern emerges. We could assume that relationships progress in particular ways because of some cultural rule or genetic predeterminism that biases the progress of the relationship in favor of one or the other individual. In the last chapter I rejected such facile solutions because they merely take what is observed about the existing types of relationships and then hypothesize some discrete unit – a gene or a rule – that carries the code for the pattern. The genetic and cultural models that arise are merely one-to-one mappings backward from the behavior to its presumed cause.

There is another approach, although it may seem radical to many readers.

That approach is to assume that there is no such rule or code but that differences between relationships emerge, are created in the process of interaction. Complex systems, by their very nature, will converge after a period of time toward a relatively stable and identifiable pattern of functioning because of the ways in which the elements of the system constrain each other to act.

At the beginning of any relationship, the number of possible forms of communication between individuals, the number of degrees of freedom in the communication system, is very high, set by the potentials of the participants' bodies and their ability to form communicative actions. Individuals enter into relationships with particular predispositions, temperaments, in the form of varying degrees of attentiveness, fussiness, activity level, and thresholds for stimulation and emotional arousal.[4] Because these starting points are different, and because even through change some temperamental features will continue to enter into what gets co-regulated, relationship patterns will be unique to each co-acting group of individuals.

In spite of the many possible ways two or more individuals could co-regulate, a relatively small set of patterns of interaction emerge that have order and regularity as well as variability. How, then, does a communication system go from an initial condition of high uncertainty with many possible degrees of freedom to a more organized pattern of interaction?

Recall from Chapter 4 that the patterned behavior of collective organization in a system has a smaller number of degrees of freedom than the total number of degrees of freedom of its members, or in Weiss's words, 'the component activities have many degrees of freedom, but submit to the ordering restraints exerted on them by the integral activity of the "whole" in its patterned dynamics.'[5]

In these terms, by entering into a communication one's many action possibilities (degrees of freedom) are in fact *reduced*. Out of the expectations that one may have had before the encounter, out of the multiple actions that might have shaped the encounter, out of all the ways one's body can move that make communicative sense, a particular and specific set of actions selectively emerges in the *actual* encounter. *Information is created when the degrees of freedom are reduced.* How can this happen?

I can illustrate the initial phases of self-organization in a communication system by returning to the example of wolf communication, shown in Figure 3.1. In the first frame of Figure 3.1, the first wolf walks past the second wolf, say from east to west, while the second wolf remains seated. In the next frame, the first wolf continues on this trajectory and both begin to turn their heads toward each other. In the third frame of Figure 3.1, the first wolf begins to execute a turn toward the north, while the second wolf begins to move toward the east: the circling pattern is taking shape.

Now, we can begin to see how the *creation* of information is related to the *reduction* of degrees of freedom in the action dynamics. A head turn constrains subsequent degrees of freedom precisely because its meaning to the other individual is to create a pattern of action (a matching head turn and a body turn) whose meaning to the first individual is continued vigilance. In other words, once the first wolf turns his head toward the second, the second's actions reduce the first wolf's possibilities: he must continue to keep his head turned to maintain his gaze at the second wolf. He can't walk off cavalierly without risking attack. Something is meaningful because it informs me about how to regulate the dynamics of my next action, about how to choose my next action.

Thus, in a very short time, a consensual frame emerges with only a few degrees of freedom left to each animal: continue walking in a circle, continue looking at the partner. We can formalize the description of the frame, therefore, as the set of degrees of freedom that have been consensually constrained, via the initial co-regulated negotiation, while the remaining degrees of freedom in the system are currently part of the negotiation process.

Information, therefore, is created when degrees of freedom are compressed, when one 'submits' to the restraints of the collective, of the discourse. Co-regulation as the continued compression of degrees of freedom is experienced by each individual as the continuous ceding of regulatory control from the self to the interaction. This may feel good, or it may feel miserable, depending on the nature of the discourse.[6]

There are a number of important conclusions to be derived from this simple example. First, we can see how information arises when the dynamics of action are co-regulated and how information leads to consensus. Second, the inevitable consequence of reducing degrees of freedom in a consensual communication system – or synonymously, the inevitable consequence of creating meaning in a communication system – is that frames coalesce spontaneously. The wolves, as explained in Chapter 3, don't have to plan this out and they don't have to have a rule system in their heads for making a circling pattern. Yet, they may circle each other many times before they mutually withdraw, and they may do the same thing the next time they pass each other so closely. Repeating patterns in a relationship are *symptoms of information creation*, not the proof of the existence of a rule or of the guidance of one partner by the other.

If I would otherwise have done one thing but because of my relationship with you I allow myself to be constrained to do something else, I allow the relationship to define what is meaningful for me. If I do this consistently during each of our repeated encounters, I am also acting responsibly with respect to the relationship as I choose to enter anew into a co-regulated contract that re-creates this responsibility. Responsibility to a partner is not necessarily represented in the mind, it is a characteristic of action-in-relation to another individual or thing.

A dynamic model of consensual framing in relationships

One model of how repeating patterns, such as consensual frames, form in a complex system is derived from a dynamic systems perspective. In certain systems, a stable resultant pattern can sometimes be modeled as a mathematical construct called an *attractor*. Attractors are not to be taken metaphorically to mean something like interpersonal attraction. Rather, given a family of curves generated by a system of equations in a complex n-dimensional space of component variables, the word attractor refers to the mathematical property of these curves to converge to specific points or trajectories as a function of time. Point attractors converge to a single point, limit cycle attractors represent oscillatory systems and chaotic attractors represent a repeating movement over similar, but never precisely the same ground.[7]

I find dynamic systems models extremely heuristic for the purpose of understanding relationship development because they suggest that complex systems can converge toward a stable pattern of behavior without a pre-scription or plan, merely by the mutually constraining influences of the components. The concept of attractors suggests that it is mathematically possible to model a system in which such convergence occurs spontaneously. Mathematicians have further demonstrated that it is possible to generate attractors from a system of equations, none of which specifies the final form of the attractor.

Such models are also useful because they assume that dynamic systems are inherently variable. Most of this variation, however, tends to return the system to the attractor configuration. In the example of wolf-circling, we can imagine that on each new meeting of this pair they may approach from different directions and at different speeds, and individual actions will be somewhat different. Yet in spite of these differences, the system is likely to converge into the same general pattern.

Sometimes, however, the range of variation exceeds that which is most conducive to creating a circling pattern. Circling occurs when one wolf is moving toward another who is sitting. If, however, the wolves are both moving in the same direction and initially in visual contact, a different stable pattern emerges called 'following,' shown in Figure 7.1. In following, the wolves maintain roughly the same distance between themselves at all times, a larger distance than for circling. They also maintain a similar body orientation toward each other, but that orientation is slightly different than for circling.[8]

Besides these two stable consensual frames in the two-wolf system,

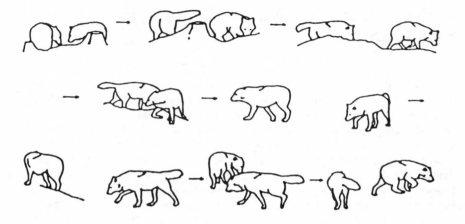

Figure 7.1 Another example of wolf co-regulation is the 'following' pattern. Following is similar to circling (Figure 3.1) except that the wolves have a different mutual orientation at the onset of the pattern. (*Source*: Moran, G. *et al* 'A description of relational patterns of movement during "ritualized fighting" in Wolves', in *Animal Behaviour*, 1981, 29, 4, reprinted by permission of Academic Press Inc. (London) Ltd. and the authors.)

there are a number of others that Moran and colleagues have described. Consistent with the mathematical model of an attractor, each pattern has movement and variability, yet converges toward a repeatable and recognizable stability. Also, the relationship system moves from one type of stable pattern to another by different variations of the *same features* that maintain the initial stable pattern: in this case, distance between the partners and mutual orientation. Thus, the maintenance of a stable pattern and the changes between stable patterns are *co-regulated by the same set of system components*. Both stability and change, therefore, arise spontaneously and are part of the natural functioning of this particular system. Innovation leading to the emergence of new stable patterns is an inherent feature of any dynamic system assuming that variation occurs across the range of system activity. Some variations will return the system to a stable configuration, while other variations will shift the system to another and perhaps entirely new stable pattern.[9]

In spite of the sophistication of such models and their potential applicability to social relationship processes, I can only use them as metaphors rather than as specific models of relationship formation for the following reasons. First, the mathematical modeling of a system's behavior can only be done for relatively simple systems in which all the movements and system variables can be defined and their relationships quantified. We are nowhere near this kind of specificity in the social sciences. Second, mathematical models have only been worked out for a small number of dynamic systems in which the equations have exact solutions. Many systems of equations can only be solved by approximation and their theoretical behavior is unknown.

Finally, and perhaps the most critical problem for me, is that dynamic systems approaches are models of the macroscopic behavior of the system. A model of fitness, for example, tells you that heart rate and temperature co-vary in limited ways, it tells you where and when the systems converge toward stable patterning. The model does not tell you why or how this happens. To understand that one would have to examine the specific systems within the body responsible for the linkages between these variables. In other words, one would have to examine the way in which heart rate is constrained by temperature and vice versa, the type of information that the temperature regulation system needs in order to respond meaningfully with respect to the cardiovascular system.

Dynamic systems models are heuristic because they are general, that is, not specific to the nature of the information-creation process that sustains the patterning of the system over time.[10] They also focus attention on the possible emergence of pattern without prescription. These kinds of systems metaphors have been applied to the mother–infant interaction system by several authors, including myself. For example, one of the first to speak of a non-prescriptive systems model of the parent–infant relationship was Louis Sander.

> We believe it useful to consider the infant and caretaking environment together as a biological system and to focus on the aspects of the regulation of exchange in the system as a way of approaching the problem of mutual adaptation . . . We take for granted the notion of the life process as an ongoing synthesis in an open-ended dynamic, one which is resolving basic polarities but leaving us with an 'in-between' in the open endedness of the present moment – an open endedness that our living activity resolves in new organization.[11]

Dynamic systems models of development have led to the emergence of a research strategy that focuses on the individual mother–infant dyad and its transformations over time, and on an unwillingness to ascribe causal primacy to mother or to infant in the organization of developmental change.[12]

Nevertheless, without some connection to the way in which these patterns are related to the specific information created by individuals within such systems, these perspectives fall short of being a generative theory of early development. We need to understand that social systems create stable patterns in the form of consensual frames and that they change between such patterns, but we also need to know why and how this happens, and the ways in which the patterns are meaningful to the participants.

Just as discrete state theorists have had a tendency to reify their models to search for similar units in the brain that correspond to their constructs, dynamic systems theorists may also succumb to such temptations. Attractor models, for example, may lead to the assumption that individuals are motivated to discover such attractors or to explore the limits of an attractor region in the state space defined by their body in the environment. Information creation is the primary motivation for action and for development. Although individuals may somehow sense the inherent stability of certain patterns of action, they typically do not set out in search of those patterns.

Information within consensual frames

The painter described in the last chapter who is gazing at the same landscape day after day is exhibiting a stable frame in his or her engagement with the environment: go each day to the same spot, set up the easel and paints, examine the subject, and paint. How can we grasp the stability of this frame from an informational perspective? Although the painter re-creates the same frame each day, there is continued variability within the frame regarding the discovery of information about the relationship of the paints to this particular landscape, about the gradations of shade and color where the mountains meet the sky and how that is translated into the dynamics of applying the paint to the canvas or to mixing and juxtaposing the colors.[13] The frame preserves the main topic while the variations induce elaborations and possibly innovations that may lead to changes in the frame.

Many observers of parent–infant relationships have found that couples create one consensual frame at a time. The consensual frame is maintained for some minutes or even longer, followed by another frame that may be related in some way to the first.[14] Frames revolve around actions like rocking and walking, mealtimes, physical or verbal games, and bedtime routines.

For example, parents often play games in which they loom their faces or hands in toward the baby's face and then zoom them away. We found this type of game more frequent in Japanese compared to American mother–infant dyads at 3 months.[15] If we analyze this game from the perspective of visual perceptual information, we see that it is related to a single invariant of expansion and contraction (see Table 5.1). Other examples are games involving exchanges of facial expressions that create information related to shape and surface deformation, and peek-a-boo in which information is related to the dissolution and emergence of visual and auditory forms.

This kind of informational analysis of consensual frames suggests that games and other routines are stable in part because the degrees of freedom in the system have been reduced to focus on one or a small number of information themes. A peek-a-boo game explores the many ways in which information can be created about the theme of dissolution and emergence of form.

Relationships develop unique consensual frames because each of the individuals has a preference or desire for the exploration of certain kinds of information themes. This preference may arise in the types of actions the body is capable of producing or perceiving, and also in the ways in which the culture makes certain types of consensual frames available to individuals. Information themes may be discovered spontaneously by the participants and then elaborated over time into stable consensual frames that have single information themes.

In the previous chapter I discussed the metaphor of adults as guides for their infants. According to Bruner and Rogoff, for example, adults introduce and maintain particular formats into which their infants come to fit their own activity. From their point of view, these game formats, and similar consensual frames for all kinds of routines such as eating and bedtime, are jointly negotiated, co-regulated communication systems in which partners agree about information themes they wish to create together.

The role of the adult, therefore, is to participate in the co-creation of consensual frames making the environment informative for the infant. Sometimes this occurs because of intentional guidance on the part of the adult. Sometimes the adult relies on cultural tools and practices to highlight the information. Sometimes making the environment informative occurs during spontaneous play and without the goal of doing so. Adults can also help this process by continuing to participate in consensual frames with themes that interest the infant and by letting the infant take responsibility for action when appropriate.

The formation of differences between relationships

To summarize the conclusions of this chapter so far, I propose that relationships are systems engaged in the creation of consensual frames having themes of information. The result of the mutual exploration of one theme at a time, followed by a shift to another theme, corresponds to a process over time in which stable consensual frames of co-regulated action persist and then shift abruptly to different consensual frames. Relationships not only move between different themes, they also repeat the same themes many times until such themes are dropped from the repertoire. They may try out the same themes within different consensual frames. The theme of emergence and dissolution, for example, appears in frames like peek-a-boo, hide-and-seek, and object-hiding games. By participating in such related consensual frames, individuals may come to discover new invariants related to sub-themes and combinations of themes as they are set against the background of different frames.

The primary source of stability, change and diversity of consensual frames and themes is the motivational salience of information-creation for the participants. Information themes persist so long as they are informative and are lost when they cease to be informative. Although one or another participant may play a leading role in the introduction of a theme and its maintenance over time, both partners must participate in some way to keep the theme alive.

This brings us back to the main purpose of this chapter, the process by which differences between parent–infant relationships emerge. Relationships with a parenting figure are the first long-term relationships in which babies are participants. Thus, the information themes that emerge in such relationships, and the consensual frames that support them, are the primary means by which those infants experience their world.

Example: Motor development as a social process

In order to illustrate how different patterns of relationships form because of differences in the emergence of information themes I shall use the example of infant acquisition of the ability to reach voluntarily for objects. The hand can be used to play a musical instrument, to write, or to sculpt and no one would deny that these cultural activities require interaction with a teacher who makes the medium of the piano, pen or clay informative with respect to the potential and actual creativity of the child's hand. Some people would argue, however, that many of the infant's early motor skills such as reaching are culture-free and can be acquired without a social partner.[16] It would be impossible, however, for infants to develop such skills without the active support of adults who at a minimum supply the baby with objects that are graspable and attractive.

What is the adult's role in relation to reaching in a 3-month-old? To guide the infant through some curriculum of how to use objects at an early age? To be supportive of infants' desires to use particular objects? To reinforce their efforts? My guess is that the agenda for parents of infants this young is just to participate, just to do something together without an explicit goal for guidance. An alert 2-month-old infant lying on her back is probably a wonderful but incomprehensible sight to most young parents and it is not clear that the baby can be guided to do anything very useful. According to one literary description, when babies

> are a few months old, they lie and look around and wave and smile and undergo a constant gentle agitation, as though they were sea anemones, gently waving in some other element, delicately responding to currents we cannot feel.[17]

Many of the actions of young infants are not recognized by their parents as being systematic. For example, I and others have discovered that infants as young as 1 month of age can display index finger extension movements and these movements occur when infants are attentive and not smiling or distressed.[18] Parents, however, do not recognize index finger extensions as expressions of interest until the infant is almost 1 year of age because these early extensions are not as perceptually salient for the parents as the later ones that occur with the arm outstretched that we call *points*.[19] Thus, it is difficult to argue that parents intentionally guide the infant when the parents themselves are often uncertain about the meaning of the infant's actions.

Research that I conducted collaboration with Lisa West[20] shows that infants acquire different patterns of hand usage and attention to objects depending upon the type of information created about hand use during their co-regulated interactions with their mothers. Some infants are more likely to direct their attention to the object the mother is demonstrating during the weeks before they manipulate objects on their own. Once they are able to hold on to the object that the mother places in their hands, they look at the object as they hold it. At the same time, their mothers continue to touch the object, and to support not only the child's manual actions, but also the child's attention to the object. In the later sessions after reaching is acquired, the mother will simply place the object within reach and stay out of the infant's way while the infant explores the object. For these infants, their exploration of the object is related to their gazing at the object; they seem systematically to combine information across several sensory modalities (vision and touch, mouthing and touch, mouthing and action).

Mark Reimers and I[21] worked out the following description of the consensual frames supporting object exploration in one such infant, Jerry, and his mother, in one observation session after the infant begins reaching for objects. The mother presents objects to the baby while the baby lies on his back, watches and tries to reach for the objects. This mother alternates between demonstrating the object's properties and then moving the object in so the baby can easily contact the object with his hands. She helps the infant grasp the object and helps to pick it up when dropped. She seems focused on highlighting the object's physical features and on maintaining the infant's attention to the object. Her voice is distinctively different for each of these object-related actions, helping to mark the different pieces of her action for the infant. The infant remains alert, attentive to the object, and smiles and brightens in a modulated way that is co-regulated with the mother's actions and voice. She seems content to wait until the infant loses interest in an object before introducing another one, thus changing the theme within the same consensual frame. When she introduces objects to the baby she rarely persists for more than ten seconds unless the baby shows some interest.

In other infants we find very different consensual frames for action and attention *vis-à-vis* the mother. For these infants, the mother's demonstrations of object properties are not sequentially related to infant attention. Their early interactions with objects are short-lived, rapidly dissolving into bouts of face-to-face play, during which the mothers gradually try to integrate the infant's attention to objects via their attention to the mother. These infants are slow to attend to the object. Even when they begin to grasp and hold the object, they look elsewhere. In later sessions, their actions on objects tend to focus on mouthing the objects without any systematic looking at or acting on the objects, leaving relatively few opportunities for their mothers to intervene in object-related discourse, and no option but for them to engage in face-to-face play.

Reimers and I described such a consensual frame in infant Andrew during one session with his mother at 4 months. In their consensual frame, the object is informative with respect to attention to the mother, rather than with respect to attention to and manipulation of the object. Like Jerry's mother, this mother also demonstrates the physical affordances of objects but in a rather different manner. She moves the object continuously in the same position as the infant gets excited, but rarely follows up by putting the object in the infant's hand. She touches the infant's face and body with the object and when Andrew loses visual contact, he becomes visibly frustrated and over-agitated, calming only when mother puts the object down. The mother's voice is similar in its tonal characteristics regardless of the activity. Even when Andrew is holding an object, his mother touches or distracts him with a different object, a theme change that gives the child little opportunity for focused and socially supported visual and manual exploration. His elaboration of information about objects, that is, the mother–object communication system, appears to be more fragmentary than Jerry's. Attention to objects and their visual and auditory properties is not systematically linked to exploratory action.

At 12 months our first pair, Jerry and his mother, go on to establish consensual frames for cooperative play. In a typical play frame, the infant initiates exploration with an object and often pauses to allow mother to become involved in the play. She responds by following up on Jerry's initiative, elaborating the theme introduced by him. In other instances, Jerry will become involved in play with mother, but she won't persist with her theme if he shows no interest.

For this pair during the first year, the dyad has gone from consensual frames in which attention and action on objects are facilitated by maternal support and vocal encouragement, to the development of consensual frames for cooperation requiring more than one to play. During solitary exploration with objects, this infant looks rather focused and intent, showing object-appropriate examining actions. The mother is content to wait for pauses in

Jerry's activity, which occur frequently with looks to mother to get involved in the play, and he responds to mother's bids, as in petting a toy cat the mother holds out.

At 1 year Andrew, the second infant, and his mother do not have consensual frames for cooperative play. She persists in introducing her own agendas while he is working on something else. She will place objects next to ones he is playing with, she vocalizes similarly whether the play objects are her own or the ones Andrew is using. When Andrew does not pause to allow her to intervene, she attempts to take away his objects to introduce herself into the action. Co-regulated consensual frames almost never occur around objects *per se*, but rather during highly stimulating encounters such as tickling or having a tug-of-war.

Thus, there is either solitary play in which Andrew attempts to ignore the mother and compromises his ability to examine objects unhindered, or play with mother in which she is the main actor on the objects or on him. When his activity is disrupted by mother, he often resorts to non-exploratory actions such as absently banging or mouthing an object without systematic examination. He provides his mother with few or no opportunities for her to become involved in his play.

These infants differ in the relationship of the dynamics of action with respect to the object, that is, in the information about objects created by the encounter. For one infant, the meaning of the object is to act directly on it. For the other, the object means a social routine in which mother is a part. The adult's role in both cases is to co-regulate consensual frames in which the objects are informative with respect to the infant's prehensile potential, yet the consensual frames and the type of information created are different for each dyad.[22]

Note also that information is being created for the mothers in these situations. It would not be correct to infer that the mother is imposing her style on the infant. It could be the case that some infants at 3 months are intently focused in their attention to the object, thus informing their mothers to hold the object closer to them, which in turn leads to more opportunities to reach and to the construction of an object-centered consensual frame. Other infants may appear less focused, providing less information regarding object-specific interest to their mothers. These infants leave their mothers with more degrees of freedom, and hence mothers may introduce themselves into co-regulated routines more often.

Whatever the explanation, very small differences in the early negotiation process may create lasting consensual frames that are preserved over long periods of time. It may be that in her early attempts either to demonstrate properties of objects or to get the infant involved with objects, the mother found the infant relatively more or less perceptive or skilled, relatively more or less focused or attentive. Differences between relationships in patterns of exploratory play are likely to be emergent from the whole dynamic system of two individuals of different skills and abilities, with different goals in relation to the physical and cultural context.

Conclusions: Two patterns of relationship formation

The preceding analysis suggests some new ways of thinking about the formation of early relationships, why they differ and why the participants differ as a result of their involvement. Whenever communication is co-regulated, the process by which degrees of freedom are constrained is mutually negotiated. However, our examples suggest that not all consensual frames in a relationship lead to continued co-regulation and creativity. In some cases, as in Andrew's interactions with his mother at age 1 year regarding objects, the actions of the partners are not mutually creative. In fact, the partners seem to act in ways that curtail avenues for negotiation: both partners attempt to control the access and use of objects and leave few or no opportunities for the other to get involved. Although this pair is creative around other themes and in other frames, part of their unique character as a team is their lack of co-regulated discourse about particular kinds of object play.

Stable consensual frames for creativity and innovation. Some consensual frames that persist over time in relationships are maintained by continued co-regulation, characterized by inventiveness and creativity. There are themes, and each time those themes are mutually engaged something new emerges. The participants want to interact about these themes, they are motivated by the potential for creativity in the relationship about these themes. As long as the relationship pattern is creative, negotiated and mutually maintained, stability is a dynamic and mutually engaging process that embodies the seed of change.

Stable consensual frames for rigidity and dissolution. Other consensual frames that persist over time are not inventive or creative. They are marked by rigidity and sameness, by a motivation to avoid creativity around particular themes, by a sense of obligation without pleasure. Rigid consensual frames, once established, may persist for long periods in a relationship. A parent or child may insist on introducing a topic that the other wishes to avoid. There may be activities that are maintained because of familial or cultural factors, regardless of their usefulness for the particular couple (see Chapter 10). These rigid patterns co-exist with creative ones in most relationships.

I speak here of differences in patterns of information creation around particular themes, rather than about the quality of a relationship as a whole. In some cases, rigid themes are mere annoyances to one partner (as in reading the same book with the baby again and again) and in others they are disruptive and destructive (as in consistently denying a partner access to a resource or emotional support for an information theme that relates to adaptive functioning in that culture). In some cases, however, the maintenance of rigid consensual frames is useful for the individuals, as in ritualized greetings that may lead into more creative consensual frames.

All relationships need a process by which some frames are limited in creative scope. Dyads cannot be creatively intense in all aspects of their co-action. Thus, some frames may be curtailed into perfunctory rituals while others may dissolve entirely. By means of these two relationship processes – creativity and rigidity – differences will emerge between relationships with respect to the frames that become elaborated, ritualized or dropped, and also with respect to the type of information-theme creation that occurs within the frame. Within the more creative frames, co-regulated innovations cannot be planned and their spontaneity introduces yet another source of variability between relationships.[23]

The continued creative elaboration of particular consensual frames and themes may be consonant with respect to the culture (as in the development of pleasurable and instructive games and routines) or dissonant (as in parent–infant-negotiated and mutually consenting participation in picking up and holding the infant who cries in a family or culture where this is not considered acceptable). In this case, it may be more culturally appropriate to rigidify the crying–picking up consensual frame in such a way as to eliminate it in the future.

There are many ways in which consensual frames and themes in a relationship may evolve. Social psychologist Starkey Duncan refers to such frames as composed of *conventions* that are mutually constructed and mutually dissolved by the participants through a process of *ratification*.

> In order for a convention to be adopted within an interaction, it must be initiated by one participant and ratified by the other. Once adopted, for a convention to continue in use, it must be continually ratified by both participants ... For a convention to be changed, the change must be initiated by one participant and ratified by the other. Finally, the ending of some conventions requires the same process of initiative and ratification ... The process of initiative and ratification provides one important sense in which interaction must be regarded as an achievement involving the joint, coordinated action of both participants.[24]

The concepts of initiative and ratification are similar to my constructs of innovation and co-regulation. Ratification is the process by which consensual frames achieve dynamic stability via co-regulation. Duncan's view of initiative within a relationship seems to suggest, however, that one individual is primarily responsible for introducing a change which must then be ratified by the other. In my view, innovation is often the result of mutual creativity. Innovation is probably emergent and jointly constructed even when it appears to originate from a single individual, since the innovation is created in the context of some ongoing consensual frame.

Duncan proposes a number of change processes for conventions that are consistent with the model of co-regulation. Conventions may change in intensity and timing, in the use of different actions, in streamlining or expanding, and in a change in the role of actors permitted to display the convention. His model of convention variability and change offers some specific conceptual tools with which to study relationship development, as long as one is clear that these mechanisms of change must be jointly co-regulated, that they are not imposed unilaterally by one participant on the other. These processes fall under the heading of what I have called · elaboration or creation of information within a co-regulated relationship system.

The reader, therefore, should resist the temptation to be evaluative about the different patterns of relationship formation discussed here: toward creativity and toward rigidity, toward innovation of new patterns and dissolution of old patterns. Both types of relationship process are part of a viable relationship system. The elaboration of informative themes and their maintenance within the relationship by consensual frames is a fundamental characteristic of co-regulating communication systems over repeated encounters. The saliency of information-creation in a social system is the source of stability and change, stage and sequence, similarity and difference. In the next two chapters I turn to the problem of how this process of information co-created in relationships becomes part of a sense of self and a unique individuality.

Notes

1. Hearne (1987).
2. Sroufe (1989).
3. Hinde (1977, pp. 347–8).
4. Hearne (1987); Kagan (1989).
5. See Note 16, Chapter 4.
6. In literature, drama and films there is no end to stories of relationships that evolve into situations of dramatic urgency, often ending in tragedy.
7. See Gleick, 1987, for an admirable explanation of attractors and chaos. See also, Abraham & Shaw (1982).
8. Moran, Fentress & Golani (1981).
9. Dynamic systems theory offers a rich set of mathematical models for the time course change from one stable pattern to another (Kelso & Tuller, 1984). These so-called phase shifts are typically abrupt compared to the time the system spends in one stable state or another. For example, if temperature is increased steadily, matter spends most of its time in one or another of its stable states: solid, liquid or gas. Phase shifts between states, such as

between ice and water, occur over a very small temperature range at about 0 deg. centigrade – small compared to the range of temperatures over which the system is either ice or water. Similar phase transitions occur in the gait patterns of animals as speed is increased and in developmental transitions in locomotor performance during infancy as muscle strength and coordination is increased (Kelso & Tuller, 1984; Thelen, Kelso & Fogel, 1987; Thelen, 1989). The application of these concepts and models of change to social systems is wide open.

10. Thelen & Ulrich (1991).
11. Sander (1977, pp. 152–3); see also Sander *et al.* (1979). Sameroff (1984), Thoman *et al.* (1979) and Patterson and Bank (1989) have expressed similar ideas about the parent–infant system. Motor development in the context of social systems was described by Thelen (1989) and Wolff (1987).
12. Fogel (1989); Sander (1977); Thoman *et al.* (1979). Single-subject research strategies are highlighted in this book, although they are used infrequently in developmental psychology, which is surprising because it has often been pointed out by methodologists that the individual or the relationship is the unit of developmental change (Wohlwill, 1973).
13. I am referring to the direct relationship between action and information here. There is no need to invoke attractors as explanations of the individual's behavior, even though attractors are potentially appropriate mathematical models of the convergence of action patterns over time.
14. Fogel (1977; 1982); Fogel, Toda & Kawai (1988); Stern *et al.* (1977).
15. Fogel, Toda & Kawai (1988).
16. Beek & Hopkins (1992); Burnham & Dickinson (1981); Piaget (1952); Savelsbergh & van Emmerik (1992); Thelen (1992); von Hofsten (1984); White & Castle (1964).
17. Drabble (1982).
18. Fogel & Hannan (1985); Service, Lock & Chandler (1989); Trevarthen (1977).
19. Hannan (1987); Service, Lock & Chandler (1989).
20. Fogel (1990b); West & Fogel (1990). Similar differences have also been reported for infants under 6 months by Gray (1978). Others have also found that an infant's interactions with objects is related to interaction with adults. Infants become more skilled at object play if they have been exposed to higher amounts of adult touching, holding and carrying (White & Castle, 1964); pre-term infants progress faster in motor skills with objects if their mothers play participatory games with objects (Landry, Chapieski & Schmidt, 1986); infants display different hand movements as a function of the type of object presented, its proximity, size and animation (Fogel & Hannan, 1985; Legerstee, Corter & Kienapple, 1990; Trevarthen, 1977); and infant's attention to and actions on objects is more focused if mothers time their interventions with respect to the infant's level of engagement with the object (Parrinello & Ruff, 1988).
21. Reimers & Fogel (1992).
22. Fogel (1990b); Lock (1980); Lyra & Rossetti-Ferreira (in press).

23. See also Sroufe and Jacobvitz (1989) for a similar perspective on the development and remediation of early forms of psychopathologies in parent–child relationships.
24. Duncan (1991, p. 345).

Chapter 8

The self in relation: embodied cognition

Cognition, as I use the term, refers to the subjectivity of activity. Cognition is in the arms and legs, on the lips and tongue, and in the head. It is feeling and thinking, body and mind, perception and action. It is not entirely inside us, since part of cognition is our perception of the world around us. Cognition is completely mundane yet completely mysterious. It is necessary to understand the cognitive aspects of participating in a relationship because the central feature of relationships is the creation of information, through perceptual and cognitive process.

Embodied cognition

In a discrete state model of cognition, action, thought, memory and intention are separate information–processing units. Information in the form of messages is processed and interpreted by these different components of the discrete system. In traditional information–processing models, information flows between discrete units in a sequential fashion. The message is altered by each unit and passed on to the next.

In a recent version of the discrete state model, called a parallel processing network or a connectionist model, all the components may be active at the same time and information may flow freely between them. Connectionist models avoid a central planning agent and allow cognitive activity to emerge from the multiple transactions of the system. In spite of their obvious improvements over linear information-processing models, connectionist models have not escaped being essentially discrete state systems.[1] Information is directly transmitted between components, and each component in the model has a designated function whose possibilities are set before anything ever happens.[2]

In earlier chapters I spoke about the importance of the body in understanding communication and its development. I return to this theme now because the body also plays a crucial role in cognition. Progress in the modeling of cognitive systems is occurring when modelers attempt to incorporate bodily processes – perception and action – into their models and when the nodes of the models are free to co-regulate with each other in a system that creates its own rules as it acts in a real environment.[3] For example, an insect-like robot named Genghis, designed by Rodney Brooks and his group at MIT, can walk over rough terrain and avoid obstacles in an unfamiliar situation – one of the first robots ever to function outside of a perfect and predictable laboratory environment. In these types of robots,

> There was no central model of the world explicitly represented within the systems. ... There was no central locus of control. In general, the separation into perceptual system, central system, and actuation system was much less distinct than in previous approaches, and in these systems there was an intimate intertwining of aspects of all three of these capabilities. There was no notion of one process calling on another as a subroutine ... as the systems relied heavily on the dynamics of their interactions with the world to produce their results.[4]

Brooks's robot works the way a Gibsonian continuous process model of action would have predicted. It has a motor system that relates directly to a sensory system. The more sensory experience the robot has, the more skilled the motor system becomes. The robot does not learn by storing rules of action in an abstract represented memory, but by tuning its motor system directly to the demands of the environment. For Brooks and colleagues a robot must be 'embodied' to function intelligently.

In 1744, the Italian philosopher Gianbattista Vico published the following statement in his work *Scienza Nuova*,

> the human mind is naturally inclined by the senses to see itself externally in the body, and with only great difficulty does it come to understand itself by means of reflection ... words are carried over from bodies and from the properties of bodies to signify the institutions of the mind and spirit.[5]

This view is fundamentally different from the Platonic conception of words and thought as representations that directly encode the real world without reference to the nature of the perceiver. Vico's idea is that we understand and know the world through our actions in it and our thought and language is a way of encoding the perception–action relationship between the self and the environment. Cognition is therefore embodied and relational, a reflection of our participation in a dynamic perception–action system, not a record of objective or represented contents of 'reality.'

A more recent and more extensive treatment of the embodied and relational nature of cognition comes from philosopher Mark Johnson.[6] Johnson suggests that we understand and remember our experiences via metaphors that are based on the body and its relationship to the environment. He gives the example of how the mental construction of emotion is understood with respect to the metaphor of physical balance and physical pressure.

> Emotions can *simmer, well up, overflow, boil over, erupt,* and *explode* when the pressure builds up ... One can *express, release,* or *let out* the emotions (*blow off steam*) to lessen the strain. One can try to *repress, suppress, hold in,* or *put a lid on* one's emotions, but they will not thereby disappear ... we tend to seek a temporary homeostasis where we are emotionally *balanced, stable,* and *on an even keel.*[7]

According to Johnson, cognition is the history of the experiences in which our bodies have engaged with the world. Higher forms of abstract thinking are built up out of these embodied metaphors.

In contrast to the traditional information-processing perspective in which the memory of an experience is stored in some abstract manner in a specific location of the brain, cognitive psychologist Paul Kolers suggests that the processes of memory are closely associated with the processes of performing actions. A vast number of experimental studies on human memory, for example, have been done on the recognition and recall of words. The assumption is that the meaning of the word is what the subject remembers, the word's abstract content.

Experiments have shown, however, that subjects are more likely to recognize words if they are presented in the same typeface during testing as during training. Color, size and the location of a word on a page influence the way it is remembered.[8] According to Kolers,

> knowledge is means dependent ... knowledge is expressed in activities, techniques, procedures – skilled ways of relating to the stimulus ... the means of acquisition, even motoric means, often form a part of whatever a person knows ... Consciousness does not report on what is in the world, but on how the person's sensing organs respond to events.[9]

Knowledge, or what is remembered, is not simply an abstract representation of a list of contents, but it is knowledge of how to do something or how to perceive something, knowledge of our body's relationship to things. When making skilled movements, sighted individuals appear to rely primarily on visual cues, while the congenitally blind use movement cues under the same circumstances.[10] When I remember a rose, I remember the way a rose looks and the way it smells, that is, I remember the rose through the perceptual modalities by which I initially gained information about roses.

There is another way in which I can remember a rose, a more direct way. When I go out to the garden and I see and smell a rose, it is familiar to me and I recognize it as a rose. My memory of the rose is not lodged in the recesses of my brain: it comes alive as my perception and action systems engage with the rose. In other words, skilled action and perception, performing knowledgeably in familiar situations, is also a form of cognitive remembering.

Participatory cognition

I call this *participatory cognition* because it is created in the individual's ongoing transactions with that environment. James Gibson's theory of perception and action, and the current work on embodied cognition, suggest that memory is an integral part of a perception–action system in the present.[11] *Imaginative cognition*, on the other hand, is a process that occurs when we are thinking about transactions with the environment that are not presently occurring.

I can illustrate the differences between participatory and imaginative remembering with novelist Marcel Proust's description of a moment in his protagonist Swann's love affair with Odette, from the novel *Remembrance of Things Past*.

> This new manner, indifferent, offhand, irritable, which Odette now adopted with Swann, undoubtedly made him suffer; but he did not realize how much he suffered ... this change was his deep, secret wound, which tormented him day and night, and whenever he felt that his thoughts were straying too near it, he would quickly turn them into another channel for fear of suffering too much. He might say to himself in an abstract way: 'There was a time when Odette loved me more,' but he never formed any definite picture of that time.[12]

Swann's current memory of Odette is a participatory memory that directly affects his frame of mind. He cannot conjure Odette as an imaginative memory even though he was able to do so freely in the past. Swann's current perception of Odette is colored by his past relationship with her. Whatever Odette is actually doing or saying in the present is of little consequence. The information created when Swann perceives her amounts to indifference and irritability. Yet, Swann can't bring himself actually to imagine his prior relationship with Odette. Swann's remembering is experienced as miserableness. In Proust's account, this is different from the period just after Swann first meets and courts Odette, when his memory was more imaginative as he compared her to images from Renaissance paintings.

There is a resemblance between participatory memory and the concept of recognition memory, and similarly between imaginative memory and recall memory. Recognition memory occurs when we experience something perceived as familiar or similar to something perceived in the past. Recall memory is more like an evocation of a past event for which a similar cue is not currently available. I reject these terms from individualistic psychology because they take the environment's role in memory to be only with respect to the 'cue,' the stimulus that is associated with the 'real' memory stored in the brain. In addition, participatory and imaginative memories are re-creations of a perception–action system, embodied procedures of acquiring knowledge and not simply context-free contents.

Like physical actions such as driving a car, mental actions like thinking and remembering are perception–action systems constituted by their activity. To be sure, the brain, body and environment all contribute to the creation of the memory, but memory is a living thing, like the performance of an actor, the stroke of a tennis expert or the arpeggio of a concert pianist. Memories are not stored intact, they become intact and coherent only when we actively experience them in action or in thought. Experiencing a memory is not simply reading out a whole image stored in the brain. Rather, the individual takes whatever is stored in the brain in relation to what is going on in the world, and creates information from the resulting transactions.[13] The neural patterns are not fixed and finalized, not burned in like images in the silver nitrate of a film negative. The neural patterns are open systems, co-regulated by the cognitive process and by the stream of actions and sensations in which the individual is continuously bathed.[14]

The concept of participatory memory is similar to the term 'involuntary' memory developed by the Russian psychologists A. A. Smirnov and P. I. Zinchenko.[15] Involuntary memory is when remembered information is directly incorporated into the individual's ongoing goal-oriented activity. Smirnov and Zinchenko's experiments showed that people remembered things better when they actively had to perform some kind of task, such as actually using Morse code to send a message rather than simply having to recognize Morse code symbols. 'Voluntary' memory occurs when the individual's specific goal is to remember something for its own sake. Thus, whether memory is involuntary or voluntary depends on what the person is trying to do. The Russian psychologists were especially influential in establishing the idea that all forms of cognition could be understood with respect to the individual's activity or goal, which led to currently used contextual approaches to cognition.[16]

However, the activity theorists often leave out an essential component to activity: the fact that it is embodied. The way we think, experience, and remember action is intimately tied to the way in which our perception–action systems create information through their engagement with the environment. A more embodied approach is offered in the concepts of 'autocentric' and 'allocentric' perception described by the psychoanalyst Ernest Schachtel.[17] According to Schachtel, autocentric perception is involved in the direct control of behavior and the immediate experience of acting, while allocentric perception involves reflection and understanding of objects and other people. He calls autocentric memory 'passive re-sensing,' and allocentric memory 'voluntary recall' and sees them both as creative activities.

Schachtel also makes the observation that certain sensory systems are more involved in autocentric perception, including the sensations of temperature, passive touch, taste and smell. Sight, hearing, and active touch (exploration) are more likely to become objects of reflection and active thought. For example, it is much more difficult voluntarily to evoke a memory for smell, temperature, or taste than for something seen or heard.

Schachtel speculates that adults are not voluntarily able to recall infantile memories because infant activity primarily involves the autocentric senses. Daniel Stern[18] also suggests that certain kinds of perceptions, such as for body movement, fail to become linguistically encoded and thus cannot be voluntarily recalled. These memories, however, may remain with the individual as participatory memory, memory that is constituted as action. It may be that the adults' typical postures, patterns of facial expression and sensitivity to smells and touches are organized with respect to their infantile participatory memories.[19]

The participatory future

Our relationship to the future is identical to our relationship to the past and present: through participation and imagination. Information about the future is generated in two ways: by actually moving toward the future in the immediate present through participatory activity, and by imagining oneself in some future state.

The participatory future is analogous to participatory memory. It is a way of acting *in the present* that moves the individual toward another activity, but without the need for a future state to be represented in consciousness. The participatory future is experienced as *direction* rather than as an imagined goal.

The psychologist Dankert Vedeler[20] proposes that intention is directed action that is not necessarily future-oriented in the form of a goal toward which one is guided. Intention, in his view, is part of action and need not involve any mental representation of a desired future state. His reasoning is also influenced by Gibsonian thinking and by the phenomenologists. Vedeler reviews the work of mid-nineteenth century psychologist Franz Brentano who believed that intentionality concerned the 'aboutness' or 'object directedness' of action, which is not the same as having a goal. Husserl considered objects as 'targets' of intentions rather than mental representations. And Vedeler quotes Merleau-Ponty (1962, p. 160) as follows: 'In the action of the hand which is raised towards an object is contained a reference to the object, not as an object represented, but as that highly specific thing toward which we project ourselves . . .'

For animals, direction is observed in potentially threatening situations[21] as one animal takes steps to avoid another before a confrontation. It is not necessary to assume that the individual animal has a representation or imagination of the threat. Instead, there is information available in the present situation that calls forth in the animal some anticipatory directionality, either to approach or avoid.

In greetings, individuals anticipate a communicative engagement with the person they are saluting, yet the greeter remains vigilant with respect to the possibility that the interaction will not develop, that the person being greeted, on closer approach, will turn out to be mistaken for another more familiar person. During informal conversations there is often a smoothly flowing topic progression, yet 'one does not get the impression that speakers *plan* to proceed in any particular way, or know in advance what they are going to say or for what reason.'[22] Even when individuals are involved in deliberately planning some joint activity, planning is a process that involves both improvisation and flexibility with respect to changing circumstances and ideas that emerge spontaneously during conversation.[23]

Because direction is not a separate faculty of the mind, but is integral to participatory activity, direction changes as action is being executed, much like the perceptual flow field changes as a function of one's own movements. During greetings, one's actions may smoothly flow into open conversation if the person greeted expresses a willingness to become involved. On the other hand, in the event that this does not happen, there is an abrupt shift in the greeter's behavior and a corresponding change in direction. Stated simply, direction is not a static initial condition, not an executive giving orders that guide action, it is a fluid part of a dynamic perception–action system.

Imaginative cognition

Participatory cognition is part of ongoing action, bringing prior experience to bear on current actions and goals. When I write this book, I do not have to remember all of the articles and books I have worked on in the past. Participatory memory allows me to incorporate that experience into the problems of writing in the present, without the intermediary of bringing all those experiences to mind. Independent of actually writing this book, however, I can remember a particular experience of writing something else in the past. I can remember the problems I was trying to solve, the time and place of writing, some of the other events going on at the same time. This is *imaginative memory*, memory that has the purpose of remembering something done, seen, felt or heard before.

In principle, imaginative memory is no different from participatory memory.[24] When I imagine something from the past it is part of some ongoing thought process, or it is evoked by some event in the current physical or social environment. Imaginative memory, like participatory memory, is a re-creation and a re-experiencing *in the present* of something previously experienced. That re-creation may not necessarily be identical to the earlier experience. It is related to the goals of the present time and to the whole history of experiences I have since had. In addition, imaginative memory like participatory memory is embodied. I remember the way in which I experienced something, and not just the thing itself. For example, I don't remember my childhood home in the abstract. I remember looking at it from different places in the yard, I remember walking through it, I remember hugs or scoldings that took place in particular locations.

Clearly, not every event in the present evokes imaginative memories.

> It is ecologically adaptive that familiar objects do not automatically remind us of previous experiences. If they did, our minds would be deluged with experiences ... On the other hand, events do sometimes seem to spontaneously remind one of previous experiences . . . a theory [of memory] must not only explain how internally generated or explicitly presented cues *do* help one recreate past experiences, but it must explain why potential cues *do not* always prompt one to remember.[25]

Thus, even for imaginative memories, the remembered past is co-regulated with respect to the present situation and appears as a meaningful present experience in relation to that situation.

Without resorting to a memory faculty, how do we know the difference between when we are actually participating in the present in relation to a present task or situation, compared to when we are participating in the present with respect to a past situation? The French phenomenologist Merleau-Ponty suggests that the ability to imagine an event does not by itself tell you whether the event is in the past, present or future.

> If my brain stores up traces of the bodily process which accompanied one of my perceptions, and if the appropriate nervous influx passes once more through these already fretted channels, my perception will reappear, but it will be a fresh perception, weakened and unreal perhaps, but in no case will this perception, which is present, be capable of pointing to a past event which enables me to recognize it as memory.[26]

Merleau-Ponty suggests that the information about whether an event is past, present and future is not 'in' the mind or brain alone. Rather, information about an imagined event's temporal relationship to us must arise as part of the process of active remembering.

According to Merleau-Ponty, the present is uniquely experienced in consciousness as an unfolding, as a creation out of what was, immediately before, the future. The present is created as information about the substantiation of mental or physical action. The past, on the other hand, has already been substantiated. The information unique to a past event is that we can imagine not only the event, but the related events that preceded and followed it. The event is precluded from change forever. Information indicating the future, on the other hand, is the lack of specificity, the lack of a concrete prior sequence and of an outcome.

One characteristic of fantasy and delusion is the belief in the imaginary as substantial, or in a remembered past that can be changed at will. In pretend play, children will alter the past and re-create it to suit their own purposes.

That does not mean that their ability to remember or imagine is flawed, but rather that information created in those memories is strongly colored by the motives of the present context of remembering.

In one research study, 4 and 6 year-old children were questioned about their beliefs about monsters. When psychologists asked questions like – 'That monster that wags its tail and comes chasing after you in your head. Can I see it . . . is it a real one?' – the children overwhelmingly said the monster was not real. On the other hand, when asked – 'That monster in your head, were you really scared when it came chasing after you, or just pretend scared?' – most children admitted being afraid.[27] Is this any different from an adult's terror after a bad dream, or emotional reaction to an imaginary relationship with a film star or sports figure?[28]

For most adults, imaginative memories of the lived past are experienced as unalterable. After I had been driving no more than a year I skidded out of control on the wet overpass of a highway, spun around and fortunately stopped, but just short of going over the edge of the bridge. The experience tempers my driving on slick surfaces even today as part of participatory memory. In imaginative memory, however, I sometimes think about that particular incident. I think about what might have happened had I tumbled to the roadway below, or about how I might have prevented the incident from occurring at all. I re-live the incident in the present, but I perceive it as past because it is beyond reach, completed for better or worse. I can accept it, deny it, suffer from it, or rejoice in it in the present, but I cannot change it. I can only change what I am doing right now, on this wet pavement under my wheels, and I can imagine in the future how I might behave should such a situation again arise. These imaginings are all relational, my conduct in relation to the driving surface, but they are experienced as part of me and as part of my own past.

The important point is that memories are not merely traces in the brain that are accessed and re-played like a videotape. Memories are active experiences in the present and they mean something different each time they are remembered. Whatever traces the brain does store they do not contain a fixed quantity of information. Rather, those brain traces become informative only during the act of remembering. I can learn more about myself in the past by repeated imaginative remembering because each time I remember I perceive different information that restructures my understanding of the past event.[29]

The view expressed here is that imaginative memories are perceived as part of my own past because they contain information about the sequence of events before, during and after the remembered events, events that belong to me because my body experienced them. This perspective on imaginative memory as a sequence of temporally related events is similar to the notion of *episodic* or *scripted* memory, that is, memory for the flow of real experiences as they occurred in time.[30] After the age of 3 years, children's memories are structured around episodes such as going to school, going to a birthday party, or talking with a friend, and children remember events best if they can relate them to an episode.[31]

A problem occurs, however, when the concept of episodic memory is extended to explain how such memories relate to current actions. Those who take the view that memory is a discrete faculty of the mind reason that in order for episodic memories to have an impact on current experience, such memories have to become generalized episodes, an average over all similar episodes. Thus, in going to school, one should get up, get dressed, eat breakfast, travel from home to school, and go into one's classroom. This *generalized event structure* has elements that typically occur every day, but it does not include any specifics of individual occurrences.[32] Applied to a child's experience in relationships with other people, such memories have been called *representations of interactions that have been generalized* (RIGs)[33] or *internal working models*.[34]

In this view, the individual stores generalized memories in some memory faculty or store, and when in a similar situation the individual calls up the generalized memory and follows the script by adapting it to fit the present situation. Each time such a situation occurs, the generalized memory is changed somewhat and put back into storage. In other words, participation in the current situation is viewed as a separate faculty from the faculty of remembering such situations. Somehow the individual must send information from the present perception to memory, find the correct script, and then generate the appropriate actions; a discrete state model of the mind. Even though the discrete elements here are episodes rather than single events, the problem remains.

Another problem is the need to invent a cognitive process of generalization and a cognitive faculty to store the generalizations. Actions are attuned to information by virtue of past experience, but this is not by means of a generalization or averaging across past instances. It is a change in the relationship between the self and the environment, between the senses and the muscles, as easy as maintaining balance when riding a bicycle. To do this I don't have to remember my experiences of imbalance, or even my early successes at balance. When I get on the bike the dynamic forces created by my body are perfectly attuned to the forces that destabilize it. Balancing is direct, not mediated by memory in the traditional sense of a generalized store of information.[35]

Infant cognition and its development

Participatory cognition in early infancy

The concept of participatory cognition that is linked to perception and action, and that is constructed with respect to the body, is well suited to explain cognition and the development of the self in infancy. Infants as young as several months have a remarkable participatory memory for procedures in which they are active participants. For example, if they learn to kick a particular leg in a particular way in order to make a mobile move over their heads, they will re-enact the same kicking pattern up to two weeks later when placed in a similar situation.[36] Infants can also remember by reproducing a series of complicated head turns that they have been trained to perform, and they can bring a slide projector into focus by sucking either faster or slower on an automated nipple.[37] Remarkably, newborns can recognize their mother's smell and the sound of her voice, and they can also recognize songs their mothers were asked to sing to them in the two weeks prior to birth.[38]

Piaget observed instances of infant action becoming increasingly skilled and proposed the concept of *scheme* in which cognition, including memory, was entirely in the realm of action during early infancy. He used infant activity and purpose as the central organizing feature of infant cognition, a view that was also taken up by the activity theorists. Other students of infant cognition have suggested that memory formation is directly related to the individual's attempt to create meaning by pursuing goals and updating action.[39] Indeed, it would be difficult to find a student of infant cognition today who thought otherwise.

If the infant's memory is totally bound up with patterns of skilled action, then the infant's entire cognitive experience is defined by the particular forms of action and the particular modalities of perception that are used in these tasks. If the theory of embodied participatory cognition is correct, we have to assume that the cognition of young infants is not a world of visual images and verbal narrative – these are aspects of adult cognition.[40] It is certainly a world of activity in which smells, sounds, tastes and touches are remarkably salient, filling practically the entire cognitive sphere.[41] When we consider that these perceptual activities are in a living body that tingles and shudders, that feels pleasure and tension, that becomes aroused and relaxed, we can begin to get a sense of the quality of infant experience.

Freud, for example, remarked on the voraciousness with which babies attacked the nipple. For Freud, this was due to the overwhelming press of the hunger drive. For me, it is due as much to hunger as to the sensory primacy of the lips and tongue and the information in the form of pleasure and mastery that is created when those organs co-regulate with a soft nipple and sweet warm milk. Research has shown that the mouth of a small baby is adept at adjusting to different shape nipples, the tongue will explore and detect differences in shape, and oral stimulation and sucking serve a variety of exploratory and soothing functions, not just nutritive intake functions.[42] For the baby, at that moment, there is nothing but smell, warmth, taste and touch: no distracting visual or verbal images. This primacy of perception and direct action, of participatory cognition, is more likely to be the source of the oral eroticism with which Freud endowed infants, not the drive to eat.

Infant participatory cognition, therefore, is clearly embodied. It is also rooted in the situation in which the infant experiences the activity, as shown by research related to the infant's memory for procedures necessary to make a mobile move by kicking. In a variant of the studies reported earlier, if infants cry when the initial training takes place they fail to remember how to make the mobile move on later occasions in which they were not crying. Or, if the experimenter changes the decorations in the crib between training and testing the infants fail to remember. That is, the infants re-enact the action sequence with respect to the entire context in which they first acquired their action with respect to moving the mobile.[43]

In the previous chapter I reviewed research on the development of the infant's relationship to objects that evolves out of a history of interactions between mother and infant around the topic of object play. I concluded that the meaning of objects for the infant was related to the way information about objects was created with the mother over the course of the first year. In the language of this chapter, the infant's participatory cognition of objects includes all the procedures that were used during those social interactions. Thus, for infants, the cognition of objects is inherently social because infants acquire object-related procedures in a social situation. Indeed, it is the differences between the social relationships in the two dyads that I described that captures the differences in infant cognition about objects.

Daniel Stern expresses a very similar view with his concept of the *evoked companion*.

> For instance, if a six-month-old, when alone, encounters a rattle and manages to grasp it and shake it enough so that it makes a sound, the initial pleasure may quickly become extreme delight and exuberance [that is] not only the result of successful mastery, which may account for the initial pleasure, but also the historical result of similar past moments in the presence of a delight- and exuberance-enhancing (regulating) other. It is partly a social response, but in this instance it occurs in a nonsocial situation ... It is in this way that an evoked companion serves to add another dimension to the experience ... so that even if actually alone, the infant is 'being with' a self-regulating other in the form of an activated memory of prototypic lived events.[44]

Stern's concept of the evoked companion is similar to the concept of participatory memory in the sense that the memory of the other person occurs as part of ongoing action. Stern thinks of early infant memory not as imaginative or purely ideational, but as the relationship of the whole body – involving perception, action, and emotion – to the context. Stern's view also suggests that participatory memory is not limited to the particular event, like shaking a rattle, but to the entire sequence of actions and events that have occurred with mother when shaking the rattle in the past.

Stern points out that the concept of the evoked companion is similar to the original Freudian notion of infant 'hallucination,' as when the infant feels hunger and re-creates, at that moment, the experience of nursing with the mother because in the past hunger and mother tended to occur together.[45] The evoked companion is also similar to the psychoanalyst D. W. Winnicott's concept of 'illusion' in which the infant creates the mother in relation to her typical presence at times of need.[46] Unlike Stern and Freud, however, Winnicott elevates creativity to a central role in the formation of illusions, and suggests that the infant's creation of the mother arises in co-regulated activity.

> The infant cannot be said to know at first what is to be created. At this point in time the mother presents herself. In the ordinary way she gives her breast and her potential feeding urge. The mother's adaptation to the infant's needs, when good enough, gives the infant the *illusion* that she is an external reality that corresponds to the infant's own capacity to create. In other words, there is an overlap between what the mother supplies and what the child might conceive of. To the observer, the child perceives what the mother actually presents, but this is not the whole truth. The infant perceives the breast only in so far as a breast could be created just there and then.[47]

Winnicott is talking about the creation of information: the infant's participatory cognition of the present situation. Winnicott believes that imagination arises only later, when there has been a controlled 'disillusionment' process by which the mother withholds immediate comfort allowing the infant to self-comfort via imaginative re-creation.

Stern's evoked companion is not created by the infant 'there and then.' Stern's views evoked companions as stored, individualized memories and as generalized event structures. He explains the association between the evoked companion and the infant's action when alone with an object as 'cued recall.' Stern has a discrete state model of the infant in which memory is separate from action, and in which there are dedicated and separate parts of memory for self and for mother.[48] The only differences between his view and the discrete state concept of internal working models is that he focuses more on specific incidents and endows them with feeling.

The concept of participatory memory suggests that there is no stored or generalized memory that exists separate from the procedures by which experience is acquired. The infant is fully relational at all times, and the experience of the other person is completely in relation to the procedures of action by which one co-regulates with that person. This is true even later in infancy and childhood, when individuals begin to engage in imaginative cognition and can talk about their own cognition.

The origins of imaginative cognition

When do infants begin to engage in imaginative cognition? In order to understand what form of imagination is available to infants, it is useful to examine relational theories suggesting that adult imaginative cognition is entirely encompassed by *imaginative dialogues*.[49]

These dialogues are with one part of the self and another part of the self: the self imagined at different times, in different places, or taking different narrative perspectives. In thinking, in other words, one is always telling or showing something to oneself. We do this because the inherently social nature of our experience leads us to create multiple mental perspectives that are the parties to a mental discussion. Adults also imagine dialogues with other people, dialogues with imaginary figures in imaginary situations, and dialogues with the non-social environment. Data to support this perspective comes from the pervasiveness of narrative dialogues found in literary formats, psychological research data, clinical case material, and the near universality of relational metaphors in private and in social speech.[50] In most cases, adult cognitive narratives take on a linguistic form.

Personal narrative dialogues using language apparently do not begin until the middle of the second year of life.[51] We know this because until about the age of 5 or 6 years, children think out loud. This form of cognition, called private speech, is a monologue that typically occurs when children are alone or think that they are alone.[52] It is unlikely that imaginative narratives using speech occur earlier than the second year since the developmental onset of private speech is coincident with the developmental onset of speech during social interaction. Katherine Nelson taped the private narratives of 2-year-olds while in their cribs. Here is one example from a child named Emily.[53]

> Go to library. I sat in Mormor's lap. I went to the library. Probably that's what we did in the *bus*! I sat on top of the bus and I wait for my bus. Cause the . . . I did sit in the regular bus I not in school bus. I wait for the school bus. I waited and waited and waited and waited and waited. The last buses are for . . . that's too much outside. But mostly . . . But mostly one more time.

Among other things, Emily is telling herself about having to wait for a bus. She seems to be remembering a particular feeling, using her narrative as cognition. The disjointed sequence of events suggests that Emily's purpose was not to remember for its own sake, but because the narrative occurs in the present, just before bedtime, its purpose may be to settle Emily's feelings about the situation before falling asleep.

Nelson's interpretation, however, is somewhat surprising.

> Strictly speaking, we cannot call these memories at this point because they seem to be neither remembered or anticipated. Rather they form a general undifferentiated knowledge base that serves as a background for present experience . . . Under this account, we can speak of experientially based representation in infancy, but not of memory *per se*.[54]

Nelson's view of an 'experientially based representation' that guides present experience is close to the idea of participatory memory. However, Nelson assumes that this experiential memory is stored somewhere as a representation of the contents of reality, and that because Emily's narrative is not strictly sequential in its re-creation of events, her representations of reality must be stored in a confused or 'undifferentiated' way. Nelson, like Stern, insists on a discrete memory faculty that represents, more or less faithfully, the 'real' world.[55]

To understand the developmental origins of imaginative cognition we have to examine it as an active cognitive process, not as the recall of the contents of a generalized memory store. Imaginative cognition is, in fact, one form of participatory cognition because it is mental action in the present, it is related to our purpose for imagining (to comfort ourselves, to remember an event, to plan, to solve a problem, or to help us fall asleep), and because in imagination we use the same perceptual and motor modalities that are the procedures for participatory cognition.

This participatory aspect of Emily's narrative is revealed by her meaningful use of words and grammar, by how she forms her lips and throat and tongue into conventional sounds, by her use of emphasis to express emotion (not shown in the transcript), and by her ability to tell herself about things that are important to her in the form of private speech created in the present.

A surprisingly large number of children's first words are emotion-related such as *tired* (fatigue), *ouch* (pain), *sad* (distress), *yuk* (disgust), *love mommy* (affection) and *good/bad* (value), and a considerable amount of early pretend play with language focuses on feelings.[56] By the age of 2½ years, children can talk about their feelings and label emotional states correctly,[57] they can discuss past and future emotions and the sequentially related causes and consequences of emotions (*It's dark, I'm scared; Mommy, you went away. I was sad*),[58] and they can recognize emotional sequences in themselves and in other people.[59]

Language also has the ability to describe events that are not currently present – what Roger Brown refers to as the *displacement* property of language.[60] Thus, once children begin to use language as a mode of action they become capable of referring to that which is not present. A number of developmental psychologists have suggested that the ability for cognitive displacement, or imagining, begins around the age of 2 years as evidenced not only by the onset of language, but also by delayed imitation, in which the child copies another's action at some later time when the model is no longer present.[61] Because this is the age at which children begin to recognize their own image in a mirror, it is assumed that they have an 'objective' sense of self and that they can form mental representations of self and other, and hence perhaps multiple narrative perspectives within the self.[62]

Almost everyone agrees, therefore, that the infant can imagine once language is acquired. But can the infant imagine before language is acquired? Recall from my example in Chapter 7 that when infants play with objects on their own, their cognition of the object is related to how they related to the object with their mother. The participatory memory is the re-enactment of procedures used with objects in the past, procedures acquired in the mother's company. The mother at this point is not, contrary to what is suggested by the evoked companion metaphor, created as an imaginary play partner.

However, if the infant begins to have enough experience with objects when alone it is inevitable that the infant will discover, by creating information through action, procedures for interacting with objects when alone that are different from those procedures acquired in the company of the mother. Thus, when the infant returns to the mother's company and enacts the participatory cognition based on the solo experiences with objects, information will be created that differentiates these new procedures from the old context.

To put this in the language of communication, the infant is a participant in two frames that share similar themes of information. One of the frames is consensual, the result of co-regulated negotiation with the mother. The other frame is created through a non-social communication with the physical environment. Because the infant is a participant in both frames, information can be created through perception and action. Not only can the infant detect invariants within each frame, but the opportunity exists to detect invariants between frames, particularly since the information themes are closely related.

What results is a *participatory cognitive dialogue* in which perception and action are compared between several different frames in which similar information is created.[63] The dialogue is participatory in the sense that when participating in one frame, the other frame is present as a procedural memory. This comparative activity has all the elements of a narrative mental dialogue, except that it does not occur imaginatively: the infant has to be involved in one or the other frame. The object-related action created in one frame is one cognitive perspective while the action created in the other frame forms another cognitive perspective. The infant does not have a Platonic view of the context, the object, the mother or the self as real objective entities. Neither, for that matter, does an adult.

In other words, *every action embodies a relational dialogue between one's past and the present*.[64] Thus, through participatory dialogical cognition the infant begins to create information about what is not present in relation to what is actually present. The not-present becomes part of participatory cognition and thus, from its inception, stands in a dialogic relationship to the present. Imaginative cognition probably develops as images coalesce around the co-participating frames of a cognitive dialogical relationship. To the extent that cognitive dialogues are co-regulated forms of communication between different cognitive frames or positions, these images created are cognitive processes, not cognitive contents. Thus, imagination begins as a participatory dialogue between cognitive frames and does not have to await the acquisition of language.

In conclusion, infants are capable of a relational cognitive activity from a very early age. Because cognition is always the experience of being related to something or to someone, and because infants are capable of detecting invariant information in complex situations, cognition contains all the necessary attributes for discovering a sense of self in relationships.

Notes

1. McClelland & Rummelhardt (1988).
2. For these conclusions, I gratefully acknowledge my many discussions with Mark Reimers on the philosophy of science and the nature of computer modeling of behavior. See also, Beek & Bootsma (1991).
3. cf. Aloimonos & Rosenfeld (1991), Linsker (1986), Skarda & Freeman (1987), van Geert (1991), among others.
4. Brooks (1991, pp. 1229–30).)
5. Bergin & Fisch (1968, p.78). For a discussion of some of the implications of Vico's work for psychology, see Hermans *et al.* (1992) and Shotter (1981).
6. Johnson (1987).
7. Johnson (1987, p. 88). My colleagues and I argue in a recent paper that the concept of emotion 'expression' is a metaphor that assumes that emotions are 'inside' and need to be let out or controlled. We suggest instead that emotions are not 'in' the person at all, but like cognitions and perceptions, they are created as part of a process of engagement with the environment (Fogel *et al.*, 1992). Due to the pervasive and insidious tendency to believe our metaphors as if they were real entities, even among the scientific community, this kind of talk about emotions, cognitions and perceptions is certain to induce anxiety and skepticism. This is perhaps because it shakes us out of our comfortably embodied metaphors, at least until we can find some other embodiment for our concepts.
8. Kolers & Roediger (1984).
9. Kolers & Roediger (1984).
10. Miller & Ittyerah (1991).
11. Bransford *et al.* (1977), Gibson (1966), Jenkins (1977), Michaels & Carello (1981), Ruff (1984).
12. Proust (1981, p. 350).
13. There are a number of evocative metaphors that ecological psychologists have used to describe what happens when one remembers. To emphasize the active aspect, they prefer remember*ing* rather than memory. Other metaphors are *recreating, re-experiencing, attunement* and *resonance*. The latter two terms refer to the idea that prior experience of the individual is thought to attune the person to particular types of information available in the environment, information that would not be perceived without such experience. This is not the same as having a stored memory that is associated with current perception. Rather, it is more like what a skilled pianist does with piano keys. The pianist doesn't remember all of his or her music lessons when playing a concert piece. Rather, experience has attuned the pianist's mind and body to perceive certain affordances in the keyboard that create certain types of sounds. See Bransford *et al.* (1977), Michaels & Carello (1981).

14. See Miller, Li & Desimone (1991). Recent work on the brain is entirely consistent with this view of neural processes as open and dynamic systems that better fit the notions of a continuous process model of communication than a discrete process model. Odor recognition, for example, cannot be traced to a single cell or group of cells. Instead, as a result of a body action (inhaling) all the neurons in the olfactory bulb actively oscillate in a receptive mode that leaves them free to form into a more defined pattern of combined activity in response to the environment, to the chemical information in the odor. The memory of the odor is somehow contained in all the cells and recognition is a self-organizing transaction between the cells, the body and the odor chemical from the environment. Every time a new odor is experienced, the entire pattern of cell oscillations changes subtly and that changes the individual's response to the next odor (Freeman, 1990; Skarda & Freeman, 1987). Similar processes have been observed in the visual system (Eckhorn & Reitboeck, 1990).
15. Smirnov & Zinchenko (1969).
16. Rogoff (1982); Valsiner (1987); Wertsch (1985).
17. Schachtel (1959).
18. Stern (1981).
19. I can't imagine how this proposition could ever be tested empirically because these memories are not subject to reflection or linguistic description. It nevertheless comforts me to think that my infantile experiences are in some way a part of my adult sensorimotor cognition.
20. Vedeler (1987; in press).
21. Examples of the importance of anticipation in co-regulation are discussed in detail in Chapters 2 and 3. In Chapter 4, Collis' concept of interaction synchrony specifically highlights anticipation. See also, Bowlby's (1969) concept of a control system.
22. Foppa (1990, p. 184).
23. Baker-Sennett, Matusov & Rogoff (in press).
24. Kolers & Roediger (1984).
25. Bransford *et al.* (1977, pp. 442–3).
26. Merleau-Ponty (1962, p. 413).
27. Harris *et al.* (1991).
28. Caughey (1984).
29. Psychotherapeutic reconstructions always occur in the present. According to Carroll Izard, Freud's use of free association during psychotherapy may be a way of using memories that are primarily participatory as a trigger for opening up new realms of imaginative self-reflection.
30. Nelson (1973), Shank & Abelson (1977), Tulving (1972).
31. Nelson (1973).
32. Nelson & Greundel (1981).
33. Stern (1985).
34. Bowlby (1969).
35. Stern (1985) refers to examples like riding a bicycle as 'motor memory,' one of several memory systems that operate without language. He also includes 'perceptual memory' and 'affect memory.' Motor memories 'reside in voluntary muscular patterns and their coordinations' (p. 91), and are similar to Bruner's (1967) concept of 'memories without words,' and Piaget's (1962) concept of

'sensorimotor scheme.' This is similar to participatory memory, but different in two ways: participatory memories are not confined to non-linguistic actions and can also apply to thought processes, and participatory memories are not 'in' muscular coordinations as Stern would have it, but are created as information when muscular coordinations are engaged with the environment.

36. Rovee-Collier *et al.* (1981).
37. Papousek, H. (1967).
38. Cernoch & Porter (1985); DeCasper & Fifer (1980); DeCasper & Spence (1986); MacFarlane (1975). Infants also have been shown to have long-term auditory memory for up to two weeks following exposure to particular sounds in the second week of life (Ungerer, Brody & Zelazo, 1978).
39. Bruner (1990); Olson & Strauss (1984).
40. Hermans, Kempen & van Loon (1992). See Fogel (1991) for a review of sensory development in infants.
41. Human newborns can see with a visual acuity of about 20/800, not enough to detect more than outlines of highly contrasted shapes. The eyes of rat pups are completed covered by the lids until they open at 14 to 16 days. Thus, the pups' normal sensory world is even more centered on tactile, auditory and olfactory perception than human infants. Developmental psychobiologists have done experiments in which the pups' eyes are surgically opened for varying amounts of time prior to 14 days. The experimental animals, introduced out of normal sequence to the entirely different sensory modality of vision, began to structure their actions with respect to visual cues much earlier than the control animals. On the other hand, the experimental pups failed to develop certain kinds of motor skills typically associated with olfactory and auditory orientation to the environment (Foreman & Altaha, 1992; Kenny & Turkewitz, 1986). Although such experiments seem at first far removed from the human case, the experimental rats are similar to premature human infants who begin to receive patterned light stimulation weeks and months before full-term infants. We can't assess the consequences of these alterations of the sensory sequence because of other complicating factors of prematurity.
42. See Fogel (1991) for a review of the extensive literature on oral activity in infants.
43. Butler & Rovee-Collier (1989); Fagen *et al.* (1989); Hayne, Rovee-Collier & Perris (1987); Rovee-Collier *et al.* (1981).
44. Stern (1985, pp. 113–14).
45. Freud (1900).
46. Winnicott (1971).
47. Winnicott (1971, p. 12).
48. In the next chapter, we will return to Stern's view of the self and other and show how discrete state constructs of cognition lead inevitably to views of the self as non-relational. As Philip Cushman (1991) argues in his critique of Stern's theory of the self, objectively distinct cognitive faculties and objectively different concepts of the self and the other is part of a distinctly Western cultural view of individuals as independent and separate.
49. Hermans *et al.* (1992).
50. Bruner (1990); Hermans *et al.* (1992); Sarbin (1986). See earlier review of embodied cognition and the work of M. Johnson (1987).

51. Eisenberg (1985); Nelson (1984).
52. Furrow (1984).
53. Nelson (1985, p. 122).
54. Nelson (1985, pp. 122, 127).
55. This leads Nelson to conclude that the reason adults cannot remember their infancy is because the generalized representations before the age of 3 years are incomplete and disorganized (Nelson & Greundel, 1981). Contrast this with Schachtel's view, like my own, that there are participatory memories of infancy that are expressed in particular action and perceptual modalities that were most salient during infancy.
56. It may help to understand the participatory nature of speech about current and past events by imagining the emphasis, body movement and facial expression that might accompany a toddler's use of these words. Language is not just a discrete state program for producing syntax and semantics, it is part of many of the child's perception–action systems. Bloom & Beckwith (1989); Bretherton *et al.* (1986); Dunn, Bretherton & Munn (1987); Ridgeway, Waters & Kuczai (1985).
57. Denham (1986); Lewis & Michalson (1983).
58. Bretherton *et al.* (1986).
59. Bretherton *et al.* (1986); Hoffman (1975); Radke-Yarrow & Zahn-Waxler (1984).
60. Brown (1973).
61. Golinkoff (1983); Piaget (1954).
62. Lewis and Brooks-Gunn (1979); Kagan *et al.* (1978). We will return to the topics of imitation and mirror self-recognition in the next chapter as we discuss the infant's cognition of self and other. These developmental events have taken on importance in the minds of psychologists because they appear to hint at an objective, stored self-representation that fits a discrete state model of cognition. I shall argue that there is a continuous process interpretation of these developmental phenomena, and that we can find evidence for a dialogical self well before these events.
63. Infants only weeks old can compare a present situation with one that has immediately passed, as shown by the phenomenon of habituation. Habituation occurs when the infant's attention to the same stimulus wanes over repeated presentations. If a different stimulus is placed in the series, the infant's attention will recover to initial levels, assuming the infant can detect the differences perceptually. This ability for comparison between present and non-present is used routinely by researchers to illuminate the infant's perceptual and cognitive processes (Bornstein, 1985; Colombo *et al.*, 1987). Infants can also show recognitory responses to familiar stimuli in the first month.
64. Most developmental psychologists think of the emergence of linguistic narrative and self-recognition as a great cognitive leap because of a presumed emergence of objectivity. For me there is no particular mystery here since objectivity in the traditional sense never occurs. We simply develop by elaborating different types of relational systems of action and cognition. Thus, I see the cognitive processes of the infant as similar to those of the adult.

Chapter 9

The self in relation: self and other

What is the self? More than a body, or a history, or a set of feelings: the self can't be completely encompassed because it is always re-making itself. Individuals that have stopped making themselves become shadows cast by a former self, they speak to themselves and others in a single voice of pain or compulsion or sentimentality.

> Human identities are considered to be evolving constructions; they emerge out of continual social interactions in the course of life ... Narrative constructions are the socially derived and expressed product of repeated adventures and are laid over a biological life progression that often extends beyond its storied span ... the athlete retiring after a long and successful career is often ill-prepared to meet the challenges of continuing to structure a life story ... The typical dramatic progression is that of tragedy.[1]

The self is the set of one's personal stories, or narratives, told in inner speech or told to others. Selves, like relationships, are collections of story themes, some of which are creatively changing in the re-telling, while others become rigidified vestiges from the past.

V. S. Naipaul describes his experiences of travel, followed by his attempts to write stories about those experiences.

> To arrive at a place without knowing anyone there, and sometimes without an introduction; to learn how to move among strangers for the short time one could afford to be among them; to hold oneself in constant readiness for adventure or revelation; to allow oneself to be carried along, up to a point, by accidents; and consciously to follow up other impulses – that could be as creative and imaginative a procedure as the writing that came after ... However creatively one travels, however deep an experience in childhood or middle age, it takes thought (a sifting of impulses, ideas, and references that become more multifarious as one grows older) to understand what one has lived through or where one has been.[2]

Every human life is a journey into the unknown, often with guides but rarely without taking risks and grasping opportunities. The self is seldom settled or known completely. We travel through time as creative participants. Later, we re-create it imaginatively as participants in dialogue. The self, in both the living and the enlivened telling, is relational. The self is both parts of the dialogue, it is a continuously re-created co-regulated process. And there are many dialogues and many parts to the self. When the dialogue on a topic turns into a monologue, when it becomes a thing about which everything seems known or knowable, when the story is unchanging, that part of the self becomes a rigid frame that is no longer a participant in an otherwise unfolding personal tale.

The dialogical self in adults

In the previous chapter, I embraced the notion of cognition as embodied narrative dialogue. Hubert Hermans, Harry Kempen and Rens van Loon, two psychologists and one philosopher from the Netherlands[3] argue that the self emerges from that dialogue. Psychologists beginning with William James at the end of the nineteenth century and continuing to the present time have made a distinction between the *I* as the part of cognition that is the thinking agent, and the *me* as the object of that thought.[4] The *I* imagines things or makes metaphors (thinking about taking a walk), while the *me* is what the *I* imagines (picturing oneself actually walking).

If cognition is a narrative between two or more imagined positions, the cognitive process seems spontaneously to assign multiple narrative voices that can engage in a discussion and that can be perceived as parts of ourselves.[5] Position, as a dynamically changing process, is a more appropriate metaphor than that of role to suggest the different perspectives which constitute dialogue.[6]

> we conceptualize the self in terms of a dynamic multiplicity of relatively autonomous *I* positions in an imaginal landscape. ... The *I* has the possibility to move, as in a space, from one position to the other in accordance with changes in situation and time ... the *I* has the capacity to imaginatively endow each position with a voice so that dialogical relations between positions can be established ... As different voices, these characters exchange information about their respective *mes* and their worlds, resulting in a complex, narratively structured self ... The *I* in one position can agree, disagree, understand, misunderstand, oppose, contradict, question and even ridicule the *I* in another position.[7]

One need not retain the conceptual distinction between *I* and *me*. It is sufficient to conceptualize the self as a dialogical process between multiple cognitive positions.

According to Hermans and his colleagues, the dialogical self has a number of characteristics that make it different from the traditional Western (or Cartesian) notion of the self, some of which are summarized in Table 9.1.

Table 9.1. Characteristics of the adult dialogical self, based on the work of Hermans, Kempen and van Loon

Dialogical self	Rational/objective self
The self has multiple *I* positions, each of which has a different perspective	The self is unitary, with a single *cogito* responsible for reasoning
The self is embodied such that the *I* positions must occupy an imaginary time and space. Thus, cognition must participate in a dialogue and cannot transcend those positions, except from some other embodied position	The self is disembodied and thought can transcend its material boundaries by taking an abstract stance
The self is social, and can act 'as if' it were another person as one of the positions the *I* can occupy. The other position may or may not be the actual perspective of another person; it could be an imaginary person or an imagined point of view of another person.	The self is individual even though one can think about interacting with another, or take the role of another
The self as dialogical is decentralized; it is not one particular position but all of them combined and the dialogue between them.	The self is the centralized or ideal center of control with defined boundaries
The self is defined with respect to its historical and cultural context	The self is context free, without reference to society and culture, and can stand outside its own history

(Adapted from Hermans, H.J.M. *et al* 'The dialogical self', in *American Psychologist*, **47**, No 1, January 1992, copyright © 1992 by the American Psychological Association, adapted by permission.)

The dialogical self is not an objectively specifiable entity. The self is not entirely 'in' the individual, since it embodies the positions of others and can imagine itself in times and places that are not here and now. The self is not a single locus of control, since it is composed of multiple positions, none of which is more correct or real than any other. The self is never entirely defined, but is always in the process of creation through dialogue. This dialogue can occur with another person, or it can occur between the different cognitive positions, or between one or more imagined narrative voices. In any case, the form of the dialogue is identical to the form of social discourse.

In answer to the question 'who am I?' I can describe myself in terms of linguistic-cultural categories. I am of medium height, I have grey hair, I am a father and husband, I am a psychologist, I have particular religious and political beliefs, and the like. But none of these categories is myself, they are descriptors of external features or of completed actions.[8] If I were to describe myself in continuous process terms, I would have to talk about all of my cognitive debates and discussions. I would have to admit that I am not a single and permanent entity, but rather a set of choices, possibilities and uncertainties. I would have to describe all of the identities I take on in both actual and imagined social relationships.

Frankly, I could never finish this description because of the multiplicity of the self and because it continues to change as I am thinking about it. I could never entirely know myself objectively, I could never trace all the historical connections, alternative cognitive positions, or even all of the facets of the self here and now. I can't do it partly because of the complexity, but also partly because every time I think or remember, I create a different point of view as my participatory cognition engages with one embodied position from the perspective of another.[9]

It is easier in the end to think of myself categorically, because in Western culture we are encouraged to simplify our experience, to achieve a single identity and an independent point of view. The concept of the ideal, stable, unified self is a distinctly Western cultural concept and Western readers may balk at the notion of the self as an inherently open-ended dialogical process.[10]

Jerome Bruner refers to the dialogical self as the 'distributed' self and makes the claim that such a self is known only through a lifelong interpretive procedure.[11] Bruner finds the roots of this view of self in current trends in philosophy, sociology, anthropology and psychoanalysis. The self is always created in the present, it only exists with respect to the interpretive activity of creating a story in the here and now. Bruner's studies of autobiographies found that almost one-half of the narrative units are in the present tense. The authors seem not merely to be recounting the past but 'deciding what to make of the past narratively at the moment of telling.'[12]

The dialogical self in infancy

I propose that the infant self is dialogical and that it is experienced primarily in the realm of participatory cognition rather than imaginative cognition. Instead of a dialogue between actual or imagined points of view or between different voices, the infant self emerges as a result of the cognition of alternative action possibilities and the resulting dialogue in action between them. These action possibilities are perceived directly by the infant as self-produced actions, and therefore the self is experienced by the infant as the relationship between the different self-produced activities.

Multiple action possibilities as dialogical positions

From an individualistic perspective, one would argue that the self is located in the body. A relational perspective suggests that the self is distributed as the relationship between the body and the environment. According to James

Gibson's theory of ecological perception, individuals perceive themselves at the same time that they perceive the environment.[13] In the process of visual perception, for example, one looks out and observes the visual flow field and at the same time perceives one's own location with respect to the flow. Humans, for example, can see their nose at all times in the visual field. Depending upon one's posture and the direction of gaze it is possible to see other body parts in the field. Thus, in order to perceive what is out 'there,' one at the same time automatically perceives what is 'here.'

According to Gibson, the hands as visual images expand and contract as they move closer or farther away from the body. Babies can determine the spatial limits of the body because the hands can get only so small as a visual array, while other objects can recede until they disappear. Because the production of force in the arms is precisely coupled with changes in the visual array for the hands, the infant perceives the hands as part of the self, but only with respect to the co-perception in the background of the visual field of things that are clearly not under one's control. Those things that are part of my body have a different visual array, different patterns of motion, and different connections to proprioception than things that are not part of my body.[14]

Thus, one always observes from a location, and the point of observation is located by virtue of its relationship with everything else in the visual field. The self is not merely the point of observation, nor is it merely the sense of convergence between the motor control and the visual image of the body. It is the *dialogic relationship* between the point of observation, the rest of the body, and the perceptual flow field in which the body is immersed. *The self, from the beginning and by the very nature of perception, is relational.*

There is a wide range of converging evidence that young infants perceive the self as the dialogical relationship between the perception of self-produced action and aspects of the environment that are not self-produced. Self-produced motion —like crawling or walking – enhances infant skill in acting on objects, and their knowledge of out-of-sight object locations: knowledge of the environment, in other words, is directly tied to self-motion.[15] Similarly, kittens who have acquired visually guided locomotion are better at reaching at objects with their paws than those who cannot locomote.[16] Human infants of 7 months who are skilled at reaching are more likely to reach for a sound-making object in the dark if it is within reach compared to out of reach. Thus, forms of skilled action and knowledge of object locations are intimately associated with the movement of the individual within the spatial environment.

According to George Butterworth,[17] infants also have a range of dialogue-like self-directed action, similar to the idea of the *I* that acts and the *me* that is the focus of that action. Newborns will exert strong pushing movements if they are in danger of suffocation. In the first few hours of life, newborns touch their own head in an ordered sequence beginning with the mouth, then moving to the face, the head, the ear, the nose and the eyes. This occurs only when the infant is awake.[18] Prior to hand-to-mouth contact, newborns open their mouths. Such patterns of hand-to-mouth and hand-to-head contacts occur in fetal development in both humans and other species.[19] As infants become more skilled at reaching, touching and grasping, they begin to self-explore by touching different parts of the body beginning with the fingers and ending months later with the toes.[20]

These self-directed actions seem analogous to the adult *I* telling something to the *me*. In some ways, it seems curious that adults have mental dialogues at all. If the self were some central and coherent all-knowing entity, why would it have to talk to itself? It should know itself directly and immediately, making imagined *I-me* dialogues unnecessary or even ridiculous.[21] The Cartesian mind is transparent to itself, is completely rational and can never deceive itself. It is only from the Cartesian point of view that one is confirmed as a self by means of rational certainty. There is no certainty in dialogue in which knowledge is always relative to other cognitive points of view. Selves are open systems and never entirely complete.

The fact that we do talk to ourselves is an indication that there is not a higher-order point of view: *we are the dialogue and not one voice or another.* Indeed, to the extent that one voice takes over and ceases to participate in the dialogue, that part of the self becomes rigidified. Some forms of psychopathology may be found either in the absence of dialogue when a single inner voice compels, or when the dialogue becomes ritualized and constraining. The Cartesian mind of absolute certainty is a Western myth and a psychotic's reality.

Similarly, why should babies have to touch themselves to know their own bodies? This can only be explained by the different perspectives gained as an action dialogue between the position taken by the act of touching and the position taken by the act of perceiving the area that is touched.

The idea of a pre-linguistic or pre-conceptual sense of self is relatively recent in the history of psychology, and represents an important turn in our thinking about infancy. However, the scholars who propose that infants have a self have not conceptualized that self as dialogical or relational. The infant self they construct has an objective existence as a stored representation and a unity of purpose, control and organization. These scholars take the same data that I have reviewed and interpret it differently.

For example, they note that the infant can both see the hands and feel the proprioception coming from that location of the body. This coherence of perception, feeling and the control over activity is what they call the self. They propose that the self is built up as a generalized representation of coherence between perception and control: the self is the experienced locus of control and of feeling.[22]

For example, Robert Emde agrees that the infant self develops via

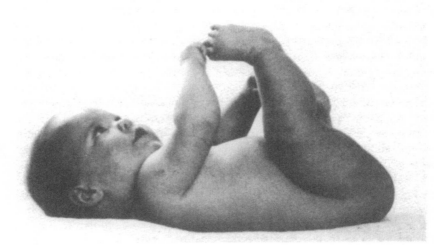

Figure 9.1 A 2 or 3–month-old infant touching and looking at the hands and feet. (Copyright © Ace Photo Agency/Vibert-Stokes.)

procedural knowledge, what I have called participatory cognition. Yet he states that 'a sense of coherence and of agency are the cardinal features of the self system along with a fundamental sense of control (i.e. ownership) of body and action.'[23] Ulrich Neisser develops the Gibsonian idea of an 'ecological self' that is embodied, but then speaks of a remembered self, a private self, and a conceptual self. These different selves are not the same as the different narrative locations in the dialogical self. Rather, they seem to be different types of stored representations each of which has an independent developmental course.[24]

Daniel Stern also relies on Gibsonian notions of the detection of invariants and their relationship to one's sense of self-produced action. The infant's sense of self is experienced directly in feeling, action and perception and is not linguistic or conceptual. But Stern, like Emde, suggests that the self is the infant's sense of coherence or organization across the various perceptual and motor realms. Infants are seen as creating order and organization. The 'sense of a core self results [because] the infant has . . . the ability to integrate all of these self-invariants into a single subjective perspective.'[25]

Of course, infants experience a coherent link between perception and action, but one should not stop there. As I have tried to show, it is impossible to perceive coherent self-action without reference to a corresponding perception of the self in a location, in a body, in an environment. Thus, coherence of perception and action is always relational, always with respect to a context, and never part of a context-free objective core.

What is the problem with defining the infant self simply as the sense of coherence between perception and action? One problem is that the dialogical self of the older child and adult seems to emerge as if by some developmental magic. Every one of these self theorists recognizes, as I do, that dialogical narrative is central to the self of the older child. How can the self transform from coherence to dialogue, from unity to multiplicity? How can a core self that exists encased in a generalized form change into the narrative, open and questioning self of the older child and adult? These theorists all assume that the ability to take narrative perspectives is brought in by the *deus ex machina* of neural maturation, cognitive sophistication, and linguistic skill. If, as I propose, the dialogical self exists from the beginning in the inherently relational form of perception and action, the developmental change is no longer mysterious.

A second problem occurs when these theorists try to connect the self to other people. How can a core, objectively defined self be related to anything? The answer varies, but it seems to be by mere associationism between objective representations of self and other. Stern's concept of the evoked companion is an example in which the absent other exists as a separate coherent mental representation associated with the mental representation of coherent self-action. The concept of the internal working model of the mother is a similarly objective mental entity; coherent and self-contained. These metaphors are mechanistic rather than relational.

A final problem is that the coherent, objective self, if found in an adult, would be pathological. One could argue, perhaps, that what is pathological for an adult may be normal for an infant. There are many aspects of infant behavior that if displayed by adults would not be considered mature: extremes of emotion, excessive dependence on a single person, or poor motor control when eating. Yet in spite of these infantile forms of acting, I believe that infants have a self that is dialogical and relational, and that those relationships are an inherent part of the original self.

The social origins of the self

The solution to these theoretical problems is, as I have suggested, to define the infant self as the relationship between multiple points of view, between the body and the not-body, between the individual and others. The fact that the adult dialogical self is in the form of a social conversation is derived from the pervasiveness of social relationships in infancy.[26] Simply put, *the self is the individual's participatory and imaginative cognition of co-regulated relationships.*

In Chapter 2, I gave three examples in which infants may have the opportunity to detect a self in relation to the context of communication with their mother. The first example involved mother vocalizing in order to calm a crying infant, the second was being helped by mother to sit up, and the third was the transfer of an object between infant and mother. What is common across these examples is the essential ingredient for self-cognition: the dialogue that results from participation in consensual action frames in a long-term relationship with another individual.

Consider the pull-to-sit consensual frame shown in Figure 2.1. As the infant changes from a supine to a sitting position, both mother and infant are together exerting dynamic forces to create action that is related with respect to the changing perceptual information about the infant's body location. This consensual frame of a two-person action system creates a smooth movement of the infant out of the ebb and flow of forces that are continuously changing within each individual. It is this co-regulated alternation of exertion within a consensual frame that is the origin of the dynamic dialogue that we call the self.

If the infant and mother were perfectly matched in their efforts, there would not be an alternation, and without alternation there would be no dialogue. The self would not be perceived at this moment because there is no background against which the individual's efforts take on a relational form. Imagine being immersed in a water bath that is exactly at the temperature of your body. If you close your eyes you will shortly lose a sense of the boundaries of your body. For some people this corresponds to a state of blissful relaxation. For others, this perceived loss of self is startling, perhaps frightening, and they make efforts to move, surface, open the eyes or touch something solid. On the other hand, if water is colder or warmer than body temperature, or if you or the water move, the boundaries of the body and the motion of the body are spontaneously detected in relation to the difference between the body and the surround.

If the mother pulls the infant with such force that the infant is unable to resist or to provide compensatory effort, there would be no sense of self as it is absorbed into the background without an opportunity to detect the relationship between self-action and a non-responsive overwhelming force. Imagine being completely overtaken by something, as in falling off a raft in the middle of a river rapid. Nothing you do can change the situation, no force you exert can counter the power of the river. The self is also lost in this situation. One has the choice to submit to the river's urges or to continue to fight against them. In fighting the river, the self re-emerges as a palpable experience: as muscle fatigue, disorientation, fear, and if all goes well as gasping for breath in calmer water, feeling grateful for the life jacket.[27]

Hamlet's famous soliloquy, ostensibly his thoughts about suicide, is also about creating the self or submitting to its loss, 'to be or not to be,'

– that is the question: –
Whether 'tis nobler in the mind to suffer
The slings and arrows of outrageous fortune,
Or to take arms against a sea of troubles,

And by opposing end them? – To die, – to sleep, –
No more; and by a sleep to say we end
The heart-ache and the thousand natural shocks
That flesh is heir to, – 'tis a consummation
Devoutly to be wish'd.[28]

In this narrative it seems to me that Shakespeare equates the sense of self, one's being, with the embodied metaphor of a thousand natural shocks experienced in relation to the background of a sea of troubles. Hamlet, of course, is suffering and the self-story he creates from his imagined action of resistance is symbolized as corporeal pain.

The baby in my example who is pulled to sit by the mother is not suffering. The baby's self at that moment is related to the consensual frame of coming upright to view the world, experienced in the exertion of the arm and trunk muscles in relation to the mother's, in the feelings of competence due to effort, in the flow of the visual array detected by the retina, and in the changes in acceleration with respect to gravitational force detected by the semicircular canals and the otolith organs.[29] Yet, both Hamlet and the baby create the self by opposition and exertion in relation to their social surround.

The self is a metaphor for the cognition of alternative action possibilities in a particular private or social consensual frame: alternative actions of the individual, or alternative actions taken by the individual and partner. The alternatives for the baby in the pull-to-sit episode, to paraphrase Shakespeare, are to pull or not to pull, or better: to pull more or to pull less. The mother has the same choices and can also perceive herself in this transaction in relation to the baby.

Why does co-regulation have a special status with respect to the self? Earlier in this chapter I suggested that the self is perceived as the relation of the infant to the environment, whether animate or inanimate, because perception is always self-referent, always with respect to the individual's position. Even so, the infant may not always detect that relationship because information is creative and emergent, not automatically pressed upon the senses nor imprinted in the brain. Social co-regulation has a special role in human development because it enhances the individual's likelihood of detecting self-referent information, of detecting the individual's relationship to the environment.

This happens because in co-regulated communication individuals create information about their own actions in relation to another person whose actions are adjusting to the individual at the same time that the individual is adjusting to those actions.[30] Thus, the events to which one is adjusting are increasingly fitted to one's adjustive actions, making the adjustment immediately meaningful. Because co-regulation moves individuals toward each other with respect to converging upon co-created themes of information, and especially when partners have lasting relationships in which themes become created and elaborated within a stable consensual frame, the perception of the individual's own action in relation to the environment is also salient.

In the pull-to-sit example, the infant's self is perceived as the relationship between forces tied directly to proprioception and the forces to which the infant submits. The self is not one's own movement, it is how that movement in combination with this set of circumstances achieves the result of sitting upright. To put the infant's self in this example in linguistic terms it might be: I am one who, in combination with compensatory support and force, can pull myself upright.

Across time in a relationship the infant and mother may do this exercise many times. Does the infant self in this situation become the generalized representation of all of those experiences? There is another explanation. The consensual frame makes salient how to re-create his or her own participation with respect to the mother's in order to achieve an upright position. Each time they do this the precise timing and balancing of forces will differ, but this infant does not have to store and generalize all these instances. Part of the infant's memory is in the situation (lying supine, raising the arms, the mother taking hold), in the body location of the action (tighten trunk and arm muscles when in this situation), and in the sequence of co-regulated alternations that are created in this consensual frame by both participants.

Each time this discourse of forces occurs in this situation the infant self will be slightly different. The self will evolve with respect to the continued re-negotiation of the patterning of forces within the consensual frame. As the infant's trunk and muscles become stronger, perhaps through this socially mediated exercise regimen, the infant will spontaneously exert more control and the mother will spontaneously cede it, not in an all-or-nothing fashion, but by adjusting the balance of force alternation in the living process of coming upright. Eventually, the infant's sense of self with respect to this action will not include the mother but it will always be relational, including the nature of the surface from which one must arise (one gets up differently from a hard floor compared to a soft mattress).

The dialogical self is always present in every such transaction, although it is not readily observable, any more than one's inner thoughts are observable to another person. The dialogue is in the subtle interplay between one's exertion and the momentary and fleeting adjustive response of the environment to that exertion. That adjustive response is different when I am being assisted up, compared to pushing myself up from a bare floor, compared to holding on to a rigid support like a table. The self is each of those dialogues. It is re-created in each of those situations. It is not generalized across them except in so far as the actions that make one come upright may be similar in each situation.

Research suggests that the self is created with respect to social co-regulatory processes, when the partner is not merely responsive to infant signals but is an active participant in the dialogue and takes a role in the cooperative co-creation of consensual frames. For example, infant compliance and self-monitoring activities in the second year are enhanced in relationships that are co-constructed.[31] Similarly, understanding of the self's relationship to family members arises in mother–child and sibling–child discourse during the second year, as teasing, support and prohibition are co-regulated in the family.[32]

Studies of infant peer interactions in the second year are especially interesting. It is only at this time that peers can establish what appear to be co-regulated forms of communication without the intervention of an adult. They spontaneously adjust their actions with respect to each other and are able to create elaborated dialogues through mutually creative activities, first involving mimicking and later with more complementary actions in response to the partner. When investigators actually study the process and outcomes of peer play, they find that there is indeed cooperative activity in which frames are co-constructed, and that participation in consensual frames enhances the child's self-monitoring and self-regulatory actions as well as the child's understanding of self and other agency.[33]

By the age of 5 years, children define themselves linguistically with respect to their relationships to other people. The self is described, for example, as being similar to or different from other people, or in relation to actions performed with others ('We went way down by the pool'), to others ('I taught my little brother how to color'), or by others ('Jimmy hit me'). Even when describing things that happen when alone, children refer to their relationships with others ('No one was holding my hand').[34]

The behavior of adults when alone is particularly revealing in this regard. According to a review of research on emotions by Alan Fridlund,[35] when alone we treat ourselves as interactants, we act as if others are present by having both imagined and pretend conversations with them, we rehearse potential interactions and make social emotional expressions even when others are not present, and we often treat non-humans and inanimate objects as social interactants, such as in talking to pets and making faces at houseplants.

One interesting finding concerns the child's use of the word *mine*. When children first use this word around the age of 2 years it is in the context of social play and they appear to be using it in the sense of defining ownership rather than in the sense of being possessive. They are likely to say *mine* if another child approaches or picks up one of their toys, but they may not complain if the child uses the toy. Also, they often switch freely from *mine* to *me*. Thus, they seem to be defining for the other child their relationship to the toy, rather than acting as if the toy was exclusively for their own use. *Mine*, therefore, expresses the nature of a relationship rather than an absolute property of the self.[36]

Unfortunately, before infants can use language and before they can act independently in a relationship between peers, it is harder to find conclusive evidence for the social dialogical self. This may be why many observers in the past have suggested that the infant self begins around 18 months when infants appear to recognize themselvess in a mirror.[37] This developmental achievement, however, seems to be related primarily to the ability to name and describe one's own body, appearance, emotions or self agency linguistically with respect to either a mirror, a peer or an adult.[38]

There is some evidence that infants as young as several months act differently in the company of different social partners,[39] and in the presence of interactive disturbances such as simulated maternal depression,[40] interruption of maternal action,[41] changes in the animacy of the partner,[42] changes in behavior following maternal separation.[43] These differences in responding typically do not involve crying, aversion or following as they might in an older infant under such circumstances. Rather, they include subtle changes in the movements of the infant's hands, arms and legs, in the facial expression, and in the gaze direction. One has to examine the infant's whole body in relation to the specific social situation in order to detect these changes. To the extent that self-perception is automatically a part of other-perception, I suspect that these different social experiences yield different dialogical selves for the infant.

Another hypothetical mechanism for the emergence of a social dialogical self is imitation. Throughout infancy and early childhood, imitation serves as one of the primary agents in social discourse. Newborns appear to be able to imitate some simple gestures like mouth opening and tongue protrusion,[44] mothers and infants imitate each other during social play during the first year of life,[45] and when peers first begin to interact in the second year they establish play routines via mutual imitation.[46] In each of these instances, imitation serves as a simple and reliable means for the initiation and maintenance of dialogue and sharing between social partners.[47] Imitation, in other words, is often the admission ticket to a social play routine. Because of its centrality as part of social dialogue, and because of its mirror-like aspect, imitation is one way in which self-action can be made salient with respect to another person's action.

This view of the social function of imitation fits the concept of the dialogical self only if imitation, like any other social action, is creative and co-regulated. Is this the case? According to some individualistic theories of imitation, it is a capacity of the individual, based on the ability to form representations of others' actions and to match those representations with objective representations of their own actions. These representations are believed not to be tied to a specific modality of action, but rather to be amodal.[48]

On the other hand, research has shown that imitation of all sorts depends on a variety of features of the context. Newborns, for example, are more likely to imitate actions they can perform on their own (the modeler must choose just those actions that the infant is likely to imitate) and the imitation is more likely if the time between presentations is long enough for the infant to visually process and attempt to perform the action. Thus, when adults structure the situation so as to make salient information the infant can perceive and perform, in other words when adults and infants co-regulate, imitation is more likely.[49] Imitation, even newborn imitation, depends on the existence of a social context which allows infants to create information from visual or auditory displays and translate that into imitative action. Imitation, therefore, is co-regulated social action within a consensual frame for mimetic activity, not an individualistic performance by the infant. According to Kenneth Kaye, 'imitation is active and creative. An imitative act is never a perfect copy, always a novel act ... imitation is often achieved by the joint action of children and their models ... imitation does not entail representation.'[50]

Imitation does not require representation because it is created directly from perception into action. These co-regulated features of imitation occur in older infants and children. One-year-olds are more likely to imitate familiar actions than unfamiliar actions,[51] and by age 1½, children are more likely to imitate acts for which the modeler provided a verbal explanation in the context of an ongoing interaction.[52]

Thus, even the simplest of social actions, imitation, is co-regulated and therefore requires self-action to be performed in relation to the other's action. In the early months of life, imitation is dialogical because the self is perceived in relation to the other as part of participatory cognition. By the age of 2 years, and sometimes earlier, imitated actions become part of the self via imaginative cognition.

Emily, the child whose crib monologues were recorded, was also recorded during the period when the parents were still in the room and putting her to bed. An analysis of these data were conducted by Rita Watson.[53] Her father often said, 'night-night, Hon,' with a falling pitch intonation characteristic of coaxing and soothing. Just after the father leaves, Emily produces her own 'nighty-night' three times in succession with the same falling intonation pattern. Just after, she imagines the next encounter with her father, 'when Daddy come, then Daddy get Emmy then Daddy wake Emmy up ... ' This is followed by a description of herself sleeping during the night. Watson writes,

> [Emily] does not seem to be simply repeating or imitating what she has heard, or simply listing experiences in a random way. In this monologue, she casts her experience in relation to a social reality. Her effective self-regulation [calming down, getting ready to go to sleep] co-occurs with her expression of shared patterns of action ... [54]

Once again, imitation is not mere copying based on some individualistic capacity to do so. Imitation is an action created to establish a self in relation to personal history and context: I am one who, when falling asleep, am connected to my father, and to the immediate history and future sequence of events in which this period of sleep is embedded.

The dialogical self is co-regulated

The self as the history of relationships between multiple positions

In the example of Emily's monologue we can see how experiences with other people immediately become part of the dialogical self. Emily's self dialogue is partly of the I–me variety, telling herself that she will see her father when she wakes up, and partly of the other–me variety, as she repeats her father's 'night-night' it is as if the imagined position of the father is telling something to the me.

To the extent that the dialogical self is co-regulated communication, the consensual frames that make up the self are continuously being formed and dissolved in just the same way as consensual frames in social relationship formation between two separate individuals over time. The self is not a dialogue between discrete signals nor between fixed mental representations. Rather, *the meaning and character of each dialogical position must be created in the dialogue itself.* The motivation for people continuing to interact with each other is the possibility for creating new meaning through the dialogue. By analogy, *the developmental sustenance of the dialogical self is self creation.* The self is the developmental history of these participatory and imaginative cognitive relationships.

As we participate in this self dialogue we often better understand something, or better understand our relationship to something or someone. Even at our most relaxed, on a hill looking at the sky perhaps, we think about the clouds having shapes we recognize or we think about our place in nature. We don't just run stock phrases across the mind like 'save the earth,' we typically try to examine who we are or what the clouds are or what it would be like to fly among them. Our thoughts are open-ended discussions with possibilities. Most of the time, we get up from the hill with most of these thoughts and dreams unresolved but yet somehow self-renewed by virtue of having a creative experience.

Just as co-regulated social dialogues are negotiated, with each partner changing to suit the other until some kind of consensual frame or stable pattern of co-action is achieved, self dialogues often have the quality of a negotiation. As children get older their part in social dialogues, and their creation of different positions in self dialogues, become more self-corrective. During conversations, adults, for example, prefer self-repair and self-correction compared to being corrected by the partner. People generally pause and restart, repeat, or re-pronounce words and phrases in the same sentence before the partner has an opportunity to do it.[55]

As we have seen, negotiation and repair are present in early infancy in non-verbal discourse. The examples in Chapter 2 of Laura and of the crying infant show how through negotiation of initially uncertain meanings, there are self-corrective adjustments with respect to the other. By the middle of the first year, children can initiate self-repairs in speech,[56] although they have been doing this non-verbally since early infancy.[57] Indeed, in some theoretical formulations, repairs and corrections are part of the communicative process of individuals who use language and gesture to create something together.[58]

Socially co-regulated self-corrective and other-corrective dialogues have been described especially clearly in studies of remembering in the process of social discourse. Derek Edwards and David Middleton[59] recorded the conversations of eight people asked to recall together the feature film *E.T.* The people began by establishing a frame for remembering, using the word 'we' as a marker for joint activity, such as '*we'll* start by singing the theme tune.' They then constructed a narrative about the film, with each person elaborating on or contributing to the reconstruction.

K: well he goes to the fridge to get something to eat *first* doesn't he with the dog following him
D: yeah *that's it*
K: mm
D: and he finds him feeding the dog
J: *and then and then* he finds the beer
D: *and then* he finds the beer and what is it there's a link between Elliot and E.T (&)
K: Elliot's at school
J: telepathic link
D: (&) that whatever happens to E.T. Elliot feels the same effects and E.T. got paralytic (laughs) and so E.T. is sort of going
L: all a bit drunk
T: *that's right I remember*

In this excerpt,[60] the people use words like 'and then' to establish that they are filling in the sequence of events. People also correct or prime each other's memory and express a gap in their own memories with incomplete sentences or saying 'mm.' Other narrative techniques for completing the memory are saying things like 'we haven't mentioned. . . ' or 'do you remember?'

The constructed memories are not exact copies of the original. People add evaluative comments that reveal the memories to be partly constructed by their own impressions and partly by the film, such as, 'I thought the whole thing was stupid that aliens could be able to fly in bikes.' Sometimes people remember primarily those things that stood out for them, such as scenes that are 'horrible,' 'brilliant,' or 'confusing.' People try to persuade others that their own version of the story is more valid, regardless of whether it happened that way in the film, thus creating a corrected version of what actually occurred. Or alternatively, people agree too quickly on a version of the film that does not fit the original, and thus rigidify the creation of new memories. Thus, incomplete individual impressions are linked with others to create a remembered whole story.

It is common in families to re-construct a past event through group discussion. In research on the evolution of family stories, David Reiss found that story-making is always a creative and collaborative activity. Even when families are re-telling a story, 'in almost no instances did the story emerge fully formed: its retelling was always an event of re-creation, formulation, elaboration, active suppression, fresh dissent, reconciliation, or all of these.'[61] Family stories are emergent from the self-corrective and other-corrective patterns in the dialogue.

There are similar examples of research on memory constructed through corrective negotiation in which children are participants, but adults are more active than children in using such devices.

    M: Who gave it to you?
    C: Mommy.
    M: Yes.
    C: Daddy.
    M: Yeah.
    C: Mommy.
    M: Yeah.
    C: Da . . . Michelle give it.
    M: Michelle didn't give it to you. No.
         Mommy and daddy gave it to you for your birthday.

In this conversation with a 2-year-old child, the mother is asking questions and affirming the child's answers. The mother in this research study[62] used temporal questions and temporal language (when, then, before, today, this week). She also used corrective speech to alter the child's creation of his own relationship to his past. By the age of 3 years, children respond with more details and are better able to provide self-corrective monitoring for their own recollections.[63]

Thus, the self- and other-correction during social negotiation occurs both during live social dialogues and during self dialogues. Indeed, the self dialogues have the same co-regulated form as the social dialogues. Thus, all the principles of the development of relationships discussed in Chapters 6 and 7 also apply to the development of the self.

Finally, and again by analogy to the development of relationships, not all self dialogues are of this open and creative type. Some are rigidified into mental slogans that repeat and don't go away, like ritualized patterns in relationships that we somehow can't change. Even these rigid patterns are relational. If I tell myself ritually that I'm not good at making friends, that probably means to me that I am not open to developing such skills. I have closed this off from creative elaboration as part of myself.

The self is all of these multiple relationships to all of the multiple situations to which we are regularly exposed. We can never be open to all of those situations, so we have parts that are relatively more rigid and parts that are relatively more creatively predisposed. As in relationships, some individuals may experience more situations creatively or rigidly than others so that an individual's character is not a generalized representation of a superordinate self that is good or bad, it is always the self in some situation.

Self frames

I have argued for a theory of self that is parallel to a theory of social relationships; a self that is always relational and that is composed of multiple dialogical processes from multiple positions of participatory or imagined activity. I rejected the notion of the self as a coherent and generalized representation that is adopted by many scholars with respect to the self of the young infant. I suggested that the infant self is first participatory and later imaginative, first non-verbal and later verbal, but always dialogical and relational. Indeed, individuals are free to create any number of possible selves through relationships to imagined others and to imagined pasts and futures.[64]

Yet, there are times when the self seems cohesive and unified, when there seems to be a 'central' self that has the characteristics of the Western individualistic concept of the core self. Although I reject the idea of a single self representation, I suggest that the feelings of cohesion that individuals sometimes have can be explained by the same process that creates stable consensual frames and information themes within a relationship.

Informational themes are mutually created within consensual frames by both individuals in a relationship. Because the self is comprised of potentially many different private consensual frames, it may be the case that common informational themes arise across these frames. However, we do not require a 'super' self to integrate the information across each of these separate dialogical relationships within the self. Rather, all we need is participatory cognition.

The different consensual frames within the dialogical self are not split off from each other as in a multiple personality disorder. Instead, they are often connected by participation in similar information themes. One example is the development of the infant's relationship with objects in the company of mother in comparison to relationships with objects when alone. To the extent that the grasping with mother and grasping when alone yield common information about the object, the self's relationship with objects will be coherent across these frames. If, however, the information created differs, the infant will experience them as separate parts of the self. With infant Andrew in Chapter 8, for example, because social object play had a different meaning from solo object play, he had difficulty allowing mother to enter into his solo play with objects at the end of the first year and rarely engaged in cooperative activity with her.

In summary, the multiple dialogical self does not preclude a sense of self-cohesion or a sense of harmony between different aspects of one's social or private life. The concept does, however, provide a very different explanation for such cohesion from the traditional objective representational views. The experience of cohesion probably occurs when each of the relationships in which one engages are informationally consonant with each other, mutually supportive and similarly creative. A self in which one voice and one relationship dominates all others is not cohesive: it is rigidified and exclusionary, it is one that experiences disjunction between each of its real and imagined relationships. Developmental change, therefore, is the process of elaboration, dissolving, comparing and consolidating dialogical self frames.

Notes

1. Scheibe (1986, pp. 131, 144).
2. Naipaul (1984, pp. x–xi).
3. Hermans, Kempen & van Loon (1992).
4. cf. Hermans, Kempen & van Loon (1992) for a complete review. See also James (1890); Mead (1934).
5. Bakhtin (1988).
6. Harre & van Langenhove (1983).
7. Hermans, Kempen & van Loon (1992, pp. 28–9).
8. This leads to a problem in the interpretation of traditional psychological measures of the self, such as self-concept, self-esteem and the like. These measures take the self out of its historical context and treat it as a trait having a quantifiable measure (Cushman, 1991; Hermans, Kempen & van Loon, 1992).
9. Gergen (1982).
10. Bruner (1990); Cushman (1991); Hermans, Kempen & van Loon (1992).
11. Bruner (1990).
12. Bruner (1990, p. 122).
13. Gibson (1979).
14. Gibson (1979).
15. Acredolo, Adams & Goodwyn (1984); Campos & Bertenthal (1988).
16. Hein & Diamond (1972).
17. Butterworth (1992).
18. Kravitz, Goldenberg & Neyhus (1978), as reported by Butterworth.
19. Butterworth (1992).
20. Kravitz, Goldenberg & Neyhus (1978) as reported in Butterworth.
21. Apparently, even young children do not have a Cartesian theory of mind (Wimmer & Hartl, 1991).
22. See also Bruner (1989) for a critique of this objective, bounded concept of the self.

23. Emde *et al.* (1991, p. 252).
24. Neisser (1991).
25. Stern (1985, pp. 71–2).
26. Kaye (1982); Vygotsky (1978).
27. Victims of violence often recover more rapidly if their stories about such incidents reflect that they actively resisted. Or, if they could not resist, their recovery needs to include a story about why at the time it was impossible due to actions of the perpetrator and not due to perceived self-complicity in the act. Some theorists view the process of psychotherapy as narrative reconstruction, creating a story about the self that induces continuing creativity (Spence, 1986).
28. Shakespeare's *Hamlet*, III, i.
29. Benson (1990); Jouen (1990).
30. See also Kaye (1980, p. 207); Mead (1934). This is also similar to Trevarthen's (Trevarthen & Hubley, 1978) concept of primary intersubjectivity in which the self emerges as part of a mutually regulated exchange between infant and caregiver in early infancy.
31. Lutkenhaus, Bullock & Geppert (1987); Parpal & Maccoby (1985); Schaffer & Crook (1980).
32. Dunn & Munn (1985).
33. Brownell & Carriger (1990); Dunham *et al.* (1991); Eckerman (in press); Wolf (1982).
34. Miller, *et al.* (1992, pp. 53–4).
35. Fridlund (1991).
36. Levine (1983).
37. Harter (1983); Lewis & Brooks-Gunn (1979); Pipp, Fischer & Jennings (1987); Stipek, Galinski & Kopp (1990). Other research shows, however, that this may be due in part to the child's exposure to mirrors and to using mirrors for self-recognition.
38. Pipp, Fischer & Jennings (1987); Stipek, Galinski & Kopp (1990).
39. Such as between a peer and an adult (Fogel, 1979); between mother and father (Parke, 1979); between mother and an unfamiliar female (Mizukami *et al.*, 1990).
40. Cohn & Tronick (1983).
41. Cohn & Elmore (1988); Fogel *et al.* (1982); Tronick *et al.* (1978).
42. Field (1979); Legerstee, Corter & Kienapple (1990).
43. Field *et al.* (1986); Fogel (1980).
44. Meltzoff & Moore (1989).
45. Legerstee (1990); Moran *et al.* (1987); Papousek & Papousek (1984); Trevarthen (1977).
46. Eckerman & Stein (1990); Nadel & Fontaine (1989); Nadel-Brulfert & Baudonniere (1982).
47. Bavelas *et al.* (1986); Kaye (1980); Masur & Ritz (1984); Uzgiris *et al.* (1989).
48. Meltzoff, Kuhl & Moore (1991).
49. Anisfeld (1991); Kaye (1982); Meltzoff (1991).
50. Kaye (1982, pp. 186–7).
51. Masur & Ritz (1984).
52. Hay *et al.* (1985).

53. Watson (1989).
54. Watson (1989, p. 278).
55. Levelt (1983); Schegloff, Jefferson & Sacks (1977).
56. Robinson (1989); Shatz & O'Reilly (1990).
57. Golinkoff (1983).
58. Bennett (1981) takes an explicitly relational view of repairs as part of the negotiation of mutual understandings in a continuous process model of communication.
59. Edwards & Middleton (1986).
60. Edwards & Middleton (1986, p. 435), the underlined sections are as in the original.
61. Reiss (1989, p. 210); see also Ochs, Smith & Taylor (1988).
62. Lucariello & Nelson (1987, p. 233).
63. DeLoache (1983), Fivush and Hudson (1990), Ratner (1984), Rogoff (1990). This work assumes that the adults observed with the children have some knowledge of the child's past and are helping the child to review what the two experienced together. It also assumes that the adults are not trying to impose their own view on the child. Such assumptions break down in situations when children are interviewed regarding alleged incidents of abuse. The interviewer does not know the child or what happened in the situation. Some interviewers may try to persuade the child or lead the child. In addition, both the original incident of abuse and the interview itself are stressful or traumatic for the child. It would be difficult to infer anything about the social construction of memory in forensic interviews from research on the social construction of memory in parent–child play interactions.
64. Nurius (1991).

Chapter 10

Culture as communication: stability and change

Culture as a process

Co-regulation and culture

Communication, self and culture are constituted by the same process. Each is a dialogue between multiple positions, an evolving story played out on different stages. Each is governed by co-regulatory processes, by creativity and rigidity, by stability and change.

The stage of the dialogical self is the cognitive experience of a single individual. The actors are real or imagined, embodied as persons or as parts of the same person, as ideas or as emotions, as sensations or as metaphors. The stage for communicative dialogue is the space between individuals, experienced by selves and enacted in some tangible form. That form may be a conversation, a fight, an embrace, or an exchange of letters. It may occur face-to-face or separated by distance and time. The cultural stage is vast by comparison: it extends from pre-history to the future of the human species, it occupies an infinity of real and imagined universes. Cultural dialogues occur in the self and in communication between selves. They also occur every time we read a document, watch television, go shopping or to work, attend a concert, sporting event or religious ceremony. Culture is alive in its process and in its products and it lives through its use by individuals.

There is nothing I can say in this chapter about culture that I have not already said about communication in relationships and about the self: the relational process, the nature of the dialogue, is identical. Culture, as I understand it, is not a thing. It is neither a set of encoded rules nor a fixed patterning of behavior. Culture does not stand above individuals, does not guide individuals like a super self that knows all and sees all. Culture is created through communication.

Culture is the set of stable consensual frames in a social system. Cultural frames may appear fixed and rule-like because they coalesce into products like pottery, languages and writing systems, because their change is slow and distributed across time, space and social networks wider than the one in which we typically live our lives. Pots, languages and writing systems are living things, however. They change to accommodate individuals and their collective actions.

There are many cultures in a society, even in a society that is relatively homogeneous in its racial, religious and ethnic characteristics. Cultures, like selves, are comprised of multiple dialogical processes. There is a cultural frame – in the form of a distinct vocabulary and a unique set of tools and behavioral practices – for every different sport, for each religion, for different occupations and industries, and for each community. Every local communicating group has its own variation on the larger cultural frame. For example, within the culture of baseball, each team will have its distinct sub-cultural practices. Within a community, each family will share a somewhat different culture, and each dyad within a family will develop their own unique practices and vocabularies. These two points – that cultures develop through communication and that there are as many cultures as there are communities of co-participants – suggest a re-thinking of the role of culture in individual development.

Cross-cultural psychologists are concerned primarily with understanding individual behavior and development. When culture is used, it is often objectively treated as an independent variable, one of many influences on the child. According to Gustav Jahoda,

> Psychologists . . . generally have no coherent concept of culture relevant to their specific theoretical aims . . . Their usage tends to be very loose, and culture often includes 'ecology' . . . For many cross-cultural psychologists, culture appears to be a category conceptualized much like 'social class.'[1]

An alternative approach is to assume that culture is a system of meanings that mediate relationships between individuals and their environments. Culture is not a set of rules and tools, but the 'totality of . . . meanings maintained by a human population, or by identifiable segments of a population, and transmitted from one generation to the next,'[2] or alternatively, 'a system of historically evolved and socially standardized cognitive processes that provides organizational frameworks for the life of human beings within their changing environmental conditions.'[3] Culture is the active, interpretive process by which individuals create frames for meaningful relationships. Culture is created in the course of communication between the co-participants: meaning in a culture is just the extent to which communicating communities co-regulate stable themes of information.

Cultural themes and variations

If we think of culture as the frames and informational themes that emerge from a network of co-regulated relationships, then the analysis of cultural differences will follow along the same lines as the analysis of relationship differences and self differences. Co-regulation is the mutual creation of action by a negotiated process of exerting and ceding control in which self and other are relational poles of a dialogue.

Cultures differ in the perception of the individual's control in relation to others, in whether they view the self as relational or as autonomous and individualized, and in the embodiment of information in particular sensorimotor systems.[4] These differences are expressed in terms of beliefs and practices, narratives and myths, images and metaphors.

Generally speaking, Western cultures tend to perceive control as individualistic and autonomous, the individual as the center of activity. Westerners tend to think in objective terms, in what I have called discrete states and generalized objective selves and others.[5] A similar theme runs through Tibetan Buddhism in which the ultimate goal is to understand that the world is created entirely in our imagination giving license for retiring from the world into more self-absorbed states of meditation.[6]

This view of a core objective self is contrasted at the opposite extreme with the distributed or relational self of the Eskimo culture that does not even have a word for self-reference. The Eskimo phrase *tusarp-a-ra*, meaning 'I hear him,' is literally translated as 'his making of a sound with reference to me.' 'I am' is *uva-nga*, or 'the being-here mine.'[7] The Japanese and Chinese cultures also define the self in relation to others. The Japanese term *amae* and the Chinese terms *sajiao* (used for women and children) and *laugi* (used for men) express not only mutual dependency in relationships, but also the presumption of mutual responsibility between partners.[8] These cultures make explicit recognition of interpersonal responsibility with rituals expressing deep gratitude to mentors and filial piety to parents.

According to Japanese psychologist H. Befu,

> Telling children to 'make up your mind' about clothes to wear, or asking them to decide on the choice of an ice cream flavor even when children are too young is a common sight in America ... the final responsibility of making a decision is left to the person ... In reality, decision making is influenced by the views of many others, as we all know. If no one has given explicit input for a particular decision at least the decision is affected by the views and values of parents, peers, teachers and many others to whom one has been exposed through one's life. Such influences in American culture, however, are discounted when an idealized American self is under consideration.[9]

The Japanese accept their duties to others from whom they have received some benefit. Americans, on the other hand, find it difficult to receive assistance, accept gifts or to allow themselves to become dependent upon someone else. They may be taken by surprise, express embarrassment, or find it hard to think of appropriate ways of repayment.

With respect to the role of the body in cultural differences, for example, doubtful judgements about personalities in the United States are likely to refer to someone's head (I don't know what he's thinking; He must be crazy), implying a metaphor of a central location in the body that is more important than others. Among the Gahuku-Gama of New Guinea, the body is regarded as more of an integral part of the whole person and doubtful judgements may be expressed as 'I don't know his skin.' Greetings typically contain earthy phrases like 'let me eat your excreta (your urine) (your semen)' sometimes with a gesture of an open hand going to the mouth, or by grabbing the genitals or buttocks of the person being greeted.[10]

As we saw with respect to the topic of embodied cognition, many cultural categories reflect the perception and action possibilities of the human body. The metaphors used in language often reflect body processes. Words for endearment to another person, for example, often contain references to temperature, with 'warm' words signifying more emotional closeness – attachment, attraction – compared to 'cool' words. The temperature gradient is related to the mutual regulation of warmth from tactile contact between individuals across a wide variety of animal species, and the historical association of affection terms with warm terms is found in the trees of several unrelated language families over the past 1,500 years.[11]

Cultures also differ with respect to the creation of tools and practices related to the performance of particular actions. Tools and practices are cultural frames that regulate action in a context. Thus, the quality and type of tools, for example, are likely to affect the types of actions found in the culture. Tools and other cultural frames, conversely, will be shaped by the perception–action systems that they serve and the culture's preference for particular types of actions. Words must be created out of the phonological action possibilities of the oral articulators. On the other hand, cultural frames for particular kinds of body movement, including oral expression, may regulate the phonology of the language over historical time.

Culture and infancy

Macro-historical processes of cultural change

Cultural frames, practices, and tools often change but they may, however, remain stable over many years. I view these cultural frames in the same way as consensual frames in social relationships: as self-organized and created through co-regulation. As such, cultural frames are subject to innovation and change, rigidification and dissolution. Barbara Rogoff writes that 'Individuals transform culture as they appropriate its practices, carrying them forward to the next generation in altered form to fit the needs of their particular generation and circumstances.'[12] Similar points have been made by others. 'A tool creates its own environment and skills, which in turn reverberate on the tool itself and consequent effects on the society and environment it creates for its members.'[13]

Research on culture and mass communication generally support this conclusion about the role of innovation in cultural change. 'Significant innovations create new industries, alter institutional practices, and restructure the patterns of life.'[14] Once an innovation is introduced it is spread through the society via a process of diffusion. Diffusion rates depend on the similarity of the innovation to existing practices, the skill or technical requirements of the innovation, the degree of mass communication about the innovation and the extent to which recognizable and valued individuals adopt the innovation and thus model its effects for others.[15] This is true for innovations that diffuse through a single society as well as for diffusion to other societies, where the innovation may conflict with values and beliefs.

Innovations are more frequent in a society in which manufacturers of tools can advertise them through the mass media,[16] and when they are responsive to the needs of buyers and users of the tool based on feedback from market research. I found the following in the 'Family' section of my local newspaper.

> A Foldable Baby Bouncer from Playskool Baby is a parent-welcome item. This convenient, comfortable bouncer has a distinctive feature that parents will appreciate – it folds up for easy carrying and storage.
>
> This sturdy, light weight bouncer has a flexible, smooth-edged metal frame which creates a gentle, rocking motion when baby is playing or when parents are soothing baby to sleep. Non-skid grippers on the bottom prevent the bouncer from sliding and a quilted Velcro strap closes tightly to secure baby in place. It retails for about $30.[17]

This product description suggests that innovations in cultural tools evolve with respect to the concerns of the users. Note how the copy-writer appeals to values related to infant care in Western society by referring to the parents' convenience (easy carrying and storage, helpful for getting the baby to sleep) and to the infant's comfort (gentle, comfortable, soothing). Safety is also a big concern for Western parents who may leave the infant alone for brief periods in the bouncer (sturdy, smooth, non-skid). This language is meant to facilitate the diffusion of the innovation in order to benefit both the seller and the buyer: a co-regulated relationship that develops over time.

Such innovations carry with them a distinctive set of user skills and user vocabulary. Unless you are an active participant in this culture, it is unlikely that you will understand the tool-specific words like 'bouncer,' 'gripper,' and 'quilted Velcro.' Innovations in culture, therefore, like innovations in relationships, push participants to new levels of learning and expertise. This is not because the participants are guided, but because they are informed about how the innovation can be used by themselves. Skill development is emergent from participation in the co-regulated relationship within the cultural frames.

This example also suggests that there is not one culture, there are many cultures. There is a culture of infancy and of parent–infant relationships. That culture includes tools and practices for play, for caregiving (diapering, feeding, sleeping), for carrying and holding babies, and for clothing them. For each of these general domains there are entire sub-cultures creating and changing in the dialogue between users and manufacturers. Whole sections of shops are devoted to selling such merchandise and the products are continually changing, sometimes improving, sometimes disappearing, sometimes offering completely new items.

Occasionally, the user–manufacturer dialogue will become absorbed into larger social dialogues, ultimately changing the tool from some broader perspective. This occurred, for example, in the controversy over selling infant formula to Third World countries, changing both the composition of the formula and local feeding practices. This is a case of conflict between traditional cultural frames and foreign innovations. Issues have been raised about the ecological impact of soiled disposable diapers and plastic disposable baby bottles, about the shapes of nipples with respect to the growth of teeth, and about the safety issues related to the size and composition of toy materials and the use of car seats.[18]

The cultural frames for infancy also include infant care beliefs and infant care practices. Infant care practices are highly labile with respect to infant survival rates with more protectiveness and close contact in situations of high mortality.[19] In First World nations with easily accessible sources of childcare information such as television and books, beliefs and practices change so frequently that they become fads. Parents quickly become overwhelmed with a large array of often conflicting advice, much of which fails to translate into situated action at the moment the infant is crying. An inspection of the historical trends in beliefs regarding infant care in developed countries even within this century reads like a cultural roller coaster, alternating between advice for parents to punish or to praise, to coddle or to confine, to respect or to remake the infant's behavior.[20] Because of this, diffusion of innovations regarding beliefs may spread more slowly than technologies.

Generally, the culture of infancy changes with respect to the participants in the culture (parents and infants), the strategies available for childcare (parents, siblings, relatives, out-of-home care), the ecological pressures on families (food sources, safety factors) and the economic roles in the family (gender division of labor, income, resources).[21]

The culture of infancy shows a fascinating variability if one considers infancy on a world-wide scale. There is a surprisingly large amount of research documenting cultural differences in infant care practices and in infant behavior. Cultures vary in the amount of touch and handling infants receive,[22] in encouragement to explore, in access to the environment and to objects,[23] and in the quality and quantity of social interaction.[24] Not surprisingly, the skills infants develop depend on the patterns of care, the tools and the infant's access to them, and the sensorimotor modalities favored by the culture.

In Oxkutzcab, for example, a town in Mexico of 12,000 composed mostly of Yucatec Mayans, there are poor sanitary conditions and the infant mortality is relatively high. Infants are kept quiet and sheltered in the early months. In the area designated for the infant in the family's one-room home there are no infant-specific tools or furnishings except a rough infant seat. Infants spend most of their time being carried and they have little opportunity to explore.

> While mothers and other females provide very attentive care in terms of frequent feeding, body contact, quick responsiveness to distress, and absence of socialization pressure, such care does not include a great deal of the intense, vocal, affectionate interactional component that seems to be an essential part of 'good' care to Western observers ... [Mothers] do not feel themselves responsible for the child's characteristics; neither do they seek or feel able to change most infant and child behavior.[25]

Compare this to what has been observed in a city of similar size located about one hour north of Rome, Italy. Here, infants spend almost no time alone and are almost always in the company of more than one person due to the extended family structure and frequent visiting patterns between community members. The frequent social interactions

> included vigorous handling as well as teasing, both of which often resulted in more tears than laughter on the part of the infant. Games of this type involved adults playfully but forcefully spanking infants or removing an object (such as a pacifier) from the infant's grasp and holding it just out of reach ... in spite of the large amount of attention directed to the infants, play sessions as defined in U.S. studies (in which the child is in charge of the situation) were relatively infrequent ... play was initiated and terminated at the discretion of the adult.[26]

The Italian infants, like the Yucatecs, had few toys of their own.

Both the Yucatec and Italian cultural patterns evolved over centuries and continue to evolve via dynamic interactions that both stabilize certain features and eliminate others. How does this happen? Cultures evolve their frames as a result of adapting to the ecological demands of the physical and economic setting, as a result of the history of cultural narrative and belief, and as a result of the technologies available for the purpose of infant care.[27] Cultures also evolve with respect to the universal features of perception and action shared by virtually all adults and their infants, but these universally embodied features must be placed in an ecological and historical context.

An examination of cultural differences in Baby Talk (BT) reveals some of these competing sources of influence in the macro-history of a culture. BT has been found to have the universal features of exaggerated pitch range, especially toward pitches higher than in adult speech, a melodic rendering of intonation contours that emphasizes the meaning of the adult speech, a slowing down of articulation with longer pauses between sounds, and a high repetition rate.[28] The same pattern emerges even in tonal languages like Chinese and apparently is due to the perceptual salience of such speech to infants. Their changes in behavior encourage adults to continue the BT frame.[29]

Other studies have shown that although these non-semantic, more affect-laden features of BT are most influenced by infant behavior, the content and symbolic aspects of BT are more likely to be influenced by cultural formats for communication and beliefs about infants.[30] Sueko Toda, Masatoshi Kawai and I compared mothers' speech to 3-month-old infants in Japan and the United States. Based on hypotheses related to adult communicative style in Japanese compared to English[31] we found that the Japanese mothers' speech was more affect-oriented and had a much larger collection of infantized words, as shown in Table 10.1.[32] Affect vs. information salience has been found to differentiate BT between other cultures as well.[33]

In Japanese, the linguistic form used differs according to the relative sex, age or status of the speakers. Infants are more indulged in Japan, and it is more natural in that culture for mothers to empathize with the infant's needs by moving to the infant's level. Japanese mothers do not expect their baby to understand them, and seem to be using BT as a way to enhance their identification with the infant as shown by the higher rates in Japan of incomplete sentences, nonsense sounds, onomatopoeic sounds, songs and BT.[34] Studies of historical writings on infant care in the Chinese and Japanese culture reveal a remarkable continuity over centuries. Although there is no concrete data on the persistence of BT over this history, it is clear that Oriental societies have been slower to change their childrearing beliefs than has the West.[35]

Table 10.1 Examples of Baby Talk in Japanese

English equivalent	Adult speech	Baby Talk	Explanation
Are you hungry?	Onaka suita?	Onaka shuita	Phonological change
Let's play	Asobimashoo	Achobimachoo	Phonological change
Please	Doozo	Doojo	Phonological change
Eye	Me	Meme	Duplication
It hurts	Itai	Itai-tai	Duplication
Get up	Okiru	Okki	Shortening
Hiccup	Shakkuri	Hikku hikku	Mimic sound of action
Lamp	Denki	Denki-san	Use of honorific
Dirty	Katanai	Batchii	Entirely new word

Source: Toda, Fogel, and Kawai, 1990

Micro-Historical Processes of Cultural Change

It is considerably easier to study the process of micro-historical cultural change, the development over time of a single relationship system, a problem that I have discussed at length in Chapters 6 and 7. In those chapters, I spoke about the formation of dynamically stable vs. rigid consensual frames within a relationship. I did not, however, cast that discussion in terms of culture, a topic to which I will turn in the remainder of this chapter.

Even for the same infant, the culture of infancy is not uniform. The cultural tools and practices change continually with respect to the infant's development.[36] One does not use the same toys, supports or furniture for a 1-month-old as for a 1-year-old. In the space of several years, infants use and discard a series of cultural devices. Their parents change the balance of caretaking and play. Culturally available games are appropriated by the couple for days, weeks or months and then dropped in favor of others. Infants move into and out of different spatial locations and settings, expanding their range of endeavor from the bedroom to overtake larger areas of the household.

None of these changes are as simple as they may seem. They are not straightforward extensions of infant developmental change independent of anything else. They are not made possible because adults are following a curriculum for allowing infants to move into particular activities, nor because the label on a toy gives the suggested age range for its use. These changes are co-regulated between the infant, the family and the sets of tools and practices available from the society at large (the toys, games formats, furniture, childcare materials, and beliefs).

Take, for example, the issue of infant locomotor development. In some Mayan communities and other similar cultures, infant movement is restricted for several years until the infant is capable of self-monitoring. In Western homes, where infant risk for health and safety problems is minimized, infants may be permitted to move about under parental supervision, but the areas of infant travel are at first restricted. The expansion of the infant's range is negotiated, sometimes with parents encouraging more movement and sometimes with infants demanding greater access. While this is going on the parents will be gradually altering the physical environment using culturally available resources. They may remove items that pose a danger and add others, pillows and climbing toys, that are not typically part of an adult household. They can purchase devices that 'child-proof' cabinets, stairways and closets. Before long, the spatial configuration and furnishings, and the access to that space by everyone in the home, has been changed through negotiation between all involved.

Barbara Rogoff uses the term *appropriation* to signify the child's adoption of the cultural practice as part of co-participation with an adult.[37] In early infancy, it seems to me, the term may also apply to the parents in their participation in larger cultural frames related to infant care. There are many cultural frames and they are specific to their purposes. Households and other institutions are equipped by their users with the tools and practices that suit their purpose. A family with no infants or young children is not likely to have a store of infant-related cultural items. Parents-to-be begin to alter their homes and to acquire the culturally available items for a newborn. After the child is born, they continue to change the home by acquiring infant-related cultural items that are appropriate for their particular child and family situation.

I concur with Jerome Bruner's view that one of the adult's roles is to supply frames in which the child's actions can become meaningful.[38] As he points out, the culturally derived frame is only the beginning of the process. The frame comes in a particular size, shape and color, a particular sequence of actions that are the standard cultural frames for play. One size, however, does not fit all infants and their parents. Once the item or practice is appropriated by the parent from participation in the sphere of infant-related tools and expertise, it must be made into action between the parent and infant. Infants do not like or use all the toys their parents acquire, nor are they equally pleased with all the day-to-day caretaking practices the parent has appropriated from participation in one or another source of cultural inspiration.

The cultural frame must be negotiated into the relationship via co-regulation between the parent and infant. In the process, the frame changes in its structure and use by the dyadic process of mutual agreement to play a game, to use a toy, tool or word.[39]

The choice of the formats is not entirely prescriptive and certainly not automatic. As described by Jacqueline Goodnow,[40] parental choice arises in an adult cognitive and social dialogical process of selecting from many alternatives the one believed to be most suited to the task. How does the parent know what to make, buy or borrow? The parent must be guided by books, people with more experience, or commercial advertisements and shop displays in order to find just those tools and to develop just those practices that seem to be required at the moment.

How can we explain, then, the cultural gloss on the adult's BT to the infant? Adults who vocalize to and with infants do not simply start out producing random sounds that are shaped like operants into particular patterns of pitch and intensity by the infant's response. Nor is it likely that adults have a genetic program for baby talk, except perhaps in so far as the phonological range of vocal action encompasses many possible registers. It is more likely that adults have heard others talking to babies, raising their pitch and performing the usual patterns of infant-directed speech heard in that culture. They discover the format in these frames and through co-regulation with the infant the parents become skilled participants in infant-related cultural practices.

The metaphor of transmission of cultural frames between generations is just not going to capture the complexity of this process. Culture is created as much by the parents as by the infants. *The cultural frames are not rigid but malleable*; skeletons with Plasticine bones.

The metaphor of culture as cumulative and as leading to more and better things is only going to obscure the fact that the frames are specific to the situation and the task, that they are not necessarily ordered into a logical or useful sequence.[41] In what sense is playing with a rattle preparation for holding a spoon, swinging a baseball bat or a conductor's baton? – in only the most trivial sense of using a manual grip. Stirring, baseball and conducting partake of different cultural systems. The rattle may be useful and meaningful in the here and now as a cultural tool for a specific purpose. It does not have to lead to something else more grand or important. In fact, all during childhood, age-specific and culture-specific tools and practices are appropriated, negotiated and discarded.[42] *The cultural frames are not only malleable, they are disposable.*

In summary, culture is introduced within relationships by framing and co-regulation. The frames are chosen, at first by parents and later by children, from the pool of cultural resources. Culture and communication are inseparable. Culture is never 'in' the environment, it has no objective specificity. It is always embodied and negotiated, a process through which individuals form relationships and in which selves emerge.

Culture and the self

The self is the individual's experience in actual or in re-created relationships. As they are used, cultural practices and tools expand the range of the self into innovative forms of relationship.[43] Perhaps the salient feature of culture is that it carries tools and practices that create information related to actions that would not be likely to be discovered by the individual alone or within the local community. Those tools and practices, as they become co-regulated via relationships, become part of the self.[44] Our selves are defined by televisions and automobiles, for example, because these tools give us a sense of being meaningfully related to the actions and outcomes inherent in the use of those tools. A baby who is provided with a bouncer or a walker has a different sense of self than one who is carried everywhere and is not allowed free access to the environment at a distance from the adult.

Thus, even if we use the cultural item entirely on our own, without the company or help of others, we are engaging in a socially co-regulated communication. The social co-regulation arises because the tool was designed by another person and it is both malleable and disposable. It is nearly impossible for me to imagine a situation in human development that is not in some way mediated by social co-regulation, nor an environment in which infants live that has not been appropriated from some cultural resource. Even the choice of where to set up one's tent in a nomadic population is guided by whether the physical setting – the rocks, trees, grass, and natural shelter

– affords the culturally appropriate characteristics that meet the needs of the group.

Because every action we make in the environment is in relation to the self, we will choose places, practices and tools that suit us, that stand in a meaningful and informative relationship to us.[45] Should those criteria of meaning fail to operate, the relationship with that tool, practice or setting is eventually abandoned. This rigidification and dissolution process is identical in cultural frames and in consensual frames in relationships. Along with the companion process of innovation and creativity, we have enough to explain a good deal of cultural change and the macro-historical and micro-historical evolution of the self.

If transmission from culture to self is not an appropriate developmental metaphor, how are we to understand the process by which individuals participate in cultural practices and become skilled tool users? How does the self develop? I have already remarked that co-regulation and negotiation are more appropriate metaphors: they apply to the initial choice of a cultural frame and they apply as the frame is either put into practice or discarded. We don't just copy models, we embrace them as parts of our participatory selves. Even if we do seem to copy a model directly, as when a child dresses up in adult clothing and 'goes to work,' this imitation must be understood as a creative process of choice, effort and negotiation.[46]

Susan Holt and I have studied the cultural frame of a peek-a-boo game when it is first introduced to an infant by the mother, using our weekly observations of mother–infant communication within relationships. In the first instance, the adult suddenly disappears behind her hands: what is this about? The infant waits. The adult pops up with a loud noise and a wide open mouth. The infant is puzzled, perhaps, or startled, but still attentive. The adult waits for the infant to assimilate this, to re-settle, and then she hides again. The infant watches and waits. Perhaps the same thing will happen, and it does! Now isn't this interesting. After several rounds the infant loses interest, the adult introduces a different frame.

Several days later the peek-a-boo frame is re-created by the mother. The baby is again attentive. Perhaps this time he will lean over to the side to try to see behind the mother's hands, but this is useless. The baby perceives that he has no immediate control over the revealing, but that it happens anyway and unexpectedly. After several more days or weeks of this, the baby may actually smile or laugh as the mother re-appears while smiling and laughing in a way that is co-regulated with the infant. The infant begins to experience the self as delightfully connected to the social process. Weeks later, the baby will laugh when the mother begins the game, when she hides. He can now recognize the boundaries of the frame, and it has become part of himself related to mother via co-regulated perception and action.[47]

Still later the infant begins to assume some of the responsibility and initiative for the game. He may pull on the mother's hands to reveal her face. He may hide her face or his own, he may begin to use vocalizations similar to the mother's at similar junctures in the game. We can now say that the infant is a full participant in the cultural frame and has defined himself through participation.

The infant is provided with the frame in a way that is made meaningful by the adult through co-regulation. The infant does not perceive the whole frame at once, but only a small part of it, and each infant perceives a somewhat different aspect. Because the frame has a simple and compelling logic, the initial steps lead eventually to the child's fuller participation as an initiator and producer.

One has to ask, why has this game lasted in the human culture of infancy for so long? The answer is that it is particularly easy to grasp and play with only the slightest hints, those that a small baby can pick up and use. The crucial theoretical point here is that the cultural practice or tool – itself a human creation, having been improved and re-modeled over long periods of time, and having passed through many capable hands – has lasted in the culture precisely because it makes the creation of information through perception and action *readily apparent to the user*. The tool or practice reveals entirely new possibilities to the user that are implicit in its structure and revealed through use. The game, therefore, is not entirely copied by the baby nor guided by the adult, it is *re-invented* through the various hints and clues the infant first perceives as meaningful and because the sequential patterning of the frame lends itself to spontaneous creativity.[48]

Andrew Lock illustrates the concept of re-invention with the example of a child learning the number system.

> These numbers are a human construction, more importantly they are a construction of the child ... but they bring with them properties which only emerge upon their having been created ... properties such as odd or even, perfect and prime numbers ... In order to progress to the adult form of speech the infant has to realize these properties for his own use ... he has to discover these new objects which are implicit in what he has already created ... to make actual in behavior those emergent properties of a previous creation, to give explicit form to their implications.[49]

According to Lock, the adult is just as involved as the child in creating culture, but once the child picks up some of the properties of the cultural practice, the rest may emerge through use and discovery, 'through a process of guided re-invention.'[50]

To put it another way, cultural practices are initially invented and persist because they work. They carry – and here's the essential point – a structure that enhances the probability of perception and action that creates information for the next user. Thus, cultural tools and practices are exactly like persons: they are available for communication by virtue of their potential for co-regulation. This is important because it means that neither the adult nor the child has to carry all the information required for infant development, part of the information for developmental change is also in the network of relationships, tools and practices that are brought into the dyad's communication process.

This model of re-invention has been applied to the development of language as a cultural system of communication.[51] I will not review that work here, but I will point out some recent findings suggesting that language and its acquisition is always embodied in an infant's perception–action system and is co-regulated with respect to the adult's.

Language must be produced by some part of the body, and to the extent that infants have the anatomical and motor systems, they can acquire language. Recent findings show that infant babbling demonstrates intonation and articulation patterns found in the language spoken in the home, and around the same age (6 to 10 months) infants lose their perceptual sensitivity to sound contrasts. A 3-month-old can perceive sound contrasts from many languages, but by 8 months their perceptions are primarily attuned to the native language. Thus, both perception and action are changing simultaneously and with respect to the speech formats found in the home.[52] In the second year, particular phonological patterns of action constrain the degrees of freedom on the forms of syllable and word sequence that can be spoken comfortably.[53] In addition, words are distinctly related to the child's current actions and to the tools that regulate those actions.[54]

Language as a cultural frame can be adapted to any modality of perception and action. Before normal infants can articulate words, they use their babbling and intonation contours in meaningful ways that reflect the adult usages.[55] In addition, deaf children acquire a gestural language that is either spontaneous if they are not exposed to a sign language, or the sign language used in the home. Remarkably, deaf infants exposed to American Sign Language will babble gesturally in that language and they will use exaggerated gestural contours to express themselves in communicative situations.[56] Thus, the linguistic co-regulated perception–action system can either be auditory–vocal or visual–gestural.

A final piece of evidence regarding the embodiment of linguistic cultural frames comes from work on the social context in which language is typically acquired. Adults provide cultural frames that allow infants the opportunity for co-regulated re-invention, typically with games involving both action and speech. In addition, however, it appears that adult non-verbal activity while speaking is co-regulated with respect to the infant's perception–action system. Thus, when adults label objects, infants are considerably more likely to acquire the word if they are looking at the object at the same time. If, in addition to assuring joint attention, the adult points or gestures to the object, infant acquisition is enhanced.[57]

In general, this research suggests that infants play an active role, not only in perceiving language and producing it, but in establishing co-regulated frames with the adult that enhance the probability of the infant's perception and action. Thus, while adults could be said to appropriate cultural frames, they must negotiate those frames into the communication process. They do this by making the frame perceptually salient to attentive infants and creating opportunities for innovative actions by the infants within the frame. The infants create information about the cultural frame – the word, the gesture, the tool – by virtue of their available perception–action systems. Cultural frames are used by parents and infants because they enable infants to discover, to re-invent, meaningful linkages between perception and action. Culture, therefore, never loses its embodiment, never exists 'out there,' never is separate from creative co-regulation.[58]

Notes

1. Jahoda (1980, p. 115). See also Bornstein (1980); Valsiner (1989).
2. Rohner (1984, pp. 119–20).
3. Valsiner (1983, p. 6).
4. Although he does not directly discuss co-regulation or the nature of the communication process, Paul Heelas (1981a) comes up with similar dimensions of cross-cultural differences in what he calls 'indigenous psychologies,' the way a community understands the self, cognition and human relationships.
5. Bruner (1990); Cushman (1991); see also Needham (1981) who quotes Wittgenstein's condemnation of the Western philosophical search for immutable inner states and substantial categories as a 'craving for generality.'
6. Heelas (1981b).
7. Harre (1981, p. 84).
8. Doi (1973); Ho (1982); Morsebach (1980).
9. Befu (1985).
10. Read (1967, as described by Heelas, 1981b).
11. Alberts & Decsy (1990).
12. Rogoff (1990, p. 198).
13. Kirkland & Morgan (1992).
14. Bandura (1986, p. 155).
15. Bandura (1986); Rogers (1983).
16. Bandura (1986).
17. *Salt Lake Tribune*, February, 1992.
18. Fogel (1991).
19. LeVine, Miller & West (1988).
20. Fogel (1991); Goodnow (1988).
21. LeVine, Miller & West (1988) suggest that there are generally two main parenting strategies, agrarian and urban, and that parental goals are shaped by the ecological pressures and the cultural practices of the local environment. See also Agiobu-Kemmer (1986); Eibl-Eibesfeldt (1983); McSwain (1981); Super (1981).
22. Typically, touch, holding and handling increase infant alertness and enhance

motor development: Bril & Sabatier (1986); Gunzenhauser (1990); Hopkins & Westra (1988); Lusk & Lewis (1972); Sorenson (1979); Super (1981); Valsiner (1989).

23. Bornstein *et al.* (1990); Bornstein *et al.* (1991); LeVine, Miller & West (1988); Valsiner (1989).
24. Field *et al.* (1981); Fogel, Toda & Kawai (1988); Valsiner (1989).
25. LeVine, Miller & West (1988, pp. 41–2).
26. LeVine, Miller & West (1988, pp. 57–8).
27. Goodnow (1988); LeVine, Miller & West (1988).
28. Fernald (1985); Papousek & Papousek (1981; 1987).
29. Fernald *et al.* (1989); Papousek, Papousek & Bornstein (1985).
30. Blount (1972); Ferguson (1977); Penman *et al.* (1983); Snow (1977).
31. Clancey (1986).
32. Toda, Fogel & Kawai (1990).
33. Bornstein *et al.* (1992).
34. Toda, Fogel & Kawai (1990).
35. Kojima (1986).
36. Rogoff (1990); Valsiner (1987).
37. Rogoff (1990).
38. Bruner (1983).
39. Haight & Miller (in press); Vandenberg (1986).
40. Goodnow (1988).
41. Kagan (1989).
42. My mother often reminisces about the games we used to play together, the books I liked her to read to me, and the places we visited when I was a small child. My imaginative memory can only re-create a fraction of these incidents. A similar generational memory gap has appeared with my own children. Could it be that the culture of infancy and childhood is more salient and perhaps more developmentally meaningful for the creation of the self for the parents than for the children? The parents sacrifice time and resources to create the opportunities, work to introduce and maintain the cultural innovation in the parent–child relationship system, and often feel considerably sadder at its passing than the child (McBride, 1973).
43. Bandura (1986); Vygotsky (1978).
44. According to James Wertsch (1991), cultural tools act to mediate the dialogue between the self and others, and the dialogical narrative within the self.
45. Altman & Rogoff (1987).
46. Schwartzman (1978); Vygotsky (1978).
47. Holt & Fogel (1992).
48. The term re-invention comes from Lock (1980). Kaye (1980) also alludes to the fact that cultural practices such as language must be organized in such a way that an infant can easily adopt and use them.
49. Lock (1980, p. 35).
50. Lock (1980, p. 36). Vygotsky (1978) makes a similar point about play – that it makes explicit, cultural properties that are implicit in the frame. By actually enacting the play, the players exaggerate the roles and relationships and thereby make salient for themselves the meaning of the those relationships.
51. Bruner (1983); Kaye (1980); Lock (1980); Vygotsky (1978).

52. de Boysson-Bardies, Sagart & Durand (1984); Bosma (1975); Kent (1981); Ohala (1980); Werker & Lalonde (1988); Werker & Tees (1984).
53. Donahue (1986); Matthei (1989).
54. Bates *et al.* (1979).
55. de Boysson-Bardies, Sagart & Durand (1984); Marcos (1987).
56. Bellugi (1988); Goldin-Meadow & Mylander (1983); Meier (1991); Petitto (1987).
57. Bakeman & Adamson (1986); Baldwin (1991); Dent (1990); Franco & Butterworth (1990); Harris *et al.* (1986); Schaffer, Hepburn & Collis (1983); Schmidt (in press); Tomikawa & Dodd (1980); Zukow (1990).
58. Camaioni (1989); Dent (1990); Zukow (1990).

Chapter 11

Conclusions and implications

Developmental determinism and indeterminism

Most relationships begin with a meeting, often by chance, of two individuals who are drawn to each other. According to psychologist Albert Bandura,

> A chance encounter is defined as an unintended meeting of persons unfamiliar to each other ... Some chance encounters touch people only lightly, others leave more lasting effects, and still others branch people into new trajectories of life ... The unforeseeability and branching power of fortuitous influences makes the specific course of lives neither easily predictable nor easily socially engineerable.[1]

Once a chance encounter occurs, however, the future course of events may be at least partially determined by the susceptibility of the individuals to each other and their openness to change. Within relationships there are processes that lead to the formation of stable consensual frames and those frames constitute a reduction in the degrees of freedom of individual action. Creativity and choice is possible, but within the circuit of the consensual frame. Thus, we may have historical determinism in particular epochs within the life course of an individual or a relationship. Alternatively, relationships may be partially indeterminate as they change by creative or fortuitous events that lead them into new stable frames, and indeterminacy arises in development as individuals enter relationships with others that begin either creatively or fortuitously.

In her biographical account of her own and her friend's lives, Mary Catherine Bateson discusses the use of chance opportunities and improvisation while living during a time when cultural frames for women's roles are changing. She describes her book as

> about life as an improvisatory art, about the ways we combine familiar and unfamiliar components in response to new situations, following an underlying grammar and evolving aesthetic ... A good meal, like a poem or a life, has a

certain balance and diversity, a certain coherence and fit. As one learns to cope in the kitchen, one no longer duplicates whole meals but rather manipulates components and the way they are put together. The improvised meal will be different from the planned meal, and certainly riskier, but rich with the possibility of delicious surprise. Improvisation can be either a last resort or an established way of evoking creativity. Sometimes a pattern chosen by default can become a path of preference.[2]

There is an apparent paradox in describing developmental change as both partially predictable and determinant, and partially fortuitous and indeterminate. How can humans develop similar global characteristics, yet their daily lives are often shaped by chance events that make them different from each other?[3]

My answer to the question of the balance of indeterminism vs. determinism is conceptualized within the frame of a continuous process model of relationships. Rather than thinking of some actions and events as fortuitous and others as determined or predictable, I believe that virtually every action and event is partly determinate and partly indeterminate. Events are partially indeterminate in the sense that the information we create about them is always changing, and partially determinate in the sense that they are perceived as part of ongoing action within a frame that constrains our degrees of freedom.

Chance or caprice certainly occurs in development, as in suffering from a disease or having a serious accident. But research on adult life-course development has shown that fortuitous events, if they are to play a role in changing the developmental trajectory, must be assimilable by the individual, must be informative within some frame of reference. Bandura describes how chemistry Nobel Laureate Herbert Brown decided to undertake his doctoral dissertation in the relatively obscure area of boron hydrides.

> As a baccalaureate gift, his girlfriend presented him with a copy of the book, *The Hydrides of Boron and Silicon*, which launched his interest in the subject. This was during the Depression when money was scarce. She happened to select this particular chemistry book undesignedly, because it was the least expensive one available at the university bookstore. Had his girlfriend been a bit more affluent, Brown's research career would in all likelihood have taken a different route.[4]

Now, if my girlfriend at the time of my college graduation had presented me with a book on boron chemistry, it is highly unlikely that it would have affected my career trajectory.[5] The gift Brown received was an innovation whose relative determinacy for subsequent events in his life has to be understood within the frames in which the book became informative. The book was adopted into a *self frame* in which it had some perceived affinity. Brown was already interested in chemistry, and he and his girlfriend may have maintained a *consensual frame* in which chemistry was discussed. She bought the book at a university bookstore, one of the few places one could hope to find a specialized book on boron and silicon. In other words, the girlfriend appropriated part of a *cultural frame* (the book and the bookstore) that she suspected would be co-regulated into their ongoing consensual frame (with gratitude perhaps and continued conversation about the topic) and possibly into Brown's self frame.

An innovation like a book can be rigidified as a dust collector on a shelf, it can be dissolved from the frame at the next textbook buy-back at the university bookstore, or it can be elaborated upon creatively. Brown's creative elaboration led to hundreds of his own articles and the creation of innovative consensual frames of research teams with students and colleagues, and innovative cultural frames of new concepts and new techniques adopted by other chemists. The examples I used in Chapter 2 – of Laura, of infant crying, and of runners – are essentially no different from this. They all show how innovations are incorporated into relationship frames and also how in the adoption process these innovations teeter between determinism and indeterminism, certainty and uncertainty.

Action is always partially determinate and partially indeterminate. Because the stability of a frame is created and dynamic, its future can never be entirely predicted from its past. Some frames indeed appear more stable and lasting than others, and to the extent that the frames are maintained by the creation of meaningful information by the participants they will have the appearance of a determined system. There are, however, no frames in life that cannot be altered or eliminated.

Self, communication and culture are inseparable. Self frames are inherently dialogical, between different action possibilities perceived in the present or between various imagined possibilities and positions. The action possibilities and imagined positions are modeled after our experience in relationship consensual frames and in relationship frames with non-animate features of the environment. Those frames are virtually always centered within cultural frames of beliefs, practices and tools. Cultural frames are embodied with respect to the perception and action possibilities of individual selves and are thus more easily taken up within self frames. There is no beginning and ending point in this dialogical system of relationships.

Dialogue is all there is. The dialogical process – in which actions and events are informative in relation to the history and current actions of the participants – occurs at all times within the self, between self and other, between self and environment, and between other selves that partake of the same culture. Life is a synergetic, multilayered process. An event that changes one's life direction is not a beginning, it is an innovation adopted into an existing nexus of self frames that are shaped by consensual and cultural frames.

Dialogue creates patterns that individuals can perceive as invariants within the flow of action. What I perceive as invariants within the dialogical process may not be the same as those detected by another individual. The theoretical model I have outlined here takes its particular shape in part from my perceptions of this process, in part from the actions I can execute as a scholar and writer, and in part from the cultural tools (the scientific literature, the language, the print media, the static illustrations in two dimensions) by which a book can be informative. In a relationship, it is possible that each individual may have a different perception of what is creative and what is rigid, and each may derive a different meaning from the process.

Forms of information: morality, aesthetics and affiliation

Relationships develop via dual processes of innovation and dissolution, by making and breaking frames, and by engaging in both creative and rigid dialogues. In this book I have so far avoided placing value judgements on these processes. I have not spoken of relationships as good or bad, adaptive or maladaptive, self-affirming vs. self-destructive. These values are relative to how the dialogue is framed. I have attempted, instead, to provide a general model of relationship formation that can be applied to any kind of relationship process between any individuals, at any age, and in any species.

When one moves from the stance of observer of relationships to the stance of participant, that is, when one has a vested interest in a relationship – with their children or parents, with their friends or mates, with their companion animals – issues of value inevitably arise. Participants in relationships create information that is not a cognitive content, but an embodied experience that meaningfully informs movements of the body, thoughts, and feelings.

Jean Piaget also thought of life processes as a complex system of interconnecting relationships, although he imagined that this system converged over the life course toward some Platonic ideal fittedness to 'reality' in the form of intellectual processes that mirrored the properties of the real world.[6] He expresses his view of determinacy and indeterminacy in development in relation to this system as follows.

> The concept of *totality* expresses the interdependence inherent in every organization, intelligent as well as biological. Even though behavior patterns and consciousness seem to arise in the most uncoordinated manner in the first weeks of existence, they extend a physiological organization which antedates them and they crystallize from the outset into systems whose coherence becomes clarified little by little.[7]

Piaget proposed that cognition, developed at first within physiological frames, created its own frames for logical thinking. Pure logical thought was conceived as an 'ideal equilibrium.' This ideal could never be reached, but it could be perceived by a participant in the system.

Piaget described the individual's actual experience of perceiving the ideal equilibrium as the creation of a *value*. Value is

> the expression of desirability at all levels. Desirability is the indication of a rupture in equilibrium or of an uncompleted totality to whose formation some

element is lacking and which tends toward this element in order to realize its equilibrium ... A good example is that of the norms of coherence and unity of logical thought which translate this perceptual effort of intellectual totalities toward equilibrium, and which therefore define the ideal equilibrium never attained by intelligence and *regulate the particular values* of judgement.[8]

Here, Piaget is talking about the regulation of the self frame in which logical thought occurs with the cultural frame of the norms of logic. The fundamental difference between Piaget's concept of development and mine is that he believed individuals were regulated by the ideal, but never attainable, end state of perfect logical thinking. I suggest that individuals are co-regulated within self, consensual and cultural dialogues and that the developmental trajectories are creative and emergent from the dialogue and the constraints on degrees of freedom within the frame rather than by a Platonic ideal end state.

Nevertheless, Piaget and I are thinking about the same dynamic process of action within a system of relationships. The information that one perceives as a participant in such a system has a value and desirability with respect to the frames of endeavor. I propose that there are three principal forms of informational values: moral, aesthetic and affiliative.

Moral information. Morality is the perception that some actions are better than others; that participation in some frames is more worthy than in others; that there is a choice one can make between good and not-so-good alternatives. Morality also refers to the demands one can make and the expectations one has from co-participants: the sense of responsibility and sincerity in the relationship. Because action and perception are embedded in self, relationship and cultural frames, moral information is created by individuals in relation to those frames.

Aesthetic information. Not only is action perceived as good or bad, better or worse, it is also perceived as well-formed and not so well-formed. Piaget's references to the cultural norms of coherence and unity in logical thought express aesthetic values. The artistry of performance is defined in relation to the cultural, consensual and self frames of participation. In some situations, such as in a business discussion, a more aesthetic social performance is one that is brief and to the point. In others, such as at a conversation over dinner, one expects elaborate stories with humor and contextual detail.

Affiliative information. All relationships have a dimension of liking and loving, attachment and dependency, anxiety, ambivalence or hatred. Which form of affiliative information one creates depends on the frame. In some situations, as in the study of adolescent teasing reported in Chapter 2, a high degree of threat coupled with humor may lead to a strong attachment between the co-teasers. In other situations, as in the work place between boss and employee, or between male and female co-workers, such teasing may be perceived with contempt and hatred.

It is not my goal in this book to elaborate in great detail upon the forms of information created through participation. There are vast literatures on each of these topics and they deserve a separate and more complete treatment than can be afforded here. My purpose in discussing these topics at the end of this book and in so brief a form is to point out the incompleteness of the ideas presented so far, and the realms of inquiry into which I believe those ideas may have something unique to contribute upon further analysis.

What I have to offer about these information themes is perhaps not new, but rather a way of thinking about them from the perspective of a principled and consistent theory of relationships within the self, family and community. For me, the relationship processes described in this book are elemental components of a theory of development. The relationship processes are the conflagrations out of which information is forged. Morality, aesthetics and affiliation do not exist in the Platonic sense before or after the dialogue: they emerge from its heat.

People often speak as if there are universal principles of morality and aesthetics. These principles, however, are universal only from the perspective of enduring cultural frames for morality, such as those found in legal codes, and cultural frames for aesthetics, such as in ritualized encounters like dance, athletics and warfare, and in art. There are the moral principles of the Ten Commandments, of Confucian wisdom, and of a nation's constitution. The beauty of the agon is embodied in Medea, Joan of Arc, or Martina Navratilova's volley. These things are hardly permanent but none the less powerful and compelling images for some. These cultural frames for morality and aesthetics last over time because they are not only informative to an embodied perceiver with respect to their frames, but because they also allow for creativity and interpretation, for re-invention and elaboration.

Morality

Morality is part of any activity that involves making a choice between alternatives, and alternatives are most clear within a frame in which many of the degrees of freedom have been constrained. Since the nature of dialogue is the creation of new choices, inventing actions within a frame, it follows that all dialogue is a reflection of morality. It also follows that infants make moral choices, and that there is no social endeavor – including science – that is not morally defined.

In the conventional developmental view, morality is believed to begin in the preschool period, tied on the one hand to concepts of right and wrong and on the other to behavior indicative of social responsibility such as caring and altruism. The first moral emotions are thought to appear after language is acquired, when children remark upon things that are incomplete or broken, and when they act to restore things to completeness.

There is a morality, however, even in very young infants who fuss when the nipple is removed before feeding is completed or who become upset when some routine sequence of events is interrupted. What does the interruption mean to the infant? A common psychological account is to explain this as frustration due to a failure of expectations. This, to me, seems unnecessarily cognitive. It implies that the infant 'has' a generalized expectation based on a representational memory. Even so, why should the infant become upset at the failure of expectations? Many presume that there must be some biological programming of negative emotion that leads to this more or less automatic reaction. And so discrete information is thought to flow from one representational unit to another to produce a response.

Actually, there is nothing particularly compelling about interrupting a sequence of events for a baby. There are some interruptions that mean nothing at all to a baby, such as a change in the family television viewing habits. There are some that result in extreme distress, such as removing the nipple unexpectedly. And there are some interruptions that cause aversion but not distress, which is common in the 'still-face' research manipulation described in an earlier chapter, or when the mother's interactive pace is too fast for the infant.

The interruption becomes a problem of moral choice for the baby only if it occurs in a frame in which the infant is used to having some choice and the interruption removes that freedom of choice. Infants don't choose television shows, and they typically, at least under about 5 months, don't choose to initiate play with an adult.[9] But young infants have a lot of choice with respect to sucking and eating: they are active participants in feeding interactions and the nipple is framed by a dynamic of co-regulation with the feeder. The baby who gets upset when the nipple is removed is not saying 'I didn't expect that to happen,' nor 'This is interesting, I wonder what else is going to happen.' The baby is saying 'I have the right to some control over that nipple and that right is being tampered with irresponsibly.' The baby is morally indignant because she has come to expect, not a sequence of actions, but a moral responsibility that the nipple will be provided in return for her responsible (i.e. co-regulated) temporary use of it.[10]

One could explain the infant's distress on the basis of a biological need/drive, rather than the arousal of moral information. Infants, however, seem to have such reactions to almost anything – not merely feeding – that is meaningful to them at the moment, and for which they have played their part responsibly in an ongoing co-regulated relationship. I don't mean here that infants have the same tug of responsibility toward many features of life that adults have, nor that the infant understands these acts conceptually as moral. Rather, they are moral because of a breach, from the infant's point of view, of the sincerity the infant has perceived during prior encounters. If the infant is not genuinely hungry and the mother doesn't tolerate idle play with the nipple, this is not cause for the creation of moral indignation because the baby comes to recognize that the nipple is provided only when she sincerely requires it. Through these variations on the theme of co-regulation with respect to the feeding frame and the self frame within it, the infant comes to refine the meaning of sincerity as a responsible partner in this relationship.[11]

Morality, therefore, arises within a relationship as one form of information. There are also more felicitous forms of moral information, as in the pleasure of being a responsible partner and the enjoyment of something completed within the limits of the frame. This is the sense of doing things right, the way they ought to be done, and what's right is always defined by the scope of the frame. It is possible that each frame may create different information about the rightness of a particular action.

In certain communities, premarital sex in adolescence may feel absolutely right in the consensual frame with the partner, categorically forbidden in the cultural frame, and completely wobbly within the endless dialogues of the teenager's self frame. I've discovered informally that many parents in America bring their small infants into their beds with them at night, especially if mothers are nursing. This feels just right in the mother's and infant's self and consensual frames, but is nearly taboo in the Western cultural frame. In Japanese and Mayan societies, on the contrary, it is considered immoral to let a child sleep alone.[12]

Perhaps the realms of discourse in which baby morality is created seem less important, from an adult perspective, compared to adult moral choices about life-and-death decisions, fidelity and infidelity, crime and punishment, war and peace. Certainly, removing a nipple from a baby's mouth is much less destructive than pulling a trigger or denying a civil right. Yet, all these acts have moral consequences for the victims because what has been and should be co-regulated is now unilaterally regulated, imposed rather than negotiated. The morality of freedom and its loss is part of all relationships.

Aesthetics

Aesthetics has to do with the form of the action, rather than the freedom to do it or its consequences. With a few exceptions, the aesthetics of action is not taken seriously in developmental psychology. Aesthetics is not the same as creativity. There is creativity in all aspects of relationships, including in morality and affiliation. One can create ugliness as well as beauty; it makes no difference from the perspective of creativity. Even when psychologists study children's artistic productions, such as their drawing and musical ability, it tends to be from a purely sensory, motor or cognitive perspective.

Aesthetics, however, is an integral and enduring aspect of relationships in self, consensual and cultural frames. Aesthetic information is created when one performs an action or makes something that is somehow more elegant than similar actions intended for the same purpose. Aesthetic information is created in relationships when negotiations are abbreviated into frames, that is, when something more simple is made to stand for something more complex.

A line of poetry is beautiful because of the economy of its expression as well as because of the flow of it across the tongue. Beauty in art is a combination of movement and economy, flow and the ability to represent something much bigger than the work itself. A tennis stroke is beautiful when there are no wasted movements and the force of the whole body and the arm is communicated to the ball through the racquet.

The philosopher Kenneth Burke makes the case for what he calls a poetic psychology.

> Since social life, like art, is a *problem of appeal*, the poetic metaphor would give us invaluable hints for describing modes of practical action which are too often measured by simple tests of utility and too seldom with reference to the communicative, sympathetic, *propitiatory* factors that are clearly present in the procedures of formal art and must be as truly present in those informal arts of living we do not happen to call art.[13]

The quote from Mary Catherine Bateson presented earlier in this chapter suggests that developmental change is guided by a similar aesthetic. She also states that 'composing a life has a metaphorical relation to many different arts.'[14]

In early infancy, after a period of negotiation, infants begin to abbreviate their actions. For example, after months of negotiating mutual gaze, infants will use a brief glance at the mother to indicate a readiness to participate in that consensual frame. Why does the child come to use the more elegant form instead of continuing to spend long periods negotiating who looks at whom and when? The infant probably wants to pursue other goals with the adult, and an aesthetic is required to simplify the communication system to make room for the innovations.

Take the example of infant Hannah, discussed in Chapter 6. Hannah and her mother endured weeks of laborious interchanges in which they both meant something different by their offers of objects. When Hannah finally 'got' the point of the game, she handed the telephone to the mother with obvious delight. Now the offer meant a request to play the telephone game. A cognitive explanation views Hannah as having an insight, as having been guided into the frame of the game and finally making it part of her own actions through advanced understanding.

My interpretation is that the offering was perceived, at that moment, as aesthetically pleasing. There was, for both baby and mother, a certain beauty to be experienced in the frame: everything fitted together economically; there were no wasted attempts at communication and repair. They were dancing rather than stepping on each other's toes.[15]

The evidence that infants can perceive the difference between the beautiful and the disagreeable is sparse, perhaps because few have looked for it. Some recent findings by Judith Langlois, however, suggest that infants in the first half-year prefer to look at faces that adults have judged to be attractive compared to unattractive faces.[16]

Research on the expressive behavior of preschool children by Alan Sroufe and his colleagues suggests that there is an aesthetics of communication processes that accompanies the aesthetics of physical attractiveness. Linda was not as popular as she might have been because she displayed both appealingly positive as well as ugly negative expressions.

> Linda was a beautifully expressive child. Her exuberance and flashing smile were unparalleled by any other child in her class. When she enthusiastically greeted a visitor with a 'Hi! I haven't seen you in a LONG time!' (accompanied by her ear-to-ear smile), it is no wonder that the visitor was charmed . . .
>
> Tracy, John, and Linda had been playing happily on a couch. When the three of them leave, Jerry climbs onto the couch. Linda returns to the couch and shouts at him 'You get off my couch!' She climbs on the couch and pushes him, trying to grab the pictures he is holding.[17]

John in the same class was judged as not being physically attractive based on ratings of photographs, and he scored low on tests of cognitive function.

> Yet he was rated high on social competence by teachers and was well liked by the children, having several close and warm friendships. His uniformly positive initiations and response to other children – his 'sweet nature' as one teacher put it – quite obviously played an important role in his social success.[18]

Children of lower popularity in the classroom were less expressively attractive, either affectless or showing inappropriately intense expressions. The impression that individuals are beautiful, lovely or sweet is a reflection of aesthetic information created when communicating with or watching these individuals. We know too little about the extent to which infants and young children perceive this dimension of information and we have few techniques with which to study the aesthetics of action in everyday situations.[19]

It is not the case, especially for infants, that they know what is aesthetic in advance. Rather, they create it as perception and action within a frame. A child may recognize that mumbling a word is sloppy work if the communication and self frames provide constraints for saying it more beautifully.

Affiliation

Studies of affiliation are plentiful in parent–infant and in peer relationship research, focusing on issues such as attachment, friendships and their variations. No one would deny, therefore, the importance of affiliative information in the development of relationships. Indeed, one of the most successful measures ever designed to classify individuals is Mary Ainsworth's measure of infant attachment using the Strange Situation Test.[20] The research that has been done on infant attachment is very consistent with the relationship models proposed in this book, showing that attachment may remain stable under some conditions and change under others, leading to distinctly different developmental trajectories within relationships.[21]

I say this in spite of my earlier complaints about the concept of the internal working model, a discrete representational approach that derives from Bowlby's attachment theory. I believe that data on attachment are better explained from the perspective of information within relationship frames: forms of attachment represent different qualities of affiliative information such as secure, anxious and resistant. This information is not, however, contained as a representation – a working model – within the individual infant. Rather, it is created in the dialogue of the mother–infant consensual frame, and is re-created in the dialogue of the self frame.

Research suggests that actions toward self and toward others during the preschool years are related to the security of attachment with parents measured during infancy. Securely attached children, for example, more readily and correctly identify features of themselves and their mothers, and they are facile at creating pretend narratives in which dolls play the roles of mother and child. Insecurely attached infants tend to make more incorrect and negative attributions of self and mother.[22]

I discussed earlier how increasing intimacy, a developmental change in a relationship toward new affiliative information, is created by the co-regulated constructions of new frames for affiliation and their continued mutual elaboration. Assuming that the creation of affiliative information is pleasing and arousing, one does not need an internal working model to explain its developmental transitions. The frame constrains actions into increasingly closer spheres of intimacy, or out to increasing distance and disengagement.

Relationship development is not regulated toward some Platonic ideal of perfect intimacy, no more than intellectual development is regulated toward the Platonic ideal of perfect logic. Development is created out of co-regulation in dialogue and converges toward information that is moral, aesthetic and affiliative within those frames.

In summary, the relational model of development proposed here forces one to consider information in its holistic sense, not in its purely cognitive sense. How the information is created depends upon where one is situated in the network of connected frames that comprise the on-goingness of life as a process. Life is the dialogue, stirred by creativity and warmed by the passions of participation.

Research approaches to relationship development

To study relationship systems one has to maintain a focus on the individual actors and follow them through developmental time, research that keeps life courses and relationship courses as fundamental units and that eschews group means. General or nomothetic principles are not going to be found in any collection of group statistics. According to Thorngate,

It is tempting to equate the nomothetic approach with the analysis of averages. To do so is to equate statistical models of experiments with models of people ... To find out what people do in general, we must first discover what each person does in particular, then determine what, if anything, these particulars have in common. This implies that we pay more attention to case histories, find or develop models sufficient to account for each, then examine the models for common themes or elements.[23]

Esther Thelen proposes the following.

When considerable individual differences are expected in the outcome, it is even more crucial to use *individual developmental trajectories* as the primary data source. Once individual developmental paths are identified, it may then be possible to cluster subjects, not on the basis of outcome, but on the basis of route. This means that detailed longitudinal studies are necessary to capture the times of stability and change.[24]

I have made similar points.

Typical developmental methodologies that seek independent measures of mother and infant assume that a rather sharp line can be defined between the individual and the social environment ... When investigators reify the boundary between organism and environment, they mask the dynamic processes of self-organization that constitute developmental change. *When organism and environment are conceptualized as distinct for the purpose of measurement, one cannot reconstruct from those measures alone the dynamics of the developmental process* ... Given repeated observations on the same subjects, and contextually appropriate measures, analytic approaches can be applied that preserve the integrity of the individual's life history in order to construct generalities of developmental change. *It is only when a sufficiently large sample of individual case histories are collected that longitudinal process research can be generalized to the population* ... *To study development as a dynamic phenomenon, we must observe the system in the process of changing,* and not simply before and after the change takes place.[25]

Susan Oyama proposed that rather than measuring and ranking, correlating and predicting, developmental research should

show us about the timing of events, the susceptibility of processes to various kinds of perturbation and the manner in which the regulation is achieved, if it is achieved ... what is needed to enable a particular developmental sequence to proceed, what will induce, facilitate or maintain such a sequence, how does sensitivity to these factors change with developmental state, what degree of specificity is evident in these interactions, what is the relationship among events at various levels of analysis?[26]

Research, in other words, should be open to the contingent and creative processes by which relationships form and change, that is, to the possibility for both determinacy and indeterminacy. It should be designed to see the whole elephant, not just its tail. Experimental studies have a role in process research, but only when perturbations of ongoing process can reveal something about branching developmental pathways. Thus, one would want to preserve as much as possible about a relationship frame while perturbing selected elements to observe the effects on the self-organization of the whole system.[27] Studies that compare the formation of relationships under different naturally varying conditions are also useful, especially if each relationship system is observed relatively frequently and the samples are matched on all dimensions except for the particular disturbance or difference that is being compared.[28]

The problem of research on relationships for the investigator is to enter into frames of co-participation as an outsider and to preserve as much as possible about the evolution of the process without distorting it beyond recognition. This research is time-consuming because one has to wait for development to occur with a watchful eye and most human relationships can't tolerate that degree of scrutiny without disturbance. Nevertheless, I have found that it can be done with an appropriate measure of sensitivity to the participants, respect for their courage to allow scientists to examine their secrets, and recognition of their pride that comes from collaborative participation in scientific frames of discourse.

I have felt humility and gratitude in the company of the infant and mother life histories we have collected for ongoing study. From them I have created time-lapse films, assembling a picture of relationship development by taking ten-second clips of a mother and baby playing with the same toy each week over a six-month period. This is probably not very scientific, at least not yet – not until I can afford the technology and expertise to couple these video images with computer imaging and simulation in as sophisticated a way as the local meteorologist on the evening news. But like the time-lapse films of cloud formation and flowers blossoming that I saw as a child, I watch in awe at the beauty of social systems being created, blooming and changing. I think we know less about what is between us in our everyday relationships than we know about the austere space between stars in a galactic frame.

Notes

1. Bandura (1986, p. 33).
2. Bateson (1989, pp. 3–4).
3. Bandura (1986); Sameroff (1989); Sroufe (1989); Thelen (1990).
4. Bandura (1986, p. 33).
5. I was, as I mentioned earlier, majoring in physics and mathematics, but I had an active dislike for chemistry that my girlfriend would surely have known about. We have been together since that time, possibly in part because she did not buy me a chemistry book, which would have shown a lack of sensitivity to my interests.

I chose the example of Herbert Brown because I was working at Brown's university, Purdue, at the time he was nominated for the Nobel prize. He became an instant celebrity at the university, in the community, in the state of Indiana, and indeed in the nation and world. In addition to reading weekly and sometimes almost daily articles in the local newspaper about the legendary graduation present and other stories about him, I remember being struck by how much the Nobel prize itself changed his life. For most of the next year and beyond he spent much of his time with interviews and phone calls, appearing on talk shows, giving presentations at community functions, travelling everywhere, and just generally coping with being famous outside the academic frames in which his earlier notoriety had been managed. The sudden opening of new frames can be just as important in the life course as any particular innovative event or action.

6. Haroutunian (1983).
7. Piaget (1962, p. 10)
8. Piaget (1963, p. 11), italics are mine.
9. Kaye & Fogel (1980); Cohn & Tronick (1988).
10. Cavell (1979); Hearne (1987); Winnicott (1971).
11. Sincerity is one of the maxims that Grice (1975) proposes as a necessary component of discourse: that speakers should treat each other's utterances as truthful and genuine until proven otherwise. Sincerity may be violated in consensual ways, as in humor and play.
12. Morelli et al. (1992).
13. Burke (1954, p. 264).
14. Bateson (1989, p. 4).
15. Others (Stern, 1985; Thoman & Browder, 1987) have used the metaphor of dancing in a different way, to mean something more like swaying together to the same body rhythms rather than to refer to the aesthetics of the movements. Dancing to the same rhythms can be beautiful or pitiful, depending on how it's created and perceived.
16. Langlois et al. (1987; 1990).
17. Sroufe et al. (1984, pp. 306–7).
18. Sroufe et al. (1984, pp. 306–7).
19. Burke (1954).
20. Ainsworth et al. (1978).
21. Sroufe & Jacobvitz (1989).
22. Pipp, Easterbrooks & Harmon (1992); Suess, Grossmann & Sroufe (1992).
23. Thorngate (1987, p. 75).
24. Thelen (1990, p. 39).
25. Fogel (1990a, pp. 343–4, 354).
26. Oyama (1985, pp. 160–1).
27. See, for example, research in which the mother–infant interaction is preserved while specific aspects of maternal action are changed (Cohn & Tronick, 1983; Fogel et al., 1982; Fogel, Dedo & McEwen, 1992; Tronick et al., 1978).
28. In infant development, for example, research comparing relationship differences in depressed vs. non-depressed mothers (Bettes, 1988; Field et al., 1986; Fleming et. al., 1988; Gelfand & Teti, in press; Jameson et al., 1991); comparing relationships in other forms of maternal psychopathology

to normal mothers (Schneider-Rosen & Cicchetti, 1991; Main & Solomon, 1986; Sameroff & Emde, 1989; Sroufe, 1989; Stern, 1985); comparing mother–infant relationships between pre-term and full-term infants (Barnard *et al.*, 1984; Branchfield, Goldberg & Sloman, 1980; Crawford, 1982; Easterbrooks, 1989; Oehler, Eckerman & Wilson, 1988; van Beek & Geerdink, 1989); comparing mother–infant relationships between handicapped and non-handicapped infants, as in Downs' vs. normal infants (Cicchetti & Sroufe, 1978; Jones, 1980; Stevenson, Leavitt & Silverberg, 1985); and comparing mother–infant relationships in infants with varying degrees of psychosocial risk (Rutter, 1987; Wachs & Gruen, 1982; Werner, 1979).

Bibliography

Abraham, R. H., and Shaw, C. D. (1982), *Dynamics: The geometry of behavior*. Aerial Press: Santa Cruz, CA.

Acredola, L. P., Adams, A., and Goodwyn, S. W. (1984), 'The role of self-produced movement and visual tracking in infant spatial orientation'. *Journal of Experimental Child Psychology*, **38**, 312–27.

Agiobu-Kemmer, I. (1986), 'Cognitive and affective aspects of infant development'. In H. V. Curran (Ed.), *Nigerian children: Development perspectives* (pp. 74–177). Routledge and Kegan Paul: London.

Ainsworth, M., Blehar, M. C., Waters, E., and Wall, S. (1978), *Patterns of attachment*. Erlbaum: Hillsdale, NJ.

Alberts, J. R., and Decsy, G. J. (1990), 'Terms of endearment'. *Developmental Psychobiology*, **23**, 569–84.

Aloimonos, Y., and Rosenfeld, A. (1991), 'Computer vision'. *Science*, **253**, 1249–54.

Altman, I., and Rogoff, B. (1987), 'World views in psychology: Trait, interactional, organismic, and transactional perspectives'. In D. Stokols and I. Altman (Eds), *Handbook of environmental psychology*, Vol. 1, pp. 7–40. Wiley: New York.

Altman, I., and Taylor, D. A. (1973), *The social penetration: The development of interpersonal relationships*. Holt, Rinehard and Winston: New York.

Andersen, G. J. (1990), 'Segregation of optic flow into object and self-motion components: Foundations for a general model'. In R. Warren and A. H. Wertheim (Eds), *Perception and control of self-motion* (pp. 127–41). Erlbaum: Hillsdale, NJ.

Anderson, B., Vietze, P., and Dokecki, P. (1977), 'Reciprocity in vocal interactions of mothers and infants'. *Child Development*, **48**, 1676–81.

Anisfeld, M. (1991), 'Neonatal imitation' (review). *Developmental Review*, **11**, 60–97.

Aries, P. (1962), *Centuries of childhood: A social history of family life* (trans. R. Baldick). Vintage Books: New York.

Ashby, W. R. (1952), *Design for a brain*. Chapman and Hall: London.

Austin, J. L. (1962), *How to do things with words*. Clarendon Press: Oxford.

Azuma, H. (1986), 'Why study child development in Japan?' In H. Stevenson, H. Azuma, and K. Hakuta (Eds), *Child development and education in Japan* (pp. 3–12). Freeman: New York.

Bakeman, R., and Adamson, L. B. (1986), 'Infant's conventionalized acts:

Gestures and words with mothers and peers'. *Infant Behavior and Development*, **9**, 215–30.

Bakeman, R., and Gottman, J. (1986), *Observing interaction: An introduction to sequential analysis*. Cambridge University Press: Cambridge.

Baker-Sennett, J., Matusov, E., and Rogoff, B. (1992), 'Planning as developmental process'. In H. Reese (Ed), *Advances in child development and behavior* (Vol. 24). Academic Press: New York.

Bakhtin, M. M. (1988), 'Discourse in the novel'. In N. Mercer (Ed), *Language and literacy from an educational perspective* (Vol. 1) (pp. 47–58). Open University Press: Philadelphia.

Baldwin, D. A. (1991), 'Infants' contribution to the achievement of joint reference'. *Child Development*, **62**, 875–90.

Bandura, A. (1986), *Social foundations of thought and action: A social cognitive theory*. Prentice-Hall: Englewood Cliffs: NJ.

Barnard, K. E., Bee, H. L., and Hammond, M. A. (1984), 'Developmental changes in maternal interactions with term and pre-term infants'. *Infant Behavior and Development*, **7**, 101–13.

Bates, E., Benigini, L., Bretherton, I., Camaioni, L., and Volterra, V. (1979), *The emergence of symbols: cognition and communication in infancy*. Academic Press: New York.

Bateson, G. (1955), 'The message: "This is play"'. In B. Schaffner (Ed), *Group processes* (Vol. 2). Madison Printing Co.: Madison, NJ.

Bateson, M. C. (1989), *Composing a life*. The Atlantic Monthly Press: New York.

Bavelas, B. J., Black, A., Lemery, C. R., and Mullett, J. (1986), '"I *show* how you feel": Motor mimicry as a communicative act'. *Journal of Personality and Social Psychology*, **50**, 322–9.

Beebe, B., and Jaffe, J. (1992, May), 'The dyadic regulation of mother–infant coordination'. Invited symposium, ICIS, Miami, FL.

Beebe, B., Jaffee, J., Feldstein, S., Mays, K., and Alson, D. (1985), 'Interpersonal timing: The application of an adult dialogue model to mother–infant vocal and kinesic interactions'. In T. Field and N. Fox (Eds), *Social perception in infants* (pp. 217–47). Ablex: Norwood, NJ.

Beebe, B., Stern, D. N., and Jaffee, J. (1979), 'The kinesic rhythm of mother–infant interactions'. In A. W. Siegman and S. Feldstein (Eds), *Of speech and time: Temporal patterns in interpersonal contexts* (pp. 23–43). Erlbaum: Hillsdale, NJ.

Beek, P. J., and Bootsma, R. J. (1991), 'Physical and informational principles in modelling coordinated movements'. *Human Movement Science*, **10**, 81–92.

Beek, P. J., and Hopkins, B. (1992), 'Four requirements for a dynamical systems approach to the development of social coordination'. *Human Movement Science*, **11**, 425–42.

Befu, H. (1985), 'Psychology in a non-Western country'. *International Journal of Psychology*, **19**, 45–55.

Befu, H. (1985), 'Social and cultural background for child development in Japan and the United States'. In H. W. Stevenson, H. Azuma, and K. Hakuta (Eds), *Child development in Japan*. Freeman: San Francisco.

Bellugi, U. (1988), 'The acquisition of a spatial language'. In F. Kessell (Ed), *The development of language and language researchers: Essays in honor of Roger Brown* (pp. 153–85). Erlbaum: Hillsdale, NJ.

Bennett, A. (1981), 'Interruptions and the interpretation of conversation'. *Discourse Processes*, **4**, 171–88.

Benson, A. J. (1990), 'Sensory functions and limitations of the vestibular system'. In R. Warren and A. H. Wertheim (Eds), *Perception and control of self-motion* (pp. 145–70). Erlbaum: Hillsdale, NJ.

Bergin, T. G., and Fisch, M. H. (1968), *The new science of Giambattista Vico*. Cornell University Press: Ithaca, NY.

Bernieri, F. J., Reznick, J. S., and Rosenthal, R. (1988), 'Synchrony, pseudo-synchrony, and dissynchrony: Measuring the entrainment process in mother–infant interactions'. *Journal of Personality and Social Psychology*, **54**, 243–53.

Bertalanffy, L. von. (1968), *General systems theory*. Braziller: New York.

Bettes, B. A. (1988), 'Maternal depression and motherese: Temporal and intonational features'. *Child Development*, **59**, 1089–96.

Bettleheim, B. (1976), *The uses of enchantment: The meaning of fairy tales*. Knopf: New York.

Birdwhistell, R. L. (1970), *Kinesics and context*. University of Pennsylvania Press: Philadelphia.

Blake, J., and de Boysson-Bardies, B. (1989), 'Patterns in babbling: A cross-linguistic study'. Paper presented at ISSBD, Jyvaskyla, Finland.

Bloom, L., and Beckwith, R. (1989), 'Talking with feeling: Integrating affective and linguistic expression in early language development'. *Cognition and Emotion*, **3**(4), 313–42.

Blount, B. (1972), 'Parental speech and language acquisition: Some Luo and Samoan examples'. *Anthropological Linguistic*, **14**, 119–30.

Boesch, C. (1991), 'Teaching among wild chimpanzees'. *Animal Behavior*, **41**, 530–2.

Bornstein, M. H. (1980), 'Cross-cultural developmental psychology'. In M. H. Bornstein (Ed), *Comparative methods in psychology*. Erlbaum: Hillsdale, NJ.

Bornstein, M. H. (1985), 'Habituation of attention as a measure of visual information processing in human infants: Summary, systematization, and synthesis'. In G. Gottlieb and N. A. Krasnegor (Eds), *Measurement of audition and vision in the first year of postnatal life: A methodological overview*. Ablex: Norwood, NJ.

Bornstein, M. H., Tal, J., Rahn, C., Galperin, C. Z., Lamour, M., Ogino, M., Pecheux, M., Toda, S., Azuma, H., & Tamis-LeMonda, C. S (1992), 'Functional analysis of the contents of maternal speech to infants of 5 and 13 months in four cultures: Argentina, France, Japan, and the United States'. *Developmental Psychology*, **28**, 593–603.

Bornstein, M. H., Tamis-LeMonda, C. S., Pecheux, M. G., and Rahn, C. W. (1991), 'Mother and infant activity and interaction in France and in the United States: A comparative study'. *International Journal of Behavioral Development*, **14**, 21–43.

Bornstein, M. H., Toda, S., Asuma, H., Tamis-LeMonda, C., and Ogino, M. (1990), 'Mother and infant activity and interaction in Japan and the United States: II. A comparative microanalysis of naturalistic exchanges focused on the organisation of infant attention'. *International Journal of Behavioral Development*, **13**, 289–308.

Bosma, J. F. (1975), 'Anatomic and physiologic development of the speech apparatus'. In D. B. Tower (Ed), *The nervous system Vol. 3: Human communication and its disorders* (pp. 469–81). Raven Press: New York.

Bowlby, J. (1969), *Attachment and loss Vol. 1: Attachment*. Basic Books: New York.

Branchfeld, S., Goldberg, S., and Sloman, J. (1980), 'Parent–infant interaction in free play at 8 and 12 months: Effects of prematurity and immaturity'. *Infant Behavior and Development*, 3, 289–306.

Bransford, J. D., McCarrell, N. S., Franks, J. J., and Nitsch, K. E. (1977), 'Toward unexplaining memory'. In R. Shaw and J. Bransford (Eds), *Perceiving, acting, and knowing: Toward an ecological psychology* (pp. 431–66). Erlbaum: Hillsdale, NJ.

Braunwald, S. R. (1978), 'Context, word and meaning: Toward a communicational analysis of lexical acquisition'. In E. A. Lock (Ed), *Action, gesture, symbol: The emergence of language* (pp. 485–527). Academic Press: New York.

Brazelton, T. B. (1982), 'Joint regulation of neonate–parent behavior'. In E. Tronick (Ed), *Social interchange in infancy: Affect, cognition, and communication*. University Park Press: Baltimore, MD.

Brentano, F. (1973), *Psychology from an empirical standpoint* (trans. L. L. McAlister). Routledge and Kegan Paul: London. (Original work published 1874.)

Bretherton, I., Fritz, J., Zahn-Waxler, C., and Ridgeway, D. (1986), 'Learning to talk about emotions: A functionalist perspective'. *Child Development*, 57, 529–48.

Bril, B., and Sabatier, C. (1986), 'The cultural context of motor development: Postural manipulations in the daily life of Bambara babies (Mali)'. *International Journal of Behavioral Development*, 9, 439–53.

Bronfenbrenner, U. (1979), *The ecology of human development: Experiments by nature and design*. Harvard University Press: Cambridge, MA.

Brooks, R. A. (1991), 'New approaches to robotics'. *Science*, 253, 1227–32.

Brown, R. (1973), *A first language: The early stages*. Harvard University Press: Cambridge, MA.

Brownell, C. A., and Carriger, M. S. (1990), 'Changes in cooperation and self–other differentiation during the second year'. *Child Development*, 61, 1164–74.

Bruner, J. (1967), 'On cognitive growth'. In J. Bruner, R. Olver, and P. Greenfield (Eds), *Studies in cognitive growth* (pp. 1–29). Wiley: New York.

Bruner, J. (1975), 'From communication to language'. *Cognition*, 3, 255–87.

Bruner, J. (1983), *Child's talk: Learning to use language*. Norton: New York.

Bruner, J. (1990), *Acts of meaning*. Harvard University Press: Cambridge, MA.

Bruner, J., Roy, C., and Ratner, N. (1982), 'The beginnings of request'. In K. E. Nelson, (Ed), *Children's language, Vol. 3* (pp. 91–138). Erlbaum: Hillsdale, NJ.

Bull, P. E. (1987), *Posture and gesture*. Pergamon Press: New York.

Bullock, D., and Grossberg, S. (1991), 'Adaptive neural networks for control of movement trajectories invariant under speed and force rescaling'. *Human Movement Science*, 10, 3–53.

Burke, K. (1954), *Permanence and change: An anatomy of purpose*. Hermes Publications: Los Altos, CA.

Burnham, D. K., and Dickinson, R. G. (1981), 'The determinants of visual capture and visual pursuit in infancy'. *Infant Behavior and Development*, 4, 359–72.

Bushnell, E. W. (1981), 'The ontogeny of intermodal relations: Vision and touch in infancy'. In R. D. Walk and H. L. Pick, Jr. (Eds), *Intersensory perception and sensory integration* (pp. 5–69). Plenum Press: New York.

Bushnell, E. W., and Boudreau, P. R. (in press), 'The development of haptic perception during infancy'. In M. A. Heller and W. Schiff (Eds), *The psychology of touch*. Erlbaum: Hillsdale, NJ.

Butler, J., and Rovee-Collier, C. (1989), 'Contextual gating of memory retrieval'. *Developmental Psychology*, **22**, 533–52.

Butterworth, G. (1981), 'The origins of auditory–visual perception and visual proprioception in human development'. In R. D. Walk and H. L. Pick (Eds), *Intersensory perception and sensory integration* (pp. 37–69). Plenum Press: New York.

Butterworth, G. (in press), 'Origins of self-perception in infancy'. *Psychological Inquiry*.

Camaioni, L. (1989), 'The role of social interaction in the transition from communication to language'. In A. de Ribaupierre (Ed), *Transition mechanisms in child development: The longitudinal perspective* (pp. 109–25). Cambridge University Press: New York, NY.

Camaioni, L., De Castro Campos, M. F. P., and DeLemos, C. (1984), 'On the failure of the interactionist paradigm in language acquisition: A re-evaluation'. In W. Doise, and A. Palmonari (Eds), *Social interaction in individual development* (pp. 93–106). Cambridge University Press: New York.

Campos, J. J., and Bertenthal B. I. (1988), 'Locomotion and psychological development'. In F. Morrison, K. Lord and D. Keating (Eds), *Applied developmental psychology*. Academic Press: New York.

Canfield, R. L., and Haith, M. M. (1991), 'Young infants' visual expectations for symmetric and asymmetric stimulus sequences'. *Developmental Psychology*, **27**, 198–208.

Cappella, J. N. (1981), 'Mutual influence in expressive behavior: Adult–adult and infant–adult dyadic interaction'. *Psychological Bulletin*, **89**, 101–32.

Caughey, J. L. (1984), *Imaginary social worlds: A cultural approach*. University of Nebraska Press: Lincoln, NE.

Cavell, S. (1979), *The claim of reason: Wittgenstein, skepticism, morality and tragedy*. Oxford University Press: New York.

Cernoch, J. M., and Porter, R. H. (1985), 'Recognition of maternal axillary odors by infants'. *Child Development*, **56**, 1593–8.

Chappell, P. F., and Sander, L. W. (1979), 'Mutual regulation of the neonatal–maternal interactive process: Context for the origins of communication'. In M. Bullowa (Ed), *Before speech*. Cambridge University Press: London.

Charny, E. J. (1966), 'Psychosomatic manifestations of rapport in psychotherapy'. *Psychosomatic Medicine*, **28**, 305–15.

Ching, C. (1984), 'Psychology and the four modernizations in China'. *International Journal of Psychology*, **19**, 57–64.

Cicchetti, D., and Sroufe, A. (1978), 'An organizational view of affect: Illustration from the study of Down's syndrome infants'. In M. Lewis and L. A. Rosenblum (Eds), *The development of affect*. Plenum Press: New York.

Clancy, P. (1986), 'The acquisition of communication style in Japanese'. In B. Schieffelin and B. Ochs (Eds), *Language socialization across cultures*. Cambridge University Press: Cambridge, MA.

Clark, H. H., and Brennan, S. E. (1991), 'Grounding in communication'. In L. B. Resnick, J. M. Levine, and S. D. Teasley (Eds), *Perspectives on socially shared cognition* (pp. 127–70). American Psychological Association: Washington, DC.

Clark, R. A. (1978), 'The transition from action to gesture'. In A. Lock (Ed), *Action, gesture and symbol: The emergence of language* (pp. 249–67). Academic Press: New York.

Clarkson, M. G., Clifton, R. K., Swain, I. U., and Perris, E. E. (1989), 'Stimulus duration and repetition rate influence newborns' head orientation toward sound'. *Developmental Psychobiology*, 22, 683–705.

Clifton, R., Perris, E., & Bullinger, A. (1991), 'Infants' perception of auditory space'. *Developmental Psychology*, 27, 187–97.

Cohn, J. F., and Elmore, M. (1988), 'Effect of contingent changes in mothers' affective expression on the organization of behavior in 3-month-old infants' *Infant Behavior and Development*, 11, 493–505.

Cohn, J. F. and Tronick, E. Z. (1983), 'Three-month old infants' reaction to simulated maternal depression'. *Child Development*, 54, 185–93.

Cohn, J., and Tronick, E. Z. (1988), 'Mother–infant face-to-face interaction: influence is bidirectional and unrelated to periodic cycles in either partner's behavior'. *Developmental Psychology*, 24, 386–92.

Collis, G. M. (1979), 'Describing the structure of social interaction in infancy'. In M. Bullowa (Ed), *Before speech: The beginning of interpersonal communication* (pp. 111–30). Cambridge University Press: New York.

Colombo, J., Mitchell, D. W., O'Brien, M., and Horowitz, F. D. (1987), 'The stability of visual habituation during the first year of life'. *Child Development*, 68, 474–87.

Condon, W. S. (1982), 'Cultural microrhythms'. In *Interaction rhythms: Periodicity in communicative behavior* (pp. 53–76). Human Sciences Press: New York.

Condon, W. S., and Sander, L. W. (1974), 'Neonate movement is synchronized with adult speech'. *Science*, 183, 99.

Cooper, R. P., and Aslin, N. R. (1990), 'Preference for infant-directed speech in the first month after birth'. *Child Development*, 61, 1584–95.

Crawford, J. W. (1982), 'Mother–infant interaction in premature and full-term infants'. *Child Development*, 53, 957–62.

Crockenberg, S., and Litman, C. (1990), 'Autonomy as competence in 2-year-olds: Maternal correlates of child defiance, compliance, and self-assertion'. *Developmental Psychology*, 26, 961–71.

Crook, C. K. (1978), 'Taste perception in the newborn infant'. *Infant Behavior and Development*, 1, 52–69.

Cushman, P. (1991), 'Ideology obscured: Political uses of the self in Daniel Stern's infant'. *American Psychologist*, 46, 206–19.

Damon, W. (1989), *The moral child*. The Free Press: New York.

Danzinger, K. (1976), 'Nonverbal communication'. In K. Danzinger (Ed), *Interpersonal communication* (pp. 57–82). Pergamon Press: New York.

De Boysson-Bardies, B., Sagart, L., and Durand, C. (1984), 'Discernible differences in the babbling of infants according to target language'. *Journal of Child Language*, 11, 1–15.

DeCasper, A. J., and Fifer, W. P. (1980), 'Of human bonding: Newborns prefer their mothers' voices'. *Science*, 208, 1174–6.

DeCasper, A. J., and Spence, M. J. (1986), 'Prenatal maternal speech influences newborns' perception of speech sounds'. *Infant Behavior and Development*, 9, 133–50.

Dedo, J. Y. (1991), 'Smiling during later infancy: Relationships among facial expressions, contexts, and other communicative behaviors'. Doctoral Dissertation. Purdue University.

DeLoache, J. S. (1983, April), *Joint picture book reading as memory training for toddlers*. Paper presented at the meetings of the Society for Research in Child Development, Detroit.

de Lyra, M., and Rossetti-Ferreira, M. C. (1992), 'Transformation and construction in social interaction: A new perspective on analysis of the mother–infant dyad'. In J. Valsiner (Ed), *Child development within culturally structured environments Vol. 3: Comparative-cultural and co-constructionist perspectives* Ablex: Norwood, NJ.

Denham, S. (1986), 'Social cognition, prosocial behavior and emotion in preschoolers: Contextual validation'. *Child Development*, 57, 194–201.

Dent, C. H. (1990), 'An ecological approach to language development: An alternative functionalism'. *Developmental Psychobiology*, 23, 679–703.

Desor, J. A., Miller, O., and Turner, R. (1973), 'Taste in acceptance of sugars by human infants'. *Journal of Comparative and Physiological Psychology*, 84, 496–501.

Diaz-Guerrero, R. (1977), 'A Mexican psychology'. *American Psychologist*, 32, 934–44.

Doi, T. (1973), *The anatomy of dependence* (trans. J. Bester). Kodansha International: Tokyo.

Donahue, M. (1986), 'Phonological constraints on the emergence of two-word utterances'. *Journal of Child Language*, 13, 209–18.

Drabble, M. (1982), 'With all my love, (signed) mama'. In S. Cahill (Ed). *Motherhood: A reader for men and women* (p. 6). Avon: New York.

Duck, S. (1991), *Understanding relationships*. The Guilford Press: New York.

Duncan, S. (1973), 'Toward a grammar for dyadic conversation'. *Semiotica*, 1, 30–46.

Duncan, S. (1991), 'Convention and conflict in the child's interaction with others'. *Developmental Review*, 11, 337–67.

Duncan, S., and Fiske, D. W. (1977), *Face-to-face interaction: Research, methods and theory*, Erlbaum: Hillsdale NJ.

Dunham, P., Dunham, F., Tran, S. and Akhtar, N. (1991), 'The nonreciprocating robot: Effects on verbal discourse, social play, and social referencing at two years of age'. *Child Development*, 62, 1489–502.

Dunn, J., and Kendrick, C. (1982), *Siblings: Love, envy, and understanding*. Harvard University Press: Cambridge, MA.

Dunn, J., and Munn, P. (1985), 'Becoming a family member: Family conflict and the development of social understanding in the second year'. *Child Development*, 56, 480–92.

Dunn, J., Bretherton, I., and Munn, P. (1987), 'Conversations about feeling states between mothers and their young children'. *Developmental Psychology*, 23, 132–9.

Dyk, W. (1938), *Son of old man hat*. University of Nebraska Press: Lincoln, NE.

Easterbrooks, M. A. (1989), 'Quality of attachment to mother and to father: Effects of perinatal risk status'. *Child Development*, 60, 825–30.

Eckerman, C. O. (in press), 'Toddler's achievement of coordinated action with conspecifics: a dynamic systems perspective'. In L. B. Smith and E. Thelen (Eds), *Dynamical systems in development: Applications*. MIT Press: Cambridge, MA.

Eckerman, C. O., and Stein, M. R. (1990), 'How imitation begets imitation and toddlers' generation of games'. *Developmental Psychology*, 26, 370–8.

Eckhorn, R., and Reitboeck, H. J. (1990), 'Stimulus-specific synchronization in cat visual cortex and its possible role in visual pattern recognition'. In H. Haken and M. Stadler (Eds), *Synergetics of cognition* (pp. 99–112). Springer-Verlag: New York.

Edwards, D., and Middleton, D. (1986), 'Joint remembering: Constructing an account of shared experience through conversational discourse'. *Discourse Processes*, 9, 423–59.

Efran, M. G., and Cheyne, J. A. (1973), 'Shared space: The co-operative control of spatial areas by two interacting individuals'. *Canadian Journal of Behavioral Science*, 5, 201–10.

Eibl-Eibesfeldt, I. (1983), 'Patterns of parent–child interaction in a cross-cultural perspective'. In A. Oliverio, and M. Zappella (Eds), *The behavior of human infants* (pp. 177–217). Plenum Press: New York.

Eisenberg, A. R. (1985), 'Learning to describe past experiences in conversation'. *Discourse Processes*, 8, 177–204.

Eisenberg, A. R. (1992), 'Conflicts between mothers and their young children'. *Merrill-Palmer Quarterly*, 38, 21–43.

Ekman, P. (1965), 'Communication through nonverbal behavior: A source of information about an interpersonal relationship'. In S. S. Tomkins and C. E. Izard (Eds), *Affect, cognition and personality*. Springer Verlag: New York.

Ekstein, M. (1989), *Rites of spring*. Doubleday: New York.

Emde, R. N. (1989), 'The infant's relationship experience: Developmental and Affective Aspects'. In A. J. Sameroff and R. N. Emde (Eds), *Relationship disturbances in early childhood: A developmental approach* (pp. 33–51). Basic Books: New York.

Emde, R. N., Biringen, Z., Clyman, R. B., and Oppenheim, D. (1991), 'The moral self of infancy: Affective core and procedural knowledge'. *Developmental Review*, 11, 251–70.

Fagen, J. W., Ohr, P. S., Singer, J. M., and Klein, S. J. (1989), 'Crying and retrograde amnesia in young infants'. *Infant Behavior and Development*, 12, 13–24.

Feldstein, S., and Welkowitz, J. (1978), 'A chronography of conversation: In defense of an objective approach'. In A. W. Siegman and S. Feldstein (Eds), *Non-verbal behavior and communication*. Erlbaum: Hillsdale, NJ.

Fentress. J. C. (1976), 'Dynamic boundaries of patterned behavior: Interaction and self-organization'. In P. P. G. Bateson and R. A. Hinde (Eds), *Growing points in ethology* (pp. 135–69). Cambridge University Press: Cambridge , UK.

Fentress, J. C. (1989), 'Developmental roots of behavioral order: Systemic approaches to the examination of core developmental issues'. In M. R. Gunnar and E. Thelen (Eds), *Systems and development, The Minnesota symposia of child psychology* (Vol. 22) (pp. 35–76). Erlbaum: Hillsdale, NJ.

Ferguson, C. (1977), 'Baby talk as a simplified register'. In C. Snow and C. Ferguson (Eds), *Talking to children: Language input and acquisition*. Cambridge University Press: New York.

Ferland, M. B., and Mendelson, M. J. (1989), 'Infants' categorization of melodic contour'. *Infant Behavior and Development*, 12, 341–55.

Fernald, A. (1985), 'Four-month-old infants prefer to listen to motherese'. *Infant Behavior and Development*, 8, 181–95.

Fernald, A. (1989), 'Intonation and communicative intent in mothers' speech to infants: Is the melody the message?'. *Child Development*, 60, 1497–510.

Fernald, A., Taeschner, T., Dunn, J., Papousek, M., de Boysson-Bardies, B., and Fukui, I. (1989), 'A cross-language study of prosodic modifications in mothers' and fathers' speech to preverbal infants'. *Journal of Child Language*, 16, 477–501.

Field, J. (1976), 'The adjustment of reaching behavior to object distance in early infancy'. *Child Development*, 47, 304–8.

Field, T. (1979), 'Visual and cardiac responses to animate and inanimate faces by young term and preterm infants'. *Child Development*, 50, 188–94.

Field, T., Sostek, A. M., Vietze, P., and Leiderman, P. H. (1981), *Culture and early interactions*. Erlbaum: Hillsdale, NY.

Field, T., Vega-Lahr, N., Scafidi, F., and Goldstein, S. (1986), 'Effects of maternal unavailability on mother–infant interactions'. *Infant Behavior and Development*, 9, 473–8.

Fivaz, E. (1987), *Alliances et mesalliances dans le dialogue entre adulte et bébé*. Delachaux and Niestle: Neuchâtel.

Fivush, R., and Hudson, J. A. (1990), *Knowing and remembering in young children*. Cambridge University Press: New York.

Fleming, A. S., Ruble, D. N., Flett, G. L., and Shaul, D. L. (1988), 'Postpartum adjustment in first-time mothers: Relations between mood, maternal attitudes, and mother–infant interactions'. *Developmental Psychology*, 24, 71–81.

Fogel, A. (1977), 'Temporal organization in mother–infant face-to-face interaction'. In H. R. Schaffer (Ed), *Studies in mother–infant interaction* (pp. 119–52). Academic Press: New York.

Fogel, A. (1979), 'Peer vs. mother directed behavior in 1- to 3-month-old infants'. *Infant Behavior and Development*, 2, 215–26.

Fogel, A. (1980), 'The effect of brief separations on 2-month-old infants'. *Infant Behavior and Development*, 3, 315–30.

Fogel, A. (1982), 'Affect dynamics in early infancy: Affective tolerance'. In T. Field and A. Fogel (Eds), *Emotion and early interaction* (pp. 15–56). Erlbaum: Hillsdale, NJ.

Fogel, A. (1989). 'Using cross-cultural research to study dynamic processes in development. Comments on Bril, Hombessa–Nkounkou, Zack and Bonnemaire's paper'. *European Journal of the Psychology of Education*, 4, 319–21.

Fogel, A. (1990a), 'The process of developmental change in infant communicative action: Using dynamic systems theory to study individual ontogenies'. In J. Colombo and J. Fagen (Eds), *Individual differences in infancy: Reliability, stability and prediction*. Erlbaum: Hillsdale, NJ.

Fogel, A. (1990b), 'Sensorimotor factors in communicative development'. In H. Bloch and B. Bertenthal (Eds), *Sensorimotor organization and development in infancy and early childhood*. NATO ASI Series. Kluwer: The Netherlands.

Fogel, A. (1991), *Infancy: Infant, family and society*. West: St. Paul, MN.

Fogel, A. (1992), 'Movement and communication in human infancy: The social dynamics of development'. *Human Movement Science*, 11, 387–423.

Fogel, A., Dedo, J. Y., and McEwen, I. (1992), 'Effect of postural position on the duration of gaze at mother during face-to-face interaction in 3-to-6-month-old infants'. *Infant Behavior and Development*, 15, 231–44.

Fogel, A., Diamond, G. R., Langhorst, B. H., and Demos, V. (1982), 'Affective and cognitive aspects of the two-month old's participation in face-to-face interaction with its mother'. In E. Tronick (Ed), *Social interchange in infancy: Affect, cognition, and communication* (pp. 37–57) University Park Press: Baltimore.

Fogel, A., Hannan, T. E. (1985), 'Manual actions of 2- to 3-month-old human infants during social interaction'. *Child Development*, **56**, 1271–9.

Fogel, A., Nwokah, E., Dedo, J. Y., Messinger, D., Dickson, K. L., Matusov, E., and Holt, S. A. (in press), 'Social process theory of emotion: A dynamic systems approach'. *Social Development*, **1**, 122–42.

Fogel, A., Nwokah, E., and Karns, J. (in press), 'Parent–infant games as dynamic social systems'. In K. B. MacDonald (Ed), *Parents and children playing.* SUNY Press: Albany, NY.

Fogel, A., and Thelen, E. (1987), 'Development of early expressive and communicative action: Reinterpreting the evidence from a dynamic systems perspective'. *Developmental Psychology*, **23**, 747–61.

Fogel, A., Toda, S., and Kawai, M. (1988), 'Mother–infant face-to-face interactions in Japan and the United States: A laboratory comparison using 3-month-old infants'. *Developmental Psychology*, **24**, 398–406.

Foppa, K. (1990), 'Topic progression and intention'. In I. Markova and K. Foppa (Eds), *The dynamics of dialogue* (pp. 178–200). Springer-Verlag: New York.

Ford, D. H. (1987), *Humans as self-constructing living systems: A developmental perspective on behavior and personality.* Erlbaum: Hillsdale, NJ.

Foreman, N., and Altaha, M. (1992), 'The development of exploration and spontaneous alternation in hooded rat pups: Effects of unusually early eyelid opening'. *Developmental Psychobiology*, **24**, 521–37.

Franco, F., and Butterworth, G. (1990), *Effects of social variables on the production of infant pointing.* Presented at European conference on Developmental Psychology, Stirling, Scotland.

Freeman, W. J. (1990), 'On the problem of anomalous dispersion in chaoto-chaotic phase transitions of neural masses, and its significance for the management of perceptual information in brains'. In H. Haken and M. Stadler (Eds), *Synergetics of cognition* (pp. 126–43). Springer-Verlag: New York.

Freud, S. (1900), 'The interpretation of dreams'. In J. Strachey (Ed and trans.), *The standard edition of the complete works of Sigmund Freud* (Vol. 3). Hogarth: London 1953. (Originally published, 1900.)

Freud, S. (1926), *Inhibitions, symptoms and anxiety.* In *The Standard Edition* (Vol. 20). Hogarth Press: London.

Frey, S., Hirsbrunner, H., Florin, A., Daw, W., and Crawford, R. (1983), 'A unified approach to the investigation of nonverbal and verbal behavior in communication research'. In W. Doise and S. Moscovici (Eds), *Current issues in European social psychology* (Vol. 1). Cambridge University Press: New York.

Fridlund, A. J. (1991), 'Evolution and facial action in reflex, social motive, and paralanguage'. *Biological Psychology*, **32**, 3–100.

Furrow, D. (1984), 'Social and private speech at two years'. *Child Development*, **55**, 355–62.

Garfinkel, H. (1967), *Studies in ethno methodology.* Prentice Hall: Englewood Cliffs, NJ.

Gelfand, D. M., and Teti, D. M. (in press), 'The effects of maternal depression on children'. *Clinical Psychology Review.*

Gergen, K. J. (1982), *Toward transformation in social knowledge.* Springer-Verlag: New York.

Gergen, K. J. (1984), 'Theory of the self: Impasse and evolution'. In L. Berkowitz

(Ed), *Advances in experimental social psychology Vol. 17: Theorizing in social psychology: Special topics* (pp. 49–115). Academic Press: New York.

Gewirtz, J. L., and Boyd, E. F. (1977), 'Experiments on mother–infant interaction underlying mutual attachment acquisition: The infant conditions the mother'. In T. Alloway, L. Krames, and P. Pliner (Eds), *Attachment behavior: Advances in the study of communication and affect* (Vol. 3). Plenum Press: New York.

Gianino, A., and Tronick, E. Z. (1988), 'The mutual regulation model: The infant's self and interactive regulation and coping and defensive capacities'. In T. M. Field, P. M. McCabe and N. Schneiderman (Eds), *Stress and coping across development* (pp. 47–68). Erlbaum: Hillsdale, NJ.

Gibbons, A. (1992), 'Chimps: More diverse than a barrel of monkeys'. *Science*, **225**, 287–8.

Gibson, J. J. (1966), *The senses considered as perceptual systems*. Houghton Mifflin: Boston, MA.

Gibson, J. J. (1979), *The ecological approach to visual perception*. Houghton Mifflin: Boston, MA.

Gilligan, L. (1978), 'In a different voice: Women's conception of the self and of morality'. *Harvard Educational Review*, **47**, 481–517.

Ginsburg, G. P. (1985), 'The analysis of human action: Current status and future potential'. In G. P. Ginsburg, M. L. Brenner and M. von Cranach, (Eds), *Discovery strategies in the psychology of action* (pp. 255–79). Academic Press: London.

Ginsburg, G. P., and Kilbourne, B. K. (1988), 'Emergence of vocal alternation in mother–infant exchanges'. *Journal of Child Language*, **15**, 221–35.

Gleick, J. (1987), *Chaos: Making a new science*. Viking: New York.

Goetzmann, W. (1987), *New lands, new men*. Donnelley and Sons: Harrisonburg, VA.

Goffman, E. (1974), *Frame analysis: An essay on the organization of experience*. Harvard University Press: Cambridge, MA.

Goldberg, J. A. (1983), 'A move toward describing conversational coherence'. In R. T. Craig and K. Tracy (Eds), *Conversational coherence: Form, structure, and strategy* (pp. 25–45). Sage: Beverly Hill, CA.

Goldin–Meadow, S., and Mylander, C. (1983), 'Gestural communication in deaf children: Noneffect of parental input on language development'. *Science*, **221**, 372–4.

Golinkoff, R. M. (1983), 'The preverbal negotiation of failed messages: Insights into the transition period'. In E. R. Golinkoff (Ed), *The transition from prelinguistic to linguistic communication*. Erlbaum: Hillsdale, NJ.

Goodnow, J. J. (1988), 'Parents' ideas, actions, and feelings: Models and methods from developmental and social psychology'. *Child Development*, **59**, 286–320.

Gould, S. (1981), *The mismeasure of man*. Norton: New York.

Gouzoules, H., Gouzoules, S., and Marler, P. (1985), 'External reference and affective signaling in Mammalian vocal communication'. In G. Zivin (Ed), *The development of expressive behavior: Biology–environment interactions* (pp. 77–101). Academic Press: New York.

Grammer, K. (1989), 'Human courtship behavior: Biological basis and cognitive processing'. In A. E. Rasa, C. Vogel and E. Voland (Eds), *The sociobiology of sexual and reproductive strategies* (pp. 147–69). Chapman and Hall: New York.

Gray, H. (1978), 'Learning to take an object from the mother'. In A. Lock (Ed),

Action, gesture and symbol: The emergence of language (pp. 159–82). Academic Press: New York.

Green, J. E. (1988), 'Loglinear analysis of cross-classified ordinal data: Applications in developmental research'. *Child Development*, 59, 1–25.

Grice, H. P. (1975), 'Logic and conversation'. In P. Cole and J. Morgan (Eds), *Syntax and semantics* (Vol. 3). Academic Press: London.

Griffin, W. A., and Gardner, W. (1989), 'Analysis of behavioral durations in observational studies of social intraction'. *Psychological Bulletin*, 106, 497–502.

Gunzenhauser, N. (1990), *Advances in touch: New implications in human development*. Johnson and Johnson: Skillman, NJ.

Haight, W., and Miller, P. (in press), *The development of pretend play in sociocultural context: A longitudinal study of everyday pretend from 1 to 4 years*. SUNY Press: Albany, NY.

Haight, W. L., and Miller, P. J. (1993). *Pretending at home: Early development in a sociocultural context*. State University of New York Press: NY.

Haken, H. (183), *Synergetics – an introduction* (3rd ed.). Springer-Verlag: New York.

Hall, E. T. (1964), 'Silent assumptions in social communication research'. *Publications of the Association for Research in Nervous and Mental Disease*, XLII, 41–55.

Hannan, T. E. (1987), 'A cross-sequential assessment of the occurrences of pointing in three- to twelve-month-old infants'. *Infant Behavior and Development*, 10, 11–22.

Haroutunian, S. (1983), *Equilibrium in the balance: A study of psychological explanation*. Springer-Verlag: New York.

Harré, R. (1981), 'Psychological variety'. In P. Heelas and A. Lock (Eds), *Indigenous psychologies: The anthropology of the self* (pp. 79–103). Academic Press: New York.

Harré, R. (1988), *The social construction of emotions*. Basil Blackwell: New York.

Harré, R., and Van Langenhove, L. (1983), 'Varieties of positioning'. *Journal of the Theory of Social Behavior*, 21, 393–406.

Harris, M., Jones, D., Brookes, S., and Grant, J. (1986), 'Relations between the non-verbal context of maternal speech and rate of language development'. *British Journal of Developmental Psychology*, 4, 261–8.

Harris, P. L., Brown, E., Marriott, C., Whittall, S., and Harmer, S. (1991), 'Monsters, ghosts and witches: Testing the limits of the fantasy–reality distinction in young children'. *British Journal of Developmental Psychology*, 9, 105–23.

Harter, S. (1983), 'Developmental perspectives on self-system'. In E. M. Hetherington (Ed), *Handbook of child psychology: Socialization, personality, and social development* (Vol. 4) (P. H. Mussen, General Editor). Wiley: New York.

Hay, D. F., Murray, P., Cecire, S., and Nash, A. (1985), 'Social learning of social behavior in early life'. *Child Development*, 56, 43–57.

Hayne, H., Rovee-Collier, C., and Perris, E. E. (1987), 'Categorization and memory retrieval by three-month-olds'. *Child Development*, 58, 750–67.

Hearne, V. (1987), *Adam's task: Calling the animals by name*. Random House: New York.

Heath, C. (1984), 'Talk and recipiency: Sequential organization in speech and body movement'. In J. M. Atkinson and J. Heritage (Eds), *Structures of social action: Studies in conversation analysis*, (pp. 247–65). Cambridge University Press: New York.

Heckhausen, J. (1987), 'Balancing for weaknesses and challenging developmental potential: A longitudinal study of mother–infant dyads in apprenticeship interactions'. *Developmental Psychology*, **23**, 762–70.

Heelas, P. (1981a), 'Introduction: Indigenous psychologies'. In P. Heelas and A. Lock (Eds), *Indigenous psychologies: The anthropology of the self* (pp. 3–18). Academic Press: New York.

Heelas, P. (1981), 'The model applied: Anthropology and indigenous psychologies'. In P. Heelas and A. Lock (Eds), *Indigenous psychologies: The anthropology of the self* (pp. 39–63). Academic Press: New York.

Hein, A., and Diamond, R. M. (1972), 'Locomotory space as a prerequisite for acquiring visually guided reaching in kittens'. *Journal of Comparative and Physiological Psychology*, **81**, 394–8.

Hermans, H. J., Kempen, H. J. G., and van Loon, R. J. P. (1992), 'The dialogical self: Beyond individualism and rationalism'. *American Psychologist*, **47**, 23–33.

Hinde, R. A. (1977), 'Changing approaches to the social behaviour of higher vertebrates'. *Natural Sciences*, **12**, 339–62.

Hinde, R. A. (1985), 'Expression and negotiation'. In G. Zivin (Ed), *The development of expressive behavior: Biology–environment interactions* (pp. 103–16). Academic Press: New York.

Ho, D. Y. F. (1982), 'Asian concepts in behavior science'. *Psychologia*, **25**, 228–35.

Hoffman, M. (1975), 'Developmental synthesis of affect and cognition and its implications for altruistic motivation'. *Developmental Psychology*, **11**, 607–22.

Holt, S. A., and Fogel, A. (May, 1982), *Infant smiles during mother–child interactions: A dynamic systems approach*. International Society for Infant Studies, Miami, FL.

Hopkins, B., and Butterworth, G. (1988), 'Concepts of causality in explanations of development'. In G. Butterworth and P. Bryant (Eds), *Causes of development: Interdisciplinary perspectives* (pp. 3–32). Harvester Wheatsheaf: Hemel Hempstead.

Hopkins, B., and Westra, T. (1988), 'Maternal handling and motor development: An intracultural study'. *Genetic, Social and General Psychology Monographs*, **114**, 379–408.

Howes, C. (1987), 'Peer interaction of young children'. *Monographs of the Society for Research in Child Development*, **57**, 1–94.

Ignjatovic-Savic, N., Kovac-Cerovic, T., Plut, D., and Pesikan, A. (1990), 'Social interaction in early childhood and its developmental effects'. In J. Valsiner (Ed), *Child development within culturally structured environments* (Vol. 1) (pp. 89–153). Ablex: Norwood, NJ.

Isabella, R., and Belsky, J. (1991), 'Interactional synchrony and the origins of infant–mother attachment: A replication study'. *Child Development*, **62**, 373–84.

Izard, C. E. (1991), 'The irrepressible phenomenon of repression: a challenge to clinicians and cognitive scientists'. *Contemporary Psychology*, **36**, 1039–40.

Jaffee, J., and Feldstein, S. (1970), *Rhythms of dialogue*. Academic Press: New York.

Jahoda, G. (1980), 'Cross-cultural comparisons'. In M. H. Bornstein (Ed), *Comparative methods in psychology*. Erlbaum: Hillsdale, NJ.

James, W. (1890), *The principles of psychology*. Holt: New York.

Jameson, P., Kulcsar, E., Gelfand, D., Pompa, J., and Teti, D. (1991), *Interactions betwen mothers and toddlers: Does depression make a difference?* Presented at the annual meeting of the Western Psychological Association, San Francisco, CA.

Jenkins, J. J. (1977), 'Remember that old theory of memory? Well, forget it!' In

R. Shaw and J. Bransford (Eds), *Perceiving, acting, and knowing: Toward an ecological psychology* (pp. 413–29). Erlbaum: Hillsdale, NJ.

Johnson, M. (1987), *The body in the mind: The bodily basis of meaning, imagination, and reason.* University of Chicago Press: Chicago.

Jones, O. (1980), 'Prelinguistic communications skills in Down's syndrome and normal infants'. In T. Field, S. Goldberg, D. Stern, and A. Sostek (Eds), *High risk infants and children: Adult and peer interactions.* Academic Press: New York.

Jones, S. S., and Raag, T. (1989), 'Smile production in older infants: The importance of a social recipient for the facial signal'. *Child Development,* **60,** 811–18.

Jouen, F. (1990), 'Early visual–vestibular interactions and postural development'. In H. Bloch and B. I. Bertenthal (Eds), *Sensory-motor organizations and development in infancy and early childhood* (pp. 119–215). Kluwer: The Netherlands.

Kagan, J. (1989), *Unstable ideas: Temperament, cognition, and self.* Harvard University Press: Cambridge, MA.

Kagan, J., Kearsley, R. B., and Zelazo, P. R. (1978), *Infancy: Its place in human development.* Harvard University Press: Cambridge, MA.

Kanki, B. G. (1985), 'Participant differences and interactive strategies'. In S. Duncan, Jr., and D. W. Fiske (Eds), *Interaction structure and strategy* (pp. 233–93). Cambridge University Press: New York.

Kato, T., Takahashi, E., Sawada, K., Kobayashi, N., Watanabe, T., and Ishii, T. (1983), 'A computer analysis of infant movements synchronized with adult speech'. *Pediatric Research,* **17,** 625–8.

Kaye, K. (1977), 'Toward the origin of dialogue'. In H. R. Schaffer (Ed), *Studies in mother–infant interaction* (pp. 89–117). Academic Press: New York.

Kaye, K. (1980), 'Why we don't talk "baby talk" to babies'. *Journal of Child Language,* **7,** 489–507.

Kaye, K. (1982), *The mental and social life of babies.* Harvester Wheatsheaf: Hemel Hempstead; University of Chicago Press: Chicago.

Kaye, K., and Fogel, A. (1980), 'The temporal structure of face-to-face communication between mothers and infants'. *Developmental Psychology,* **16,** 454–64.

Kaye, K., and Marcus, J. (1978), 'Imitation over a series of trials without feedback'. *Infant Behavior and Development,* **1,** 141–55.

Kegan, R. (1982), *The evolving self: Problem and process in human development.* Harvard University Press: Cambridge, MA.

Kelso, J. A. S., and Kay, B. A. (1987), 'Information and control: A macroscopic analysis of perception–action coupling'. In H. Heuer and A. F. Sanders (Eds), *Perspectives on perception and action.* Erlbaum: Hillsdale, NJ.

Kelso, J. A. S., and Tuller, B. (1984), 'A dynamical basis for action systems'. In M. S. Gazzaniga (Ed), *Handbook of neuroscience* (pp. 321–56). Plenum: New York.

Kendon, A. (1970), 'Movement coordination in social interaction: Some examples described'. *Acta Psychologica,* **32,** 100–25.

Kendon, A. (1975), 'Some functions of the face in a kissing round'. *Journal of the International Association for Semiotic Studies,* **15:4,** 99–334.

Kendon, A. (1985), 'Behavioral foundations for the process of frame attunement in face-to-face interaction'. In G. P. Ginsburg, M. Brenner and M. von Cranach (Eds), *Discovery strategies in the psychology of action.* Academic Press: London.

Kendon, A. (1990), *Conducting interaction: Patterns of behavior in focused encounters.* Cambridge University Press: New York.

Kendon, A., and Ferber, A. (1973), 'A description of some human greetings'. In R. P. Michael and J. H. Cook (Eds), *Comparative ecology and behavior of primates* (pp. 591–668). Academic Press: London.

Kendon, A., Harris, R. M., and Key, M. R. (1975), *Organization of behavior in face-to-face interaction*. Mouton Publishers: Paris.

Kenny, P. A., and Turkewitz, G. (1986), 'Effects of unusually early visual stimulation on the development of homing behavior in the rat pup'. *Developmental Psychobiology*, **19**, 57–66.

Kent, R. D. (1981), 'Sensorimotor aspects of speech development'. In R. N. Aslin, J. R. Alberts, and M. R. Peterson (Eds), *Development of perception: Psychobiological perspectives Vol. 1: Audition, somatic perception and the chemical senses* (pp. 161–89). Academic Press: New York.

Kessen, W., Haith, M., and Salapatek, P. (1970), 'Human infancy: A bibliography and guide'. In P. H. Mussen (Ed), *Charmichael's manual of child psychology* (3rd ed.). Wiley: New York.

Kirkland, J., and Morgan, G. A. V. (in press), 'Radical ecology'. *Early Child Development and Care*.

Kochman, T. (1970), 'Toward an ethnography of Black American speech behavior'. In N. E. Whitten, Jr. and J. F. Szwed (Eds), *Afro-American anthropology: Contemporary perspectives*. The Free Press: New York.

Kojima, H. (1985), 'Child-rearing concepts as a belief-value system of society and individual'. In H. W. Stevenson, H. Azuma and K. Hakuta (Eds), *Child development in Japan*. Freeman: San Francisco, CA.

Kojima, H. (1986), 'Becoming nurturant in Japan: Past and present'. In A. Fogel, and G. F. Melson (Eds), *Origins of Nurturance: Developmental, biological and cultural perspectives on caregiving*. Erlbaum: Hillsdale, NJ.

Kolers, P. A., and Roediger, H. L. (1984), 'Procedures of mind'. *Journal of Verbal Learning and Verbal Behavior*, **23**, 425–49.

Kravitz, H., Goldenberg, D., and Neyhus, A. (1978), 'Tactual exploration by normal infants'. *Developmental Medicine and Child*, **20**, 720–6.

Kugler, P. N., Kelso, J. A. S., and Turvey, M. T. (1982), 'On coordination and control in naturally developing systems'. In J. A. S. Kelso and J. E. Clark, (Eds), *The development of movement coordination and control* (pp. 5–78). Wiley: New York.

Labov, W. (1972), *Language in the inner city*. University of Pennsylvania Press: Philadelphia.

La France, M., and Ickes, W. (1981), 'Posture mirroring and interactional involvement: Sex and sex typing effects'. *Journal of Nonverbal Behavior*, **5**, 139–54.

Lagmay, A. (1984), 'Western psychology in the Philippines: Impact and response'. *International Journal of Psychology*, **19**, 31–44.

Lamb, M. E., (1977), 'A re-examination of the infant's social world'. *Human Development*, **20**, 68–85.

Landry, S. H., Chapieski, M. L., and Schmidt, M. (1986), 'Effects of maternal attention-directing strategies on preterms' response to toys'. *Infant Behavior and Development*, **9**, 257–69.

Langlois, J. H., Roggman, L. A., Casey, R. J., Ritter, J. M., Rieser-Danner, L. S., and Jenkins, V. Y. (1987), 'Infant preferences for attractive faces: Rudiments of a stereotype?'. *Developmental Psychology*, **23**, 363–9.

Langlois, J. H., Roggman, L. A., and Rieser-Danner, L. A. (1990), 'Infants' differential social responses to attractive and unattractive faces'. *Developmental Psychology*, **26**, 153–9.

Lee, D. N. (1990), 'Getting around with light or sound'. In R. Warren and A. H. Wertheim (Eds), *Perception and control of self-motion* (pp. 487–505). Erlbaum: Hillsdale, NJ.

Lee, D. N., and Young, D. S. (1985), 'Visual timing of interceptive action'. In D. J. Ingle, M. Jeannerod, and D. N. Lee (Eds), *Brain mechanisms and spatial vision*. Nijhoff: Dordrecht.

Legerstee, M. (1990), 'Infants use of multimodal information to imitate speech sounds'. *Infant Behavior and Development*, **13**, 347–58.

Legerstee, M. (1991), 'Changes in the quality of infant sounds as a function of social and nonsocial stimulation'. *First Language*, **11**, 327–43.

Legerstee, M., Corter, C., and Kienapple, K. (1990), 'Hand, arm, and facial actions of young infants to a social and nonsocial stimulus'. *Child Development*, **61**, 774–84.

Levelt, W. J. M. (1983), 'Monitoring and self-repair in speech'. *Cognition*, **14**, 41–104.

Levine, L. E. (1983), 'Mine: Self-definition in 2-year-old boys'. *Developmental Psychology*, **19**, 544–9.

LeVine, R. A., Miller, P. M., and West, M. M. (1988), *Parental behavior in diverse societies*. Jossey-Bass: San Francisco.

Lewis, M., and Brooks–Gunn, J. (1979), *Social cognition and the acquisition of self*. Plenum Press: New York.

Lewis, M., and Michalson, L. (1983), *Children's emotions and moods*. Plenum Press: New York.

Lilienfeld, R. (1978), *The rise of systems theory: An ideological analysis*. Wiley: New York.

Linsker, R. (1986), 'From basic network principles to neural architecture: Emergence of orientation-selective cells'. *Proc. Natl. Acad. Sci.*, **83**, 8390–4.

Lipsitt, L. P. (1979), 'The pleasures and annoyances of infants: Approach and avoidance behavior'. In E. Thoman (Ed), *The origins of the infant's social responsiveness*. Erlbaum: Hillsdale, NJ.

Lock, A. (1980), *The guided reinvention of language*. Academic Press: New York.

Lock, A. (1981), 'Universals in human conception'. In P. Heelas and A. Lock (Eds), *Indigenous psychologies: The anthropology of the self* (pp. 19–36). Academic Press: New York.

Lock, A., Young, A., Service, V., and Chandler, P. (1990), 'Some observations on the origins of the pointing gesture'. In V. Voltera and C. Erting (Eds) *From gesture to language in hearing and deaf children* (pp. 42–55). Springer-Verlag: New York.

Lockman, J. J., and McHale, J. P. (1989), 'Object manipulation in infancy: Developmental and contextual determinants'. In J. J. Lockman and N. L. Hazen (Eds), *Action in social context: Perspectives on early development* (pp. 129–67). Plenum Press: New York.

Lucariello, J., and Nelson, K. (1987), 'Remembering and planning talk between mothers and children'. *Discourse Processes*, **10**, 219–35.

Lusk, D., and Lewis, M. (1972), 'Mother–infant interaction and infant development among the Wolof of Senegal'. *Human Development*, **15**, 58–69.

Lutkenhaus, P., Bullock, M., and Geppert, U. (1987), 'Toddlers' action: Knowledge, control, and the self'. In F. Halisch and J. Kuhl (Eds), *Motivation, intention, and volition*. Springer-Verlag: Berlin.

Lyra, M. D. C., and Rossetti-Ferreira, M. C. (in press), 'Transformation and construction in social interaction: A new perspective on analysis of the mother–infant dyad'. In J. Valsiner (Ed), *Child development within culturally structured environments, Vol. 3*.

McBride, A. B. (1973), *The growth and development of mothers*. Harper and Row: New York.

MacFarlane, A. (1975), 'Olfaction in the development of social preferences in the human neonate'. In Ciba Foundation Symposium (Ed), *Parent–infant interaction*. Elsevier: New York.

MacMurry, J. (1958), *The self as agent*. Faber: London.

Mahler, M. S. (1968), *On human symbiosis and the vicissitudes of individuation*. International Universities Press: New York.

Mahler, M., Pine, F., and Bergman, A. (1975), *The psychological birth of the human infant*. Basic Books: New York.

Main, M., and Solomon, J. (1986), 'Discovery of an insecure–disorganized/disoriented attachment pattern'. In T. B. Brazelton and M. W. Yogman (Eds), *Affective development in infancy* (pp. 95–124). Ablex: Norwood, NJ.

Marcos, H. (1987), 'Communicative functions of pitch range and pitch direction in infants'. *Journal of Child Language*, 14, 255–68.

Markova, I. (1990), 'Why the dynamics of dialogue?' In I. Markova and K. Foppa (Eds), *The Dynamics of Dialogue* (pp. 1–22). Springer–Verlag: New York.

Mason, M. A. (1953), *Main currents of scientific thought: A history of the sciences*. Henry Schuman: New York.

Masur, E. F., and Ritz, E. G. (1984), 'Patterns of gestural, vocal, and verbal imitation performance in infancy'. *Merrill-Palmer Quarterly* 30, 369–92.

Mathew, A., and Cook, M. (1990), 'The control of reaching movements by young infants'. *Child Development*, 61, 1238–57.

Matthei, E. H. (1989), 'Crossing boundaries: More evidence for phonological constraints on early multi-word utterances'. *Journal of Child Language*, 16, 41–54.

Maturana, H. R. (1978), 'Biology of language: The epistemology of reality'. In G. A. Miller and E. Lennenberg (Eds), *Psychology and biology of language and thought* (pp. 27–63). Academic Press: New York.

Maxwell, G. M., and Cook, M. W. (1985), 'Postural congruence and judgements of liking and perceived similarity'. *New Zealand Journal of Psychology*, 14, 20–6.

Mayes, L. C., and Carter, A. S. (1990), 'Emerging social regulatory capacities as seen in the still-face situation'. *Child Development*, 61, 754–63.

McDowall, J. J. (1978), 'Interactional synchrony: A reappraisal'. *Journal of Personality and Social Psychology*, 36, 963–75.

McGeer, V., and Braybrooke, D. (1992), *Raising consciousness: Retrieving from personal development the lost minds of philosophers*. Paper presented at Symposium on Personal Relationships, Austin, TX.

McSwain, R. (1981), 'Care and conflict in infant development: An East-Timorese and Papua New Guinean comparison'. *Infant Behavior and Development*, 4, 225–46.

Mead, G. H. (1934), *Mind, self, and society*. University of Chicago Press: Chicago.

Mehrabian, A. (1968), 'Inference of attitudes from the posture, orientation, and distance of a communicator'. *Journal of Consulting and Clinical Psychology*, **32**, 296–308.

Mehrabian, A. (1969), 'Significance of posture and position in the communication of attitude and status relationships'. *Psychological Bulletin*, **71**, 359–72.

Meier, R. P. (1991), 'Language acquisition by deaf children. *American Scientist*, **79**, 60–70.

Melson, G., and Fogel, A. (1982), 'Young children's interest in unfamiliar infants'. *Child Development*, **53**, 693–700.

Melson, G., Fogel, A., and Toda, S. (1986), 'Children's ideas about infants and their care'. *Child Development*, **57**, 1519–27.

Meltzoff, A. N., Kuhl, P. K., and Moore, M. K. (1991), 'Perception, representation, and the control of action in newborns and young infants: Toward a new synthesis'. In M. J. Weiss and P. R. Zelazo (Eds), *Newborn attention: Biological constraints and the influence of experience* (pp. 377–411). Ablex: Norwood, NJ.

Meltzoff, A. N., and Moore, M. K. (1989), 'Imitation in newborn infants: Exploring the range of gestures imitated and the underlying mechanisms'. *Developmental Psychology*, **25**, 954–62.

Mendelson, M. J., and Ferland, M. B. (1982), 'Auditory–visual transfer in four-month-old infants. *Child Development*, **53**, 1022–7.

Merleau–Ponty, M. (1962), *Phenomenology of perception* (trans. C. Smith). Routledge and Kegan Paul: London.

Messinger, D., and Fogel, A. (1990), *The role of referential gazing in object exchange*. Paper presented at International Conference on Infant Studies, Montreal.

Michaels, C. F., and Carelo, C. (1981), *Direct perception* (Century Psychology Series). Prentice-Hall: Englewood Cliffs, NJ.

Miller, E. K., Lin, L., and Desimone, R. (1991), 'A neural mechanism for working and recognition memory in inferior temporal cortex'. *Science*, **254**, 1377–9.

Miller, G. A., Galanter, E., and Pribram, K. H. (1960), *Plans and the structure of behavior*. Holt, Rinehart and Winston: New York.

Miller, P. H. (1989), *Theories of developmental psychology* (2nd ed.). Freeman: New York.

Miller, P. J., Mintz, J., Hoogstra, L., Fung, H., and Potts, R. (1992), 'The narrated self: Young children's construction of self in relation to others'. *Merrill-Palmer*, **38**, 45–67.

Miller, S., and Ittyerah, M. (1991), 'Movement imagery in young and congenitally blind children: Mental practice without visuo-spatial information'. *International Journal of Behavioral Development*, **15**, 125–46.

Mizukami, K., Kobayashi, N., Ishii, T., and Iwata, H. (1990), 'First selective attachment begins in early infancy: A study using telethermography'. *Infant Behavior and Development*, **13**, 257–71.

Moran, G., Fentress, J. C., and Golani, I. (1981), 'A description of relational patterns of movement during "ritualized fighting" in wolves'. *Animal Behavior*, **29**, 1146–65.

Moran, G., Krupka, A., Tutton, A., and Symons, D. (1987), 'Patterns of maternal and infant imitation during play'. *Infant Behavior and Development*, **10**, 477–91.

Morelli, G. A., Rogoff, B., Oppenheim, D., and Goldsmith, D. (1992), 'Cultural variation in infants' sleeping arrangements: Questions of independence'. *Developmental Psychology*, **28**, 604–13.

Morris, T. E., McCabe, A. E., and Roberts, B. T. (1991), 'Contextual influences in mother/child conversation: Gross versus fine motor play'. Presented at the Biennial Meetings of the Society for Research in Child Development, Seattle, WA., April.

Morsbach, H. (1980), 'Major psychological factors influencing Japanese interpersonal relations'. In N. Warren (Ed), *Studies in cross-cultural psychology* (Vol. 2) (pp. 317–42). Academic Press: London.

Muir, D., and Field, J. (1979), 'Newborn infants orient to sounds'. *Child Development*, 50, 431–6.

Murray, L., and Trevarthen, C. (1985), 'Emotional regulation of interaction between two-month-olds and their mothers'. In T. Field and N. Fox (Eds), *Social perception in infants* (pp. 177–97). Ablex: Norwood, NJ.

Nadel-Brulfert, H., and Baudonniere, P. M. (1982), 'The social function of reciprocal imitation in 2-year-old peers'. *International Journal of Behavioral Development*, 5, 95–109.

Nadel, J., and Fontaine, A. (1989), 'Communicating by imitation: A developmental and comparative approach to transitory social competence'. In B. H. Schneider, (Eds), *Social competence in developmental perspective* (pp. 131–44). Kluwer: The Netherlands.

Naipaul, V. S. (1984), *Finding the center: Two narratives*. Vintage Books: New York.

Needham, R. (1981), 'Inner states of universals: Sceptical reflections on human nature'. In P. Heelas and A. Lock (Eds), *Indigenous psychologies: The anthropology of the self* (pp. 65–78). Academic Press: New York.

Neisser, U. (1991), 'Two perceptually given aspects of the self and their development'. *Developmental Review*, 11, 197–209.

Nelson, K. (1973), 'Structure and strategy in learning to talk'. *Monographs of the Society for Research in Child Development*, 38, (Serial No. 149).

Nelson, K. (1984), 'The transition from infant to child memory'. In M. Moscovitch (Ed), *Infant memory: Its relation to normal and pathological memory in humans and other animals* (pp. 103–30). Plenum Press: New York.

Nelson, K., and Greundel, J. M. (1981), 'Generalized event representations: Basic building blocks of cognitive development'. In M. E. Lamb and A. L. Brown (Eds), *Advances in developmental psychology* (Vol. 1). Erlbaum: Hillsdale, NJ.

Newson, J. (1977), 'An intersubjective approach to the systematic description of the mother–infant interaction'. In H. R. Schaffer (Ed), *Studies in mother–infant interaction*. Academic Press: London.

Nurius, P. (1991), 'Possible selves and social support: Social cognitive resources for coping and striving'. In J. A. Howard and P. L. Callero (Eds), *The self-society dynamic: Cognition, emotion, and action* (pp. 239–58). Cambridge University Press: New York.

O'Brien, M., and Nagle, K. J. (1987), 'Parents' speech to toddlers: The effect of play context'. *Journal of Child Language*, 14, 269–79.

Ochs, E., Smith, R., and Taylor, C. (1988), *Detective stories at dinnertime: Problem solving through co-narration*. Paper presented at American Ethnological Society, St. Louis, MO.

Oehler, J. M., Eckerman, C. O., and Wilson, W. H. (1988), 'Social stimulation and the regulation of premature infants' state prior to term age'. *Infant Behavior and Development*, 11, 333–51.

Ohala, J. J. (1980), 'The origin of sound patterns in vocal tract constraint'. In P. F. MacNeilage (Ed), *The production of speech* (pp. 189–216). Springer-Verlag: New York.

Olson, G. M., and Strauss, M. S. (1984), 'The development of infant memory'. In M. Moscovitch (Ed.), *Infant memory: Its relation to normal and pathological memory in humans and other animals* (pp. 29–48). Plenum Press: New York.

Oster, H. (1978), 'Facial expression and affect development'. In M. Lewis and L. A. Rosenblum (Eds), *The development of affect* (pp. 43–75). Plenum Press: New York.

Oyama, S. (1985), *The ontogeny of information: Developmental systems and evolution.* Cambridge University Press: Cambridge.

Oyama, S. (1989), 'Ontogeny and the central dogma: Do we need the concept of genetic programming in order to have an evolutionary perspective?'. In M. Grunnar and E. Thelen (Eds), *Systems and Development.* The Minnesota Symposia on Child Psychology (Vol. 22) (pp. 1–34). Erlbaum: Hillsdale, NJ.

Papousek, H. (1967), 'Conditioning during early postnatal development'. In Y. Brackbill and G. G. Thompson (Eds), *Behavior in infancy and early childhood.* Free Press: New York.

Papousek, M., and Papousek, H. (1981), 'Musical elements in the infant's vocalization: Their significance for communication, cognition, and creativity'. In L. P. Lipsitt and C. K. Rovee-Collier (Eds), *Advances in infancy research* (Vol. 1). Ablex: Norwood, NJ.

Papousek, H., and Papousek, M. (1984), 'Qualitative transitions in integrative processes during the first trimester of human postpartum life'. In H. F. Prechtl (Ed), *Continuity of neural functions from prenatal to postnatal life* (pp. 220–44). J. B. Lippincott: Philadelphia.

Papousek, H., and Papousek, M. (1987), 'Intuitive parenting: A dialectic counterpart of the infant's integrative competence'. In J. D. Osofsky (Ed), *Handbook of infant development* (2nd ed.). Wiley: New York.

Papousek, M., and Papousek, H. (1989), 'Forms and functions of vocal matching in interactions between mothers and their precanonical infants'. *First Language,* 9, 137–58.

Papousek, M., Papousek, H., and Bornstein, M. H. (1985), 'The naturalistic vocal environment of your infants: On the significance of homogeneity and variability in parental speech'. In T. Field, and N. Fox, (Eds), *Social perception in infants* (pp. 269–97). Ablex: Norwood, NJ.

Parke, R. (1979), 'Perspectives on father–infant interaction'. In J. Osofsky (Ed), *Handbook on infant development.* Wiley: New York.

Parpal, M., and Maccoby, E. E. (1985), 'Maternal responsiveness and subsequent child compliance'. *Child Development,* 56, 1326–34.

Parrinello, R. M., and Ruff, H. A. (1988), 'The influence of adult intervention on infants' level of attention'. *Child Development,* 59, 1125–35.

Pattee, H. H. (1987), 'Instabilities and information in biological self-organization'. In F. E. Yates (Ed), *Self-organizing systems: The emergence of order.* Plenum Press: New York.

Patterson, G. R., and Bank, L. (1989), 'Some amplifying mechanisms for pathologic processes in families'. In M. R. Gunner, and E. Thelen (Eds), *Systems and development,* (pp. 167–209). Erlbaum: Hillsdale, NJ.

Pawluk, C. J. (1989), 'Social construction of teasing'. *Journal for the Theory of Social Behavior*, **19**, 146–67.

Penman, R., Cross, T., Milgrom-Friedman, J., and Meares, R. (1983), 'Mothers' speech to prelingual infants: A pragmatic analysis'. *Journal of Child Language*, **10**, 17–34.

Petitto, L. A. (1987), 'On the autonomy of language and gesture: Evidence from the acquisition of personal pronouns in American Sign Language'. *Cognition*, **27**, 1–52.

Piaget, J. (1952), *The origins of intelligence in children*. International Universities Press: New York.

Piaget, J. (1954), *The construction of reality in the child*. Ballantine Books: New York.

Piaget, J. (1962), *Play, dreams and imitation in childhood*. Norton: New York.

Pipp, S., Easterbrooks, M. A., and Harmon, R. J. (1992), The relation between attachment and knowledge of self and mother in one- to three-year-old infants'. *Child Development*, **63**, 738–50.

Pipp, S., Fischer, K. W., and Jennings, S. (1987), 'Acquisition of self- and mother knowledge in infancy'. *Developmental Psychology*, **23**, 86–96.

Poyatos, R. (1975), 'Cross-cultural study of paralinguistic "alternants" in face-to-face interaction'. In A. Kendon, R. M. Harris and M. R. Key (Eds), *Organization of behavior in face-to-face interaction*. Mouton: Paris.

Prigogine, I., and Stengers, I. (1984), *Order out of chaos: Man's new dialogue with nature*. Bantam: New York.

Prothro, E. T., and Melikian, L. (1955), 'Psychology in the Arab Near East'. *Psychological Bulletin*, **52**, 303–10.

Proust, M. (1981), *Remembrance of things past Vol. 1: Swann's way/Within a budding grove*. Vintage Books: New York.

Radke–Yarrow, M., and Zahn-Waxler, C. (1984), 'Roots, motives, and patterns in children's pro-social behavior'. In E. Staub, D. Bartal, J. Karylowski, and J. Reykowski (Eds), *The development and maintenance of pro-social behaviors*. Plenum Press: New York.

Ratner, H. H. (1984), 'Memory demands and the development of young children's memory'. *Child Development*, **55**, 2173–91.

Read, K. (1967), 'Morality and the concept of the person among the Gahuku-Gama'. In J. Middleton (Ed), *Myth and cosmos* (pp. 185–230). Natural History Press: New York.

Reimers, M., and Fogel, A. (in press), 'The evolutions of joint attention to objects between infants and their mothers: Diversity and convergence'. *Analise Psicologia*.

Reinecke, M., and Fogel, A. (1988, April), *Guided interaction and the development of referential communication: An analysis of infants' offering of an object*. Paper presented at International Conference on Infant Studies, Washington, DC.

Reiss, D. (1989), 'The represented and practicing family: contrasting visions of family continuity'. In A. J. Sameroff and R. N. Emde (Eds), *Relationship disturbances in early childhood: A developmental approach* (pp. 191–220). Basic Books: New York.

Ridgeway, D., Waters, E., and Kuczaj, S. A. (1985), 'Acquisition of emotion-descriptive language: Receptive and productive vocabulary norms for ages 18 months to 6 years'. *Developmental Psychology*, **21**, 901–8.

Robinson, J. A. (1989), '"What we've got here is a failure to communicate": The cultural context of meaning'. In J. Valsiner (Ed), *Child development within culturally* structured environments: Social co-construction and environmental guidance in development (pp. 137–98). Ablex: Norwood, NJ.

Robinson, J. A., Connell, S., McKenzie, B. E., and Day, R. H. (1990), 'Do infants use their own images to locate objects reflected in a mirror?' *Child Development*, **61**, 1558–68.

Rochat, P. (1987), 'Mouthing and grasping in neonates: Evidence for early detection of what hard or soft substances afford for action'. *Infant Behavior and Development*, **10**, 435–49.

Rogers, E. M. (1983), *Diffusion of innovations* (3rd ed.). The Free Press: New York.

Rogoff, B. (1982), 'Integrating context and cognitive development'. In M. E. Lamb and A. L. Brown (Eds), *Advances in development psychology* (Vol. 2) (pp. 125–70). Erlbaum: Hillsdale, NJ.

Rogoff, B. (1989), *Children's guided participation and participatory appropriation in socio cultural activity*. Paper presented at Jean Piaget Society, Philadelphia, PA.

Rogoff, B. (1990), *Apprenticeship in thinking: Cognitive development in social context*. Oxford University Press: New York.

Rohner, R. P. (1984), 'Toward a conception of culture for cross-cultural psychology'. *Journal of Cross-Cultural Psychology*, **15**, 111–38.

Rommetveit, R. (1990), 'On axiomatic features of a dialogical approach to language and mind'. In I. Markova and K. Foppa (Eds), *The dynamics of dialogue* (pp. 83–104). Springer-Verlag: New York.

Ross, H. S., and Lollis, S. P. (1987), 'Communication within infant social games'. *Developmental Psychology*, **23**, 241–8.

Rovee-Collier, C. K., Enright, M., Lucas, D., Fagan, J., and Gekoski, M. J. (1981), 'The forgetting of newly acquired and reactivated memories of 3-month-old infants'. *Infant Behavior and Development*, **4**, 317–31.

Ruff, H. A. (1980), 'The development of perception and recognition of objects. *Child Development*, **51**, 981–92.

Ruff, H. A. (1984), 'An ecological approach to infant memory'. In M. Moscovitch (Ed), *Infant memory: Its relation to normal and pathological memory in humans and other animals*. Plenum Press: New York.

Rumelhart, D. E., McClelland, J. L., and the PDP Research Group (1988), *Parallel distributed processing: Explorations in the microstructure of cognition* (Vol. 1). MIT Press: Cambridge, MA.

Rutter, M. (1987), 'Continuities and discontinuities from infancy'. In J. D. Osofsky (Ed), *Handbook of infant development* (2nd ed.). Wiley: New York.

Sameroff, A. J. (1975), 'Transactional models in early social relations'. *Human Development*, **18**, 65–79.

Sameroff, A. J. (1984), 'Developmental systems: contexts and evolution'. In P. H. Mussen (Series Ed) and W. Kessen (Vol. Ed), *Handbook of child psychology Vol. 1: History, theory and methods* (4th ed.) (pp. 237–94). Wiley: New York.

Sameroff, A. J. (1989), 'Principles of development and psychopathology'. In A. J. Sameroff and Emde, R. N. (Eds), *Relationship disturbances in early childhood: A developmental approach* (pp. 17–32). Basic Books: New York.

Sameroff, A. J., and Emde, R. N. (1989), *Relationship disturbances in early childhood: A developmental approach*. Basic Books: New York.

Sander, L. W. (1977), 'The regulation of exchange in the infant-caretaker system and some aspects of the context–content relationship'. In M. Lewis and L. A. Rosenblum

(Eds), *Interaction, conversation, and the development of language* (pp. 133–47). Wiley: New York.

Sander, L. W., Stechler, G., Burns, P., and Lee, A. (1979), 'Change in infant and caregiver variables over the first two months of life: Integration of action in early development'. In E. B. Thoman (Ed), *Origins of the infant's social responsiveness* (pp. 349–408). Erlbaum: Hillsdale, NJ.

Sarbin, T. R. (1986), *Narrative psychology: The storied nature of human conduct*. Praeger: New York.

Savelsbergh, G. J. P., and van Emmerick, R. E. A. (1992), 'Dynamic interactionism: From co-regulation to the mapping problem'. *Human Movement Science*, **11**, 443–520.

Schachtel, E. G. (1959), *Metamorphosis: On the development of affect, perception, attention, and memory*. Basic Books: New York.

Schaffer, H. R. (1984), *The child's entry into a social world*. Academic Press: New York.

Schaffer, H. R. (1987), 'The social context of psychobiological development'. In H. Rauh and H. Steinhausen (Eds) *Psychobiology and Early Development* (pp. 239–55). Elsevier: New York.

Schaffer, H. R., and Crook, C. K. (1980), 'Child compliance and maternal control techniques'. *Developmental Psychology*, **16**, 54–61.

Schaffer, H. R., Hepburn, A., and Collis, G. M. (1983), 'Verbal and nonverbal aspects of mothers' directives'. *Child Language*, **10**, 337–55.

Scheflen, A. E. (1964), 'The significance of posture in communication systems'. *Psychiatry*, **27**, 316–33.

Schegloff, E. A. (1981), 'Discourse as an interactional achievement: Some uses of "Uh Huh" and other things that come between sentences'. In *Georgetown University round table on languages and linguistics* (pp. 71–93). Georgetown University Press: Washington DC.

Schegloff, E. A., Jefferson, G., and Sacks, H. (1977), 'The preference for self-correction in the organization of repair in conversation'. *Language*, **53**, 361–82.

Scheibe, K. E. (1986), 'Self-narratives and adventure'. In T. R. Sarbin (Ed), *Narrative psychology: The storied nature of human conduct* (pp. 129–51). Praeger: New York.

Scherer, K. R. (1982), 'Methods of research on vocal communication: paradigms and parameters'. In K. Scherer and P. Ekman (Eds), *Handbook of methods in non-verbal behavior research*. Cambridge University Press: Cambridge.

Schieffelin, B. B. (1979), 'Getting it together: An ethnographic approach to the study of the development of communicative competence'. In E. Ochs (Ed), *Developmental pragmatics*. Academic Press: New York.

Schmidt, C. L. (in press), 'The scrutability of reference: Ostensive naming events in caregiver–child interaction'. *Journal of Child Language*.

Schmidt, R. C., Carello, C., and Turvey, M. T. (1990), 'Phase transitions and critical fluctuations in the visual coordination of rhythmic movements between people'. *Journal of Experimental Psychology: Human Perception and Performance*, **16**, 227–47.

Schneider-Rosen, K., and Cicchetti, D. (1991), 'Early self-knowledge and emotional development: Visual self-recognition and affective reactions to mirror self-images in maltreated and non-maltreated toddlers'. *Developmental Psychology*, **27**, 471–8.

Schwartzman, H. B. (1978), *Transformations: The anthropology of children's play*. Plenum Press: New York.

Searle, J. R. (1969), *Speech acts*. Cambridge University Press: London.

Service, V., Lock, A., and Chandler, P. (1989), 'Individual differences in early communicative development: A social constructivist perspective'. In S. von Tetzchner, L. S. Siegel and L. Smith (Eds), *The social and communicative aspects of normal and atypical language development* (pp. 23–49). Springer-Verlag: New York.

Sexton, V. S., and Misiak, H. (1984), 'American psychologists and psychology abroad'. *American Psychologist*, 39, 1026–31.

Shank, R. C., and Abelson, R. (1977), *Scripts, plans, goals and understanding*. Erlbaum: Hillsdale, NJ.

Shannon, C. E. (1963), 'The mathematical theory of communication'. In C. E. Shannon and W. Weaver (Eds), *The mathematical theory of communication* (pp. 29–125). University of Illinois Press: Urbana (reprinted from *Bell System Technical Journal*, 1948, July and October).

Shatz, M., and O'Reilly, A. W. (1990), 'Conversational or communicative skill? A reassessment of two-year-olds' behavior in miscommunication episodes'. *Journal of Child Language*, 17, 131–46.

Shotter, J. (1981), 'Vico, moral worlds, accountability and personhood'. In P. Heelas and A. Lock (Eds), *Indigenous psychologies: The anthropology of the self* (pp. 266–84). Academic Press: New York.

Sindell, P. S. (1974), 'Some discontinuities in the enculturation of Mistassini Cree children'. In G. Spindler (Ed), *Education and the cultural process: Toward an anthropology of education* (pp. 333–49). Holt, Rinehart and Winston: New York.

Singer, J. D., and Willett, J. B. (1991), 'Modeling the days of our lives: Applying survival analysis in psychological research'. *Psychological Bulletin*, 110, 268–90.

Skarda, C., and Freeman, W. (1987), 'How brains make chaos in order to make sense of the world'. *Behavioral and Brain Sciences*, 10, 161–95.

Slade, A. (1987), 'A longitudinal study of maternal involvement and symbolic play during the toddler period'. *Child Development*, 58, 367–75.

Smith, W. J. (1977), *The behavior of communicating: An ethological approach*. Harvard University Press: Cambridge, MA.

Smirnov, A. A., and Zinchenko, P. I. (1969), 'Problems in the psychology of memory'. In M. Cole and I. Maltzman (Eds), *A handbook of contemporary Soviet psychology* (pp. 452–502). Basic Books: New York.

Snow, C. (1977a), 'Mothers' speech research: From input to interaction'. In C. Snow and C. Ferguson (Eds), *Talking to children*. Cambridge University Press: New York.

Sommerville, C. J. (1983), 'The distinction between indoctrination and education in England, 1549–1719'. *Journal of the History of Ideas*, 44, 387–406.

Sommerville, C. J. (1990), *The rise and fall of childhood*. Vintage Books: New York.

Sorenson, E. R. (1979), 'Early tactile communication and the patterning of human organization: A New Guinea case study'. In M. Bullowa (Ed), *Before speech* (pp. 289–305). Cambridge University Press: New York.

Spelke, E. S. (1976), 'Infants' intermodal perception of events'. *Cognitive Psychology*, 8, 553–60.

Spelke, E. S., and Owsley, C. J. (1979), 'Intermodal exploration and knowledge in infancy'. *Infant Behavior and Development*, 2, 13–27.

Spence, D. P. (1986), 'Narrative smoothing and clinical wisdom'. In T. R. Sarbin (Ed), *Narrative psychology: The storied nature of human conduct* (pp. 211–32). Praeger: New York.

Spitz, R. (1965), *The first year of life*. International Universities Press: New York.

Sroufe. A. (1979), 'Socioemotional development'. In J. Osofsky (Ed), *Handbook of infant development* (pp. 462–516). Wiley: New York.

Sroufe, L. A. (1989), 'Relationships, self, and individual adaptation'. In A. J. Sameroff and R. N. Emde (Eds), *Relationship disturbances in early childhood: A developmental approach* (pp. 70–94). Basic Books: New York.

Sroufe, L. A., and Jacobvitz, D. (1989), 'Diverging pathways, developmental transformations, multiple etiologies and the problem of continuity in development'. *Human Development*, 32, 196–203.

Sroufe, L. A., Schork, E., Motti, F., Lawroski, N., and LaFrenier, P. (1984), 'The role of effect in social competence'. In C. E. Izard, J. Kagan, and R. B. Zajonc (Eds), *Emotions, cognition, and behavior* (pp. 289–319). Cambridge University Press: New York.

Steele, D., and Pederson, D. R. (1977), 'Stimulus variables which effect the concordance of visual and manipulative exploration in six-month-olds'. *Child Development*, 8, 104–11.

Stegner, W. (1954), *Beyond the hundredth meridian: John Wesley Powell and the second opening of the west*. University of Nebraska Press: Lincoln, NE.

Steiner, J. E. (1973), 'The gustofacial response: Observation on normal and anencephalic newborn infants'. In J. F. Bosma (Ed), *Fourth symposium on oral sensation and perception*. Department of Health, Education, and Welfare (DHEW Publication No. NIH 73–546): Bethesda, MD.

Stern, D. N. (1971), 'A micro-analysis of mother–infant interaction: Behavior regulating the social contact between a mother and her $3\frac{1}{2}$ month old twins'. *Journal of the Academy of Child Psychology*, 10, 501–17.

Stern, D. N. (1974), 'Mother and infant at play: The dyadic interaction involving gaze, facial and vocal behavior'. In M. Lewis and L. Rosenblum (Eds), *The effect of the infant on its caregiver* (pp. 187–214). Wiley: New York.

Stern, D. N. (1981), 'The development of biologically determined signals of readiness to communicate, which are language "resistant"'. In R. Stark (Ed), *Language behavior in infancy and early childhood*, (pp. 45–62). Elsevier: Amsterdam.

Stern. D. N. (1985), *The interpersonal world of the infant*. Basic Books: New York.

Stern, D. N., Beebe, B., Jaffee, J., and Bennett, S. (1977), 'The infant's stimulus world during social interaction: A study of caregiver behaviors with particular reference to repetition timing'. In H. R. Shaffer (Ed), *Studies in mother–infant interaction* (pp. 177–202). Academic Press: New York.

Stern D. N., Hofer, L., Haft, W., and Dore, J. (1985), 'Affect attunement: The sharing of feeling states between mother and infant by means of intermodal fluency'. In T. Field and N. Fox (Eds), *Social perception in infants* (pp. 249–68).

Stevenson, M. B., Leavitt, L. A., and Silverberg, S. B. (1985), 'Mother–infant interaction: Down syndrome case studies'. In S. Harel and N. J. Anastasiow (Eds), *The at-risk infant: Psycho-socio-medical aspects* (pp. 389–95). Brookes: Baltimore, MD.

Stipek, D. J., Gralinski, J. H., and Kopp, C. B. (1990), 'Self-concept development in the toddler years'. *Developmental Psychology*, 26, 972–7.

Stoffregen, T. A., and Riccio, G. E. (1988), 'An ecological theory of orientation and the vestibular system'. *Psychological Review*, **95**, 3–14.

Suess, G. J., Grossmann, K. E., and Sroufe, L. A. (1992), 'Effects of infant attachment to mother and father on quality of adaptation in preschool: From dyadic to individual organisation of self'. *International Journal of Behavioral Development*, **15**, 43–65.

Super, C. (1981), 'Behavioral development in infancy'. In R. Munroe, and B. Whiting (Eds), *Handbook of cross-cultural human development*. Garland: New York.

Symons, D. K., and Moran, G. (1987), 'The behavioral dynamics of mutual responsiveness in early face-to-face mother–infant interaction'. *Child Development*, **58**, 1488–95.

Tannen. D. (199), 'Gender differences in conversational coherence: Physical alignment and topical cohesion'. In B. Dorval (Ed), *Conversational organization and its development* (pp. 167–206). Ablex: Norwood, NJ.

Thelen, E. (1989), 'Self-organization in developmental processes. Can systems approaches work?'. In M. Gunnar (Ed), *Systems in development* (pp. 77–118). Erlbaum: Hillsdale, NJ.

Thelen, E. (1989), 'The (re)discovery of motor development: Learning new things from an old field'. *Developmental Psychology*, **25**(6), 946–9.

Thelen, E. (1990), 'Dynamical systems and the generation of individual differences'. In. J. Colombo and J. Fagen (Eds), *Individual differences in infancy: Reliability, stability, prediction* (pp. 19–43). Erlbaum: Hillsdale, NJ.

Thelen, E. (1991), 'Is social information special?'. *Human Movement Science*, **11**, 469–74.

Thelen, E., and Fogel, A. (1989), 'Toward an action-based theory of infant development'. In J. Lockman and N. Hazen (Ed), *Action in social context: Perspectives on early development* (pp. 23–64). Plenum Press: New York.

Thelen, E., Kelso, J. A. S., and Fogel, A. (1987), 'Self-organizing systems and infant motor development'. *Developmental Review*, **7**, 39–65

Thelen, E., and Ulrich, B. D. (1991), 'Hidden skills'. *Monographs of the Society for Research in Child Development*, **56**, 6–97.

Thoman, E. B., Acebo, C., Dreyer, C. A., Becker, P. T. and Freese, M. P. (1979), 'Individuality in the interactive process'. In E. B. Thoman (Ed), *Origins of the infant's social responsiveness.* (pp. 305–38). Erlbaum: Hillsdale, NJ.

Thoman, E. B., and Browder, S. (1987), *Born dancing: How intuitive parents understand their baby's unspoken language and natural rhythms.* Harper and Row: New York.

Thorngate, W. (1987), 'The production, detection, and explanation of behavior patterns'. In J. Valsiner (Ed), *The individual subject and scientific psychology* (pp. 71–93). Plenum Press: New York.

Toda, S., Fogel, A., and Kawai, M. (1990), 'Maternal speech to three-month-old infants in the United States and Japan'. *Journal of Child Language*, **17**, 279–94.

Toda, S. and Fogel, A. (in press), 'Infant response to the still-face situation at three and six months'. *Developmental Psychology*.

Tomikawa, S. A., and Dodd, D. H. (1980), 'Early word meanings: Perceptually or functionally based?' *Child Development*, **51**, 1103–9.

Tompkins, S. (1962), *Affect, imagery and consciousness* (Vol. 1). Springer-Verlag: New York.

Tooby, J., and Cosmides, L. (1990), 'The past explains the present: Emotional adaptations and the structure of ancestral environments'. *Ethology and Sociobiology*, 11, 375–424.

Trevarthen, C. (1977), 'Descriptive analysis of infant communicative behavior'. In H. R. Schaffer (Ed), *Studies of mother–infant interaction* (pp. 227–70). Academic Press: London.

Trevarthen, C. (1979), 'Communication and cooperation in early infancy: A description of primary intersubjectivity'. In M. Bullowa (Ed)., *Before speech: The beginning of interpersonal communication* (pp. 321–47). Cambridge University Press: New York.

Trevarthen, C., and Hubley, P. (1978), 'Secondary intersubjectivity: Confidence, confiding and acts of meaning in the first year'. In A. Lock (Ed), *Action, gesture and symbol: The emergence of language* (pp. 183–227). Academic Press: New York.

Tronick, E. (1980), 'On the primacy of social skills'. In D. B. Swin, L. O. Walker, and J. H. Penticuff (Eds), *The exceptional infant Vol. 4: Psychosocial risks in infant–environmental transactions*. Bruner/Mazel: New York.

Tronick, E., Als, H., Adamson, L., Wise, S. and Brazelton, T. B. (1978), 'The infant's response to entrapment between contradictory messages in face-to-face interaction. *Journal American Academy of Child Psychiatry*, 17, 1–13.

Trout, D. L., and Rosenfeld, H. M. (1980), 'The effect of postural lean and body congruence on the judgement of psychotherapeutic rapport'. *Journal of Nonverbal Behavior*, 4, 176–90.

Tulving, E. (1972), 'Episodic and semantic memory'. In E. Tulving and W. Donaldson (Eds), *Organization of memory*. Academic Press: New York.

Ungerer, J. A., Brody, L. R., and Zelazo, P. R. (1978), 'Long-term memory for speech in 2 to 4-week-old infants'. *Infant Behavior and Development*, 1, 177–86.

Uzgiris, I. C., Benson, J. B., Kruper, J. C., and Vasek, M. E. (1989), 'Contextual influences on imitative interactions between mothers and infants'. In J. J. Lockman and N. L. Hazen (Eds), *Action in social context: Perspectives on early development* (pp. 103–27). Plenum Press: New York.

Valsiner, J. (1983), *A developing child in a developing culture: a relative synthesis*. Paper presented at the 26th annual meeting of the African Studies Association, Boston.

Valsiner, J. (1987), *Culture and the development of children's action*. Wiley: New York.

Valsiner, J. (1989), *Human development and culture: The social nature of personality and its study*. Lexington Books: Lexington, MA.

van Beek, Y., and Geerdink, J. (1989), 'Intervention with preterms: Is it educational enough?' *European Journal of Psychology of Education*, 6, 251–65.

Vandenberg, B. R. (1986), 'Beyond the ethology of play'. In A. W. Gottfried and C. C. Brown (Eds), *Play interactions: The contribution of play materials and parental involvement to children's development*. Lexington Books: Lexington: MA.

van Geert, P. (1991), 'A dynamic systems model of cognitive and language growth'. *Psychological Review*, 98, 3–35.

Varela, F. J. (1983), *Principles of biological autonomy*. North-Holland: New York.

Vedeler, D. (1987), 'Infant intentionality and the attribution of intentions to infants'. *Human Development*, 30, 1–17.

Vedeler, D. (in press), 'Infant intentionality as object directedness: An alternative to representationalism'. *Journal for the Theory of Social Behavior*.

von Hofsten, C. (1984), 'Developmental changes in the organization of prereaching movements'. *Developmental Psychology*, 20, 378–88.

von Neumann, J. (1958), *The computer and the brain*. Yale University Press: New Haven, CT.

Vygotsky, L. A. (1978), *Mind in society*. Harvard University Press: Cambridge, MA.

Wachs, T. D., and Gruen, G. E. (1982), *Early experience and human development*. Plenum Press: New York.

Waddington, C. H. (1961), *The nature of life: The main problems and trends of thought in modern biology*. Harper and Row: New York.

Waddington, C. H. (1966), *Principles of development and differentiation*. Macmillan: New York.

Walker, H., Messinger, D., Karns, J., and Fogel, A. (1992), 'Social and communicative aspects of infant development'. In V. Van Hasselt (ed.), *Handbook of social development: A life-span perspective*. Plenum: New York.

Warren, W. H., Jr. (1990), 'The perception–action coupling'. In H. Bloch and B. Bertenthal (Eds), *Sensory-motor organizations and development in infancy and early childhood* (pp. 23–37). Kluwer: Boston, MA.

Warren, W. H., Morris, M. W., and Kalish, M. (1988), 'Perception of translational heading from optical flow. *Journal of Experimental Psychology: Human Perception and Performance*, **14**, 646–60.

Wartofsky, M. (1979), 'The model muddle: Proposals for an immodest realism'. In M. Wartofsky and R. S. Cohen (Eds), *Models: Representation and scientific understanding*. Boston studies in the philosophy of science, Vol. 48. D. Reidel: Dordrecht.

Watson, R. (1989), 'Monologue, dialogue, and regulation'. In K. Nelson (Ed), *Narratives from the crib* (pp. 263–83). Harvard University Press: Cambridge, MA.

Watzlawick, P., Beavin, J., and Jackson, D. D. (1967), 'Some tentative axioms of communication'. In P. Watzlawick, J. Beavin and D. D. Jackson (Eds), *Pragmatics of human communication* (pp. 48–71). Norton: New York.

Webster's New Twentieth Century Dictionary (1979), Collins: New York.

Weisfeld, G. E., and Beresford, J. M. (1982), 'Erectness of posture as an indicator of dominance of success in humans'. *Motivation and Emotion*, **6**, 113–31.

Weiss, P. A. (1969), 'The living system: Determinism stratified'. In A. Koestler and J. R. Smythies (Eds), *Beyond reductionism: New perspectives in the life sciences* (pp. 3–55). Beacon Press: Boston, MA.

Werker, J. F., and Lalonde, C. E. (1988), 'Cross-language speech perception: Initial capabilities and developmental change'. *Developmental Psychology*, **24**, 672–83.

Werker, J. F., and Tees, R. C. (1984), 'Cross-language speech perception: Evidence for perceptual reorganization during the first year of life'. *Infant Behavior and Development*, **7**, 49–63.

Werner, E. (1979), *Cross-cultural child development*. Brooks–Cole: Monterey, CA.

Wertsch, J. V. (1985), *Vygotsky and the social formation of mind*. Harvard University Press: Cambridge, MA.

Wertsch, J. V. (1991), *Voices of the mind: A sociocultural approach to mediated action*. Harvard University Press: Cambridge, MA.

Wertsch, J. V., McNamee, G. D., McLane, J. B., and Budwig, N. A. (1980), 'The adult–child dyad as a problem-solving system'. *Child Development*, **51**, 1215–21.

West, L. and Fogel, A. (April, 1990), 'Maternal guidance of object interaction'. *Paper presented at International Conference on Infant Studies*, Montreal.

White, B. L., and Castle, P. W. (1964), 'Visual exploratory behavior following postnatal handling of human infants'. *Perceptual and Motor Skills*, **18**, 497–502.

Wimmer, H., and Hartl, M. (1991), 'Against the Cartesian view on mind: Young children's difficulty with own false beliefs'. *British Journal of Developmental Psychology*, **9**, 125–38.

Winnicott, D. W. (1971), *Playing and reality*. Basic Books: New York.

Wohlwill, J. F. (1973), *The study of behavioral development*. Academic Press: New York.

Wolf, D. (1982), 'Understanding others: A longitudinal case study of the concept of independent agency'. In G. Foreman (Ed), *Action and thought* (pp. 297–327), Academic Press: New York.

Wolff, P. H. (1987), *The development of behavioral states and the expression of emotions in early infancy*, University of Chicago Press: Chicago.

Worster, D. (1977), *Nature's economy: The roots of ecology*. Sierra Club Books: San Francisco.

Zukow, P. G. (1990), 'Socio-perceptual bases for the emergence of language: An alternative to innatist approaches'. *Developmental Psychobiology*, **23**, 705–26.

General index

abbreviation, 93, 184–6
aesthetics, 76, 180–2, 184–6
affiliation, 180–2, 186–7
appropriation, 168–9
attachment, *see* affiliation
attractor, 105–6, 108, 116 n7, 117 n13
attunement, 59
autobiography, 142

coercion, 42 n29, 158 n27
cognition, 3, 4, 12, 56, 98 n9, 119–35,
    135 n7, 140, 148, 160, 180,
    183
  embodied, 3, 15, 19, 51, 76, 111–13,
    119–21, 135 n7, 137 n50, 141,
    148, 160, 162–3, 170, 173–4,
    180–2
  imaginative, 125–8, 131–5, 136 n19,
    140–2, 152–3, 156, 175 n42
  participatory, 122–5, 128–31, 136
    n29, 138 n62, 142, 145–6,
    152–3, 156
communication
  animal, 26, 29–32 41 n10, 42 n21,
    96, 100 n36, 104, 124
  continuous process model, 5,18, 27,
    29, 54–60, 65–9, 75, 77, 87–9,
    120–2, 138 n62, 159 n58, 178
  discrete state model, 26–8, 64–5, 77,
    85–7, 90, 98 n9, 119, 138 n62,
    153
  repair, 78, 153–4, 159 n58, 185
convention, 115–16
conflict, 31–2
conventionalization, 93

co-regulation, 6, 18–21, 29–30, 32,
    34–41, 51, 54–61, 76–80, 88–9,
    91, 96–8, 99 n29, 103–4, 109,
    113, 120, 123, 126, 134, 136
    n21, 140, 146, 148–55, 160–2,
    164, 168–70, 173–4, 174 n4,
    179, 181, 183–4
creativity, 6, 11, 12, 31, 35, 36, 69–71,
    76, 88–93, 95, 103–4, 114–16,
    131–5, 140, 148–50, 153,
    155–7, 161, 163–4, 170–1, 177,
    180, 182, 184, 187
culture, 3, 6, 12–16, 22–4, 25 n18,
    39–40, 59, 62 n8, 63 n41, 81
    n19, 86, 88–9, 95–7, 98 n8,
    102, 108, 160–76, 179

degrees of freedom, 103–4, 113–15,
    177–8
determinism and indeterminism,
    177–80, 188
development, 5, 6, 7, 9 n1, 10, 16,
    24, 54, 49–51, 53, 62 n19–20,
    91, 99 n20, 117 n11, 138
    n64, 145–7, 153, 177–80, 182,
    186–7, 190 n28
  of relationships (*see* relationship-
    development)
  stage model, 85–6, 99 n20, 100 n36
dialogue, 4, 17, 20, 27, 48, 58, 93,
    131–5, 140–1, 144, 146,
    149–54, 160, 165, 175 n44,
    179, 182
dissolution, 114–15, 171, 179–80
dynamic systems
  see systems

222

Name index

Abelson, R., 136
Abraham, R. H., 116
Acredolo, L. P., 157
Adams, A., 157
Adamson, L. B., 99, 176
Agiobu-Kemmer, I., 174
Ainsworth, M., 186, 190
Alberts, J. R., 174
Aloimonos, Y., 135
Altaha, M., 137
Altman, I., 53, 63, 175
Anderson, B. 63
Anisfeld, M., 158
Aries, P. 62
Ashby, W. R., 62
Austin, J. L., 42
Azuma, H., 63

Bakeman, R., 63, 99, 176
Baker-Sennett, J., 136
Bakhtin, M. M., 157
Baldwin, D. A., 176
Bandura, A., 174, 175, 177, 178, 189
Bank, L., 100, 117
Barnard, K. E., 191
Bates, E., 176
Bateson, G., 37, 42
Bateson, M. C., 176, 185, 189, 190
Baudonniere, P. M., 158
Bavelas, B. J., 158
Beckwith, R., 138
Beebe, B., 55, 63
Beek, 117, P. J., 135
Befu, H., 25, 63, 162, 174
Bellugi, U., 176
Belsky, J., 55, 63
Bennett, A., 159

Benson, A. J., 158
Beresford, J. M., 42
Bergin, T. G., 135
Bergman, A., 98
Bernieri, F., 56, 63
Bertalanffy, L. von., 62
Bertenthal, B. I., 157
Bettes, B. A., 190
Bettleheim, B., 25
Birdwhistell, R., 27, 41, 63
Bloom, L., 138
Blount, B., 175
Boesch, C., 100
Bornstein, M. H., 25, 63, 174, 175
Bosma, J. F., 176
Boudreau, P. R., 81
Bowlby, J., 86, 87, 98, 136, 187
Branchfield, S., 191
Bransford, J. D., 135, 136
Braunwald, S. R., 99
Braybrooke, D., 63
Bretherton, I., 138
Brennan, S. E., 42
Brentano, F., 124
Bril, B., 175
Brody, L. R., 137
Bronfenbrenner, U., 62
Brooks, R., 120, 135
Brooks-Gunn, J., 25, 138, 158
Browder, S., 190
Brown, H., 178, 179, 190
Brown, R., 133, 138
Brownell, C. A., 158
Bruner, J., 40, 42, 63, 75, 81, 93, 94,
    99, 109, 136, 137, 141, 157,
    169, 174, 175
Buber, M., 63

225